MAKING SUBJECT(S)

T0352812

COMPARATIVE LITERATURE AND CULTURAL STUDIES
VOLUME 4
GARLAND REFERENCE LIBRARY OF THE HUMANITIES
VOLUME 2072

COMPARATIVE LITERATURE AND CULTURAL STUDIES
JONATHAN HART, *Series Editor*

MAKING SUBJECT(S)
LITERATURE AND THE EMERGENCE OF NATIONAL IDENTITY

ALLEN CAREY-WEBB

Routledge
Taylor & Francis Group

LONDON AND NEW YORK

First published 1998 by Garland Publishing Inc.

Published 2013 by Routledge
2 Park Square, Milton Park, Abingdon, Oxfordshire OX14 4RN
711 Third Avenue, New York, NY 10017

First issued in paperback 2014

Routledge is an imprint of the Taylor and Francis Group, an informa business

Library of Congress Cataloging-in-Publication Data

Carey-Webb, Allen, 1957–
    Making subject(s) : literature and the emergence of national
identity / by Allen Carey-Webb.
        p.   cm. — (Garland reference library of the humanities ; vol.
2072. Comparative literature and cultural studies ; vol. 4)
    Includes bibliographical references and index.

    1. National characteristics in literature.   2. Nationalism in literature.
3. Literature, Comparative—Themes, motives, etc.   4. Literature,
Comparative—History and criticism.   I. Title.   II. Series: Garland reference
library of the humanities ; vol. 2072.   III. Series: Garland reference library
of the humanities. Comparative literature and cultural studies ; vol. 4.
    PN56.N19C37   1998
    809'.93358—dc21   97-32709
                                                                       CIP
ISBN 13: 978-1-138-86438-2 (pbk)
ISBN 13: 978-0-8153-2896-4 (hbk)

Contents

Illustrations

Acknowledgments

This book could not have been written without help from many sources. I owe a debt to Western Michigan University. The Faculty Research and Sponsored Programs Fund offered grants and course reductions. The Department of English, and particularly its chair, Shirley Scott, facilitated time away from the classroom as well as making possible a graduate seminar which allowed the best kind of research, teaching and learning with students. Indeed, students in the Colonialism, Literature, and National Subjects seminar in the fall of 1994 challenged and extended my thinking at every turn. The WMU Postmodern Theory Faculty Reading Group has created an important forum for the last four years. I am especially indebted to WMU colleagues who have read portions of this manuscript and provided an intellectual community in which to work including Gwen Raaberg, Mike Jayne, John Cooley, Peter Walker, Pat Gill, Jill Larson, and Mark Richardson.

This book could not have been written without the support of the University of Oregon during the early stages. I am grateful to the Humanities Center for a graduate student research award and its financial assistance and privileges. Many ideas in this book were generated during the five years I spent in the University of Oregon's outstanding Comparative Literature Program. Steve Rendall, Irving Wolfarth, Wolf Solich, Linda Kintz, Suzanne Clark, Barbara Guetti, Elizabeth Davis, and Tres Pile significantly developed my thinking. Alan Wolfe's intellectual guidance and his unstinting help with portions of this manuscript were formative and invaluable. I learned a great deal from seminars with visiting scholars, especially Satya Mohanty and Rey Chow. The Postcolonial Discourse Reading Group, particularly Tugrul Ilter, Annuncia Escala, Paul Semonin, Yue Gang and Lifongo Vetinde sharpened my understanding of many of the issues addressed here.

Jonathan Hart, editor of this series in Comparative Literature and Cultural Studies, has provided significant freedom. Phyllis Korper's editing demonstrated her eagle eye. Throughout the publication process Garland Publishing has been helpful and expeditious.

Portions of chapter 2 appeared in the *Hispanic Issues* volume *Amerindian Images and the Legacy of Columbus* by René Jara and Nicholas Spadaccini; I appreciate permission to include them in modified and expanded form. I also appreciate the people, many of whom I don't know, who responded to portions of the manuscript presented at various annual academic conferences including those of the Modern Language Association, the Midwest Modern Language Association, the Marxist Literary Group Summer Institute, the Michigan College Education Association, the Modern Language Conference, the Philological Association of the Pacific Coast, and the Western Humanities Association.

This book could not have been completed without Nathan and Jessica's patience and Jill's support. I dedicate it to them.

SERIES EDITOR'S FOREWORD

Goethe's *Weltliteratur*—a discussion of literature as a whole rather than a partisan interest in those who are in or out of favour, and how that literature relates to other arts as well as to philosophical, historical, and cultural contexts—lies behind this series. A comparative study of literature in different contexts will be the focus of each volume. The series, whose authors and scope are international, will be pluralistic and include disparate points of view. Its only criterion is the quality of the work. Here, comparative studies will include the comparison of literary texts, as well as cross-disciplinary and theoretical inquiries. The books in this series will explore the crossing of linguistic and cultural boundaries in comparative literature, and its increasingly close relation to or overlap with cultural studies. This comparative literature will not compare European languages and literatures alone, but will also address East-West, minority, gender, and aboriginal issues. One of the goals of the Comparative Literature and Cultural Studies series is to increase consciousness or self-consciousness about methods and ideological assumptions while fostering a better understanding of specific literary, historical, and cultural texts. The volumes that constitute the series should help to improve the dialogue between theory and practice in comparative studies. Comparative literature and cultural studies are closely related, and the uniqueness of this series is that it is the only one, to my knowledge, that explores the boundaries between them. Both disciplines emphasize popular culture, visual arts, and the sociology of literature. Here cultural studies, which is also connected to cultural history, is meant as something changing, perhaps widening, its intellectual appeal. Although comparative literature and cultural studies have interesting origins, the volumes will not all be "true" to those origins. Some will be revisionary. While the Birmingham School was instrumental in contributing to cultural studies in the English-speaking world, the study of culture has undergone important changes and controversies. Another aim of this series will be to contribute to this changing debate on literature and culture. In the global village these cultural, historical, and literary comparisons may help to engender new ways of seeing in the university and the various societies in which it finds itself. How the contributors construct their visions will be, although part of a cooperative enterprise, an individual matter.

Jonathan Hart

MAKING SUBJECT(S)

CHAPTER 1

Introduction

Subjects of Empire and Nation

We have made Italy, now we have to make Italians.

Massimo d'Azeglio

I pledge allegiance to the flag of the United States of America and to the republic for which it stands, one nation under God, indivisible, with liberty and justice for all.

Francis Bellamy

Today the nation-state system is the triumphal form of political and cultural organization across the globe. Everyone on earth is a national citizen. As scholars have recently pointed out, the phenomenon of national states and cultures is, given its remarkable ascendancy, a relatively new development. Many countries are less than fifty years old, and, even in Europe, the Age of Nationalism is thought to be as close to us as the nineteenth century. Yet national peoples and national territories emerged both prior to and significantly after the 1800s. Indeed, the stage was set for the creation of modern nations in western Europe during the late sixteenth and early seventeenth centuries. With their increasing centralization of authority, ordering of regional administration, and fostering of uniform infrastructures, language, and education, European absolute monarchies were the clear forerunners of contemporary nation-states. We now recognize this transformative period as "Early Modernism," a transitional stage between medieval kingdoms and modern representative nations, and it was at this time that the first nations—Spain, France, and England—began to take form.

In ensuing centuries, as colonialism and imperialism spread European language, culture, and political forms across the globe, European rule produced significant political, social and cultural resistance. This resistance—usually coextensive with the districts of administration— eventually found expression in the rise of nationalist movements first in North and South America, and later, culminating in the mid-twentieth century, in the Middle East, Asia, and Africa.

The truly remarkable thing about the nation-state system is not its dissemination as a political form but its infusion as a deeply held consciousness, a way of feeling, thinking, and acting, accepted, even cherished, by a tremendous heterogeneity of human beings. While there remain today, at the opening of the twenty-first century, isolated pockets of peoples who may not think of themselves as "nationalized," as having—or wanting to have—an identification with a nation-state system and national territory, such peoples are increasingly rare. How the rest of us have taken on national identities, how individuals in different historical periods and vastly disparate locations across the globe have come to think of themselves as national citizens, with all the differences and commonalties this entails, is an important and interesting question in the study of culture and history.

Answering this question requires not only that we examine the formal political history of nation-states but that we look also into the complex ways in which "national peoples" are themselves "made." The problem of making Italians put forward by d'Azeglio at the first meeting of parliament of the newly united Italian kingdom has faced the leaders of all national states at one time or another, though not always in such self-conscious terms. This making is a complex activity of collective naming, of the inclusion of national selves and the exclusion of cultural and political others. In this sense the making of national subjects is a kind of "discourse," one that involves not only military conquests, political negotiations, and formal juridical institutions but also an enormous diversity of cultural and linguistic processes, from the explicit school room recitation of the Pledge of Allegiance to the establishment and institutionalization of national literary canons.

As an experiment in comparative literature, this book will explore the making of national subjects by examining literary works from different traditions and from two distinct historical moments. Although it will come up, we will be less concerned with the expression of nationalism as an explicit ideology and more interested in the ways that literature allows us to analyze national identities in their moment of emergence. We will want to see how national peoples are named, particularly in their relationship to colonial and colonizing others. More than this we will also see how literature can be read not only to name and linguistically identify national groups but, equally important, to reveal social, political and historical practices that bring national subjects and national subjectivity into being. As both literary and historical documents then, the works under discussion will help us to consider the simultaneous and mutually implicated development of state authority and national identity.

It is the contention of *Making Subject(s)* that there are significant commonalties and important mirroring oppositions in the emergence of national identity between Early Modern European states and many "third-world" nations hundreds of years later. However, as we begin, we must be aware that juxtaposing literary works from different historical periods runs the risk of sweeping generalizations that tell us more about contemporary methods of reading than about the texts, periods, or even the "discourses" that are our presumed objects of study. Care must be taken and historical sensitivity must be acute. At the same time, however, the exploration of literary texts as part of nationalist discourse ought to be both as cross-cultural and as historically ranging as is the nation-state form itself and its concomitant conception of national identity. While no two periods, nations, or national citizens are alike, attempting to connect such commonalties is the essence of informed theoretical inquiry.

Juxtaposing European and "third-world" nations and literatures also has particular pitfalls. In comparing the development of literature and nationalism in Early Modern Europe with the contemporary "third world," there is a danger in either failing to recognize or radically asserting cultural difference. There is the risk of participating in what Edward Said has identified as an orientalist narrative where the "third world" is seen as an early, arrested, or underdeveloped "stage" of European history. The issue of orientalism has also been raised in terms of the use of the term "third world," whose problematics are only partially addressed by the use of the expression in quotation marks. As is repeatedly pointed out in current discussions, the term "third world" homogenizes situations more remarkable for their diversity than their commonalty while denying internal difference.[1] Dividing the globe into distinct "worlds," the three-worlds model distances the "Other" and unifies the "Self," thus obscuring connected and mutually constitutive histories. The term "European," of course, works in similar ways, even if its swath is somewhat less encompassing. (Consequently, when the word "European" suggests radical difference from "third world," it will also appear in quotation marks.) The phrase "third world" is part of an already coded discourse, one that is established in institutional discussions, programs of "third-world" cultural study, and in "third-world literature" teaching and research positions. As Prasad Madhava explains, the term has descriptive meaning only within the context of European colonialism and its aftermath in national development. Indeed, the "third world" literature discussed in the present study is all originally written in European languages. To borrow Gayatri Spivak's phrasing, though all the texts are "(re)presentations" none are "representational," none "speak for" the "subaltern."[2]

Moreover, the association throughout *Making Subject(s)* of nations and texts is not meant to suggest that any *one* text can be representative of "its" nation of "origin." Terms such as "representative" or "origin" are not only ambiguous for "third-world" novels in European languages but also for the "European" Renaissance plays of the seventeenth century, which are more likely to still be read within unexamined constructions of "national tradition."

These reservations must be kept in mind as we place "European" and "third-world" histories and texts alongside one another. Yet, by according equal recognition of "third world" cultural products and monuments of the Western tradition it should become possible to engage in a genuinely meaningful comparative literature. By examining European and "third-world" texts together, it will become evident that the emergence of national identity is not only an issue for "third-world" writing; the very development of "the canon" and the role of canonical literature in European nation formation may also be illuminated by an investigation of "emergent literatures." Examining "first-" and "third-world" situations together reveals the profound importance of the colonial relationship and systems of national authority to the rise of the nation in both colonizing and colonized contexts. Indeed, the very problem we are addressing, the problem of the nation, requires an international perspective. Michael Sprinker points out that:

The national question, in literature and in politics, cannot be resolved except by situating it within the context of international determinations that exceed the limits imposed by the nation and national culture. (28)

The relationship of "third-world" and "European" literature is one of continuity as well as difference. The "third-world" writers discussed here were educated in systems installed by European colonizers. They write in European languages, utilize European literary forms, and are published by European presses. "First-world" readers are a part of their audience.[3] The international and historical comparisons attempted here challenge widely held notions that European nation-states are in some way more "natural" than "third-world" nation-states, or the view that "third world" revolutionary nationalism is automatically less (or more) "democratic."

As is now widely accepted, identity is coded by gender, ethnicity, class, and race. There is a growing awareness that nationality is also a form of subjectivity that requires analysis. As in the case of all identities, that of the nation is pieced together within a complex, intertwined fabric of discourse. Yet, the narration of national identity is also, in some ways, special. The nation-state comes into being in more closely defined historical moments than, say, gender, class, or race. Whether operating as an hegemonic or a counter-hegemonic undertaking, the construction of national identities can be associated with particular historical struggles and political interests. In this process we will see that literature and its institutions play a prominent role. Literary texts participate in the making of national subjects and thus are implicated in the politics of the nation. As Prasad puts it:

> Literature, or a national culture in general, is one of the representational machineries that serve to consolidate the nation-state. Its historical emergence in Europe is tied to the rise of primary capitalist nation-states; in this sense literature is "national" . . . a Marxist theory of literature cannot begin anywhere else. (72)

In recent years the enthusiastic embrace of nationality and nationhood by those countries breaking away from Soviet domination as well as by a wide cross-section of patriotic movements across the globe is often considered an anachronism, an atavistic counterpoint to a sustained global trend toward ever-greater cosmopolitanism. Such an analysis, however, entails an overly simplistic understanding of the history and culture of nations. Nation-states have always arisen in tension with international forms of social and political organization. In *Making Subject(s)* we will investigate the complex relationship of empire and nation as it is manifest in the cultural forms that have allowed the identification and development of national peoples.

SUBJECTIVITY AND SUBJECTION

This turn to the cultural aspect of the making of nations recognizes that political and historical changes cannot be understood independently of the ideological or discursive practices that define for individuals who they are and to whom and to what they owe loyalties and obligations. In bringing together an exploration of language functions with political practices, the present work is characteristic of "postmarxist" thought that recognizes the limitations of models of economic determinism in predicting and describing cultural behavior. A postmarxist perspective would seem to be especially appropriate in examining nationalism because the very resiliency of the national idea and the nation-state form itself are *the* problem of traditional historical materialist analysis. The development of internationalist socialist blocks turns out to be superseded not by worldwide class-based revolution but instead by resurgent national affiliations and increasing numbers of nation-states. Rather than greeting these developments with a simplistic return to idealist thinking, we need to complicate our conception of material practices and to recognize the way that ideology operates in the actions of everyday life. We need to see how subjection and subjectivity, subject and subjects, are made simultaneously.

In his essay "Ideology and Ideological State Apparatuses," Louis Althusser explores the surprising efficacy and persuasiveness of state power. He argues that the authority of the national state is manifest not only in the use of direct military or juridical force but also, and most importantly, in the reproduction of forms of action, ways of thinking, and habits of life that permeate all social forms including churches, schools, families, popular media, cultural institutions, and so on. Drawing partly on the thought of Antonio Gramsci, Althusser argues that ideology must be thought of not as a set of disembodied ideas but instead as concrete practices which comprise the everyday activities individuals carry out as they perform the functions laid down for them in the various institutions in which they operate. In this sense individuality itself (to the extent to which that term retains its traditional bourgeois meaning) is understood as a function of participation within accepted (always already laid-out) ideological practices. The Althusserian notion that ideology "interpellates

individuals as subjects" offers an explanation of the resilience of the
nation-state—despite the best efforts of marxists, and others, to surpass
it. Althusser's analysis inaugurates a variety of important intellectual
work aimed at understanding the relationship between ideology,
individual agency, and the effects of social institutions. The intellectual
positions influenced by Althusserian thought generally go under the
heading poststructuralist and are as diverse as the genealogies of
institution and subjectivity carried out by his former student Michel
Foucault, the cultural/political analysis of Edward Said's *Orientalism*
or *Culture and Imperialism*, and the antifoundationalist marxism of
Ernesto Laclau and Chantal Mouffe, who, instead of class struggle,
speak the language of hegemony and counter hegemony, of discourse,
articulation, and subjectivity.

These postmarxist conceptions of the mutuality of material and
ideological practices underlie the investigation of the interpellation of
subjects I undertake in both Early Modern Europe and the postcolonial
"third world." As I seek to understand the emergence of national
identities in the context of empire building and dismantling, I also draw
on recent historical and theoretical work on national subjectivity.
Benedict Anderson has been highly influential in this field. Anderson
rejects the traditional marxist notion that national affiliations are merely
"inventions" or "fabrications" (elsewhere called "false consciousness")
and claims instead that "communities are to be distinguished, not by
their falsity/genuineness, but by the style in which they are imagined"
(15). Anderson argues that the development of a capitalist marketplace
for printed books in European vernacular languages was essential to the
emergence of national consciousness; this line of argument depends
upon a profound thinking-together of ideology and material practice.
According to Anderson, when the market for texts in Latin (accessible
only to a relatively small number of bilingual readers) became saturated
in the mid-eighteenth century, the burgeoning print industry
increasingly turned to other more marketable languages. In this way
European vernacular languages were "assembled," codified, and
disseminated within a market area determined by the limits of their
intelligibility. Diverse dialects were combined, and, via print, fixed in
time.

Though Anderson does not refer to it, a suggestive example of such
an undertaking is the creation of dictionaries and encyclopedias.
Indeed, in the preface to his famous (1755) dictionary Samuel Johnson
observes, "The various dialects of the same country . . . will always be

observed to grow fewer, and less different, as books are multiplied."
Johnson's efforts at codifying the language were overtly nationalistic
and literary; "I have devoted this book," he writes, "to the honor of my
country, that we may no longer yield the palm of philology without a
contest to the nations of the continent. The chief glory of every people
arises from its authors."

Thus, creating dictionaries, printing and disseminating books, and
identifying and supporting the "people's authors" (to use Johnson's
terms) was and still is central to the development of national
consciousness. People begin to think of themselves as connected to
each other by writing even more than by spoken language in a textually
based mutual recognition of relationships between disparate readers.
Anderson argues that the modern and national conception of
subjectivity is embodied particularly in two textual genres that both
arose in the eighteenth century and that were both essential to
imagining the nation—the novel and the newspaper. The novel allows
characters who may not know each other or even have any direct
relationship with each other, not merely to exist simultaneously but to
be recognized by the omniscient reader as part of a simultaneously
construed society. Anderson uses the examples of a Filipino and a
Mexican novel and an Indonesian short story to demonstrate how
characters are supposed by the reader to be living in a single, national
community (33). Anderson further likens the newspaper to a novel
without a coherent plot, suggesting that the way a newspaper links
disparate events together because of their coincidence on a given
calendar date is rather like the novel's simultaneous juxtaposing of
different characters and events. The experience of reading a newspaper
connects anonymous people together, all consuming similar or
indentical versions of a day-by-day clocked history. The "fiction" of the
newspaper and the "fiction" of the novel are in these ways similar; they
seep "quietly and continuously into reality, creating that remarkable
confidence of community in anonymity which is the hallmark of
modern nations" (40).

Familiar documents such as newspapers and novels ought to help
us recognize that no form of identity is "original" or "given once and
for all." Instead, our collective identity is constructed within specific
historical, cultural, and political fields. Laclau and Mouffe put it this
way:

a discursive structure is not a merely "cognitive" or "contemplative" entity; it is an *articulatory practice* which constitutes and organizes social relations. (96)

While recognizing that individuals are historically situated, postmarxist analysis leaves considerable space for agency, intervention, and rearticulation. Discursive structures are always "inhabited," both producing and produced by individual subjects. Thus as we shall see, rather than viewing a national identity as made once and forever, a postmarxist approach recognizes the possibilities for alteration, complexity, and collective and unanticipated change.

For literary scholars, Anderson's work opens the door to thinking about the way in which literature has served as an important discursive form for the making of national subjectivities. Toward this end, Anderson's work is suggestive but by no means exhaustive. Despite his emphasis on print and novels, for instance, we will see that there was another literary genre developed in the formative period of state authority that incorporated diverse classes and ethnic types within a single framework. In the Early Modern period of national consolidation in western Europe, the Renaissance drama allowed the representation of a national people to a society not yet fully literate. Thus it was first via the public theater and only later through print that literary works were produced and disseminated on a national basis. Moreover, literature's select position in national identity formation ought not to be understood simply by the way it generated a readership in the open market. Literature was utilized in national systems of education and privileged by elites as an expression of national culture. With the rise in literacy and the development of markets for printed texts during the nineteenth century in Europe, the novel increasingly became the form with a national representation and dissemination both in Europe and in its colonies. Yet, the novels Anderson examines are all realist fictions written in the language of a European colonizing power by cosmopolitan "third-world" male nationalists. Given that Anderson's connecting of the novel to the nation is based on a theory of inclusiveness of characters and readers, it is necessary to ask who is included and who is excluded in the "national" novel written in Spanish in Mexico or the Philippines, or in the English short story written in Indonesia.

The present study investigates the interpellation of national identity at the point of its emergence in both European and non-European traditions through an analysis of exemplary literary works in the crucial genres of Renaissance drama and postcolonial novel. Because of the importance of the colonial relationship to the formation of nations, the plays and novels chosen for examination portray colonialism both from the perspectives of Renaissance empire building and from its twentieth-century national resistance. It will be evident in reading these selected literary works that in their specific historical contexts, they serve as narratives of national history that contribute significantly to the "making" of national subjects. The process of making subjects is always local and, simultaneously, imbricated in larger, imperial patterns of discourse. Thus while the texts under examination here may depict apparently coherent identities, by showing the national subject at the point of its elaboration, they also render its coherence problematic.

In the Renaissance dramas, for example, it will be evident that in order to identify a national Self, difference within the nation is projected outward onto a constructed Other. This process is mediated in the Renaissance texts through systems of proto-national authority, involving a progressive development of individuated subjects as members of a national order via the institutional and ideological practices of Early Modern religion, disciplinary punishment, pedagogy, and formal knowledge. In the "third-world" novels the same systems of national authority are influential, but the national subject is produced instead by a dynamic resistance to colonial domination. The questions of inclusion and exclusion in the "third-world" novel are examined in the writing of Sembène and Ngugi in Chapter IV. Inclusion and exclusion turn to questions of the stability and unity of subjectivity, and the discussion in Chapter V of Salman Rushdie's postmodern novel allows us to significantly expand upon the conclusions Anderson draws from his exploration of more traditional "realist" fiction. In the examination of these "third-world" texts, the problem of Self and Other is again prominent, but, as we shall see, in the postcolonial context, Self and Other are not resolutely separable, and postcolonial national identities are culturally hybrid.

IMPERIAL ABSOLUTISM AND THE NATIONAL DRAMA

While self-proclaimed nationalist movements arose in the nineteenth century, they marked not the commencement but the culmination of a process of national identity formation in motion, as our discussion of print and theater suggests, since the Early Modern period. Across time

1 The colonial encounter set in motion an understanding of self and others from which modern nationhoods arise. (Columbus encounters Amerindians on Hispanola, Theodor de Bry, 1594)

and geography there has been a variety of "ethnic" or "national" identifications, yet the true antecedents of what we would today describe as a national consciousness begin to appear in the sixteenth century. John A. Armstrong argues that in this period profound economic, religious, and linguistic developments were matched with an increasing centralization and bureaucratization of the state apparatus. The development of national peoples and national states took place hand in hand. An intersection of evangelizing religion and regional dialectical differences also contributed to this centralization by codifying vernacular languages that were increasingly "national" in their range and identification.[4] By the seventeenth century, the trend toward absolutism paved the way for the centralized administration of the growing nation-states. Stable polities needed central authorities, with large, stable staffs, archives, and regular, systematic administrations. Increasingly these were located in capital cities. As state systems developed from the center, their reach and rule extended into national margins.

Renaissance Spain and England were particularly important in this developmental process, which linked state formation to a growing awareness of national affiliation. Writers increasingly focused their work on explicitly national histories; the outpouring of national history plays from figures such as Lope de Vega and Shakespeare is part and parcel of the age. Walter Cohen has examined European Renaissance drama as it portrays the history of the nation-state at its moment of Early Modern consolidation. Cohen believes that even though Spain and England developed separately, the Renaissance stage in both countries can be distinguished from the theater in the rest of Europe by a rich and complex synthesis of popular and neoclassical dramatic traditions. Conscious of Greek and Roman dramatic theory, yet rejecting the ancient forms, mingling noble and base characters while attributing to lower-class characters a seriousness and autonomy, both traditions staged a tension between the popular will and the homogenizing effects of an incomplete yet stable absolutist state. Cohen asserts that in England, drama had a progressive political impact, anticipating if not preparing the conflicts of the English Revolution of the mid-seventeenth century, whereas in Spain "radical Golden Age plays lack even indirect radical effects" (28). While absolutist regimes fostered the public theater as a means of governance and social control, subsequently, when the theater's subversive effect became more apparent, oligarchs sought to undermine and control it.

Richard Helgerson has recently extended Cohen's work by arguing that despite this inclusion of the "popular, marginal, subversive, and folk," Shakespeare's history plays contributed above all "to the consolidation of central power, to the cultural division of class from class" (245) that characterized an ambitious generation of Elizabethan writers who sought to elevate English nationalism to a classical and imperial standard. This path-breaking work on the public drama draws attention to the development of national consciousness before the development of widespread literacy, the rise of a capitalist market place, and the dissemination of printed materials.

The selection of literary works for this study was also influenced by another factor: the centrality of empire to the formation of national identity. From ancient times the concept of empire has played a significant role in the legitimating myths for polities. In the transition from empire to the nation-state, an emphasis on ruling over others and on territorial, economic, and cultural expansion remained significant. A high point of imperial myth according to Armstrong was the sixteenth-century Burgundian revival, i.e., Charles V, King of Spain and ruler of a revived Holy Roman Empire (1519-56). Armstrong, Emile Beneviste, and other scholars of European nationalism recognize that constitutive myths of national identity depend not only on a common conception of Self but also, fundamentally, on the exclusion of Others; the representation of the "Other" is critical to understanding the definition of both an imperial and a national "Self."

"Holy" and "Empire" are linked terms, and certainty of religious faith and exaltation of cultural superiority go together. Cohen stresses the efficacy of the national history play in the religious justification of the nation-state:

In the first age of the nation-state and of national consciousness, belief in the continuity between past and present inherent in the providential view [of a god-directed history] found its amplest and most appropriate embodiment in the national history play. (219)

Although religious affiliation may have been the overriding identification for medieval society, the administration and practice of Christianity and Islam also had important implications for the formation of identities later construed on national grounds. As Armstrong maintains, and as we shall see in Renaissance drama, the imperial myths of a universal mission were transformed in this period into the justification for stable entities linked to specific territories. As we examine Early Modern nationalism, we will find a significant interweaving of religious faith, cultural superiority, and national pride. Close attention to specific dramatic works of Shakespeare and Lope de Vega demonstrates the complexity of Early Modern hegemony where secular languages, systems of pedagogy, and the practice of writing come together in the making of national subjects.

In particular we will examine the two literary works from the period perhaps most closely tied to the developing imperial relationship between Europe and the Americas, Lope de Vega's *El nuevo mundo descubierto por Cristobal Colon* and Shakespeare's *The Tempest*. Written and first performed only eleven years apart (1600 and 1611 respectively) and less than a generation after the Armada, the plays enter on the scene as England begins to join Spain in leadership of European colonial expansion. While *The Tempest* has become a primary text for discussion of literature and colonialism, *El nuevo mundo*, no less interesting, has received significantly less attention. Both plays center on a visionary European male figure capable of commanding obedience and bringing order in a new, untamed, and naturally beautiful world. Both plays extensively depict New World natives and are among the first imaginative works in their respective traditions to do so. Both plays also stage European violence against and betrayal of colonized peoples. In both works a native insurrection comes at the climax of the action. And, in both plays, the response to native rebellion serves to define the shape and authority of imperial and absolutist power. *Making Subject(s)* is then the first scholarly work to explore the rich intertextuality of these two very interesting plays. By bringing these works together, we are able to distinguish Spanish and English colonial texts   as well as identify common themes in the emergence of a European colonial discourse.

As much as an awareness of colonial history will guide our analysis, the significance of that history comes in the way that it helps us understand the emergence of *European*, specifically Spanish and English, national self-conception. In the analysis that follows, for instance, we will see how *El nuevo mundo*, by positioning Spaniards and Native Americans together in the New World, serves to unify an otherwise conflictive Spanish national Self in its relationship to its Other. In *The Tempest*, we will also explore the relationship of colonial encounter to the emerging authority of the European nation. A remarkable aspect of this play is the way that political authority develops contrapuntally in its aspiration for control over native *and* European subjects. A discourse of education, intellectual and technological authority, and state power infuses Shakespeare's colonial play as it does no other work by him, making it a particularly interesting site for exploring the imaginary of European absolutism. While the centrality of imperialism in determining the fortunes of European superpowers such as Spain and England must be taken up elsewhere and by others, the project of *Making Subject(s)* is to examine the way in which the colonial encounter set in motion an understanding of Self and Others from which modern nationhoods arise. As far as such a question is a matter of European nationhood, we will be seeking knowledge of the center from canonical representations of the margins, knowledge of the nation from its relations with its newly annexed far-flung territories. However, in considering modern nationhoods, it is at once necessary and insufficient to study Early Modern Europe. Thus, in examining the adversarial relationship of European and non-European identities, *Making Subject(s)* also moves us to the other side of the coin, to a consideration of literature and the emergence of nationhood from a colonized as well as colonizer viewpoint. By examining the formation of nations in Early Modern Europe together with the development of nationhood in formerly colonized regions, light will be shed in both directions. Thus the present study diverges from traditional literary analysis that maintains Europe and the "third world" as isolated categories. Cognizant of the risks involved, we will undertake a truly comparative approach, one that emphasizes that there is no resolute separation of identities in the modern world, that an understanding of Europe cannot be held apart from its Others, and vice versa.

FROM EUROPE TO THE COLONIES AND BACK AGAIN: DEVELOPMENT OF THE NATIONAL FORM

As we bring together the different contexts for national emergence in the sixteenth and twentieth centuries we will find not only difference, but intriguing similarities. For instance, national languages and literatures play a surprisingly related hegemonic role in both contexts. Indeed, writing and speaking were conducted in different languages during the Middle Ages in Europe, as they are in many "third-world" nations today. In both contexts, vernacular tongues were in a vital struggle with the language of education and imperial administration. Armstrong points out that in Europe after the year 600 "people did not again dare to write the way they customarily spoke until the tenth century in France and much later in other European countries" (253). This distance between an increasingly hegemonic "national" language and populations speaking different tongues while remaining indifferent to their "national" citizenship was a common phenomenon until quite recently in Africa, much of Asia and to a lesser but significant degree in Latin America.

While there are striking similarities between Early Modern Europe and the "third world" in terms of the role of language in the formation of national identity, there are also, as we shall see, profound differences. The development and penetration of the capitalist market and technology, the role of mass forms of communication, the formation of pedagogical systems, and the historical and cultural differences between Africa and India and Europe complicate theories of national identity formation as they seek to enclose within the concept of "nationhood" the forms of identity and authority that first emerged in Early Modern Europe with those that have become by the mid-twentieth century entirely transglobal.

The national idea, like the colonial intellectuals themselves, migrated from center to colony and back again. If national consciousness in the Americas was shaped by the print shops, newspapers, journals, and postal services that arose in the colonies in the eighteenth century, the cultural encounter taking place in the colonies also made it possible to "think of Europe as only one among many civilizations, and not necessarily the Chosen or the best."[5] Thus new perspectives and political models generated in the New World were subversive of European absolutisms and dynasties and played a role in the explosion of nationalist sentiment and nation-state building in the nineteenth century. Correspondingly, European nationalist movements inspired imperial dynasties to intensify their rule over their subjects both at home and in the remaining colonies. Ruling elites in highly diverse, multilingual polities, sought to diffuse subjected nationalist sentiments by identifying themselves with a particular central nationalism and subsequently attempting to enforce this "national" language and culture on all citizens of the empire. These polices were propagated under rubrics of "Russification," "Anglicization," "Magyarization," etc.

The establishment of English education in India following Thomas Babington Macaulay's *Minute* (address to Parliament) of 1835 offers a case in point of the way in which a forced "official nationalization" operated to inculcate the colonized citizens of the empire in the national culture of the "mother" country:

> We must at present do our best to form a class who may be interpreters between us and the millions whom we govern; a class of persons, Indian in blood and colour, but English in taste, in opinion, in morals and in intellect.[6]

As intended, colonial schools and educational systems taught European languages, culture, and administration to non-European subjects. Such schools brought the multi-ethnic and polylingual youth of indigenous elites of the colonial administrative unit into a single student body and provided them with a uniform and systematized curriculum, instruction in a single European language, and an awareness of European national histories. Reacting to a nationalist movement inspired by New World conditions, these official, imperial assertions of nationalism eventually had the ironic effect of heightening anticolonial resistance and fostering national assertion at the margins. Thus the development of nationalism in colonized Asia and Africa as well as in Europe arises out of a dynamic and complex interchange between "first" and "third" worlds.

Although colonial schools had a particular importance in developing an incipient nationalist class, they failed to penetrate to all levels of the population. Indeed, the adoption of an idea of national identity forged through the agency of a nationalist elite was derivative, borrowed from European and Creole cultural and political history. A top-down nationalism instituted by a European-educated vanguard in Africa or Asia would differ in spirit if not substance from the citizen-republican nationalism that developed in the Americas. The separation would appear all the greater when European cultural practices were utilized to advance the nationalist cause in a region with a non-European cultural heritage. Therefore, in order to examine texts of "third-world" nationalism, it is necessary to examine the complications that arise in this interchange of the national idea.

Concepts of "nationality" were often imported into colonies from European national centers where peoples, governments, and cultural institutions had become unified in ways alien to the colonies themselves; obviously this led to considerable problems—problems of both a "theoretical" and an administrative nature. While for European theorists the nation-state was often considered a necessary stage of progressive development and modernization, in various "third-world" circumstances, such a model amounted to a Eurocentric form of organization. These contradictions of "third world" nationalism are examined by Partha Chatterjee in *Nationalist Thought and the Colonial World: A Derivative Discourse*. A member of the influential Indian "subaltern studies group," Chatterjee argues that the nation-state is usually understood merely as "a stage of development" in "the story of liberty" that leads to universal "progress" and "modern democracy" (2-3). Nationalist struggles in the "backward parts of the world" have been seen in traditional Western scholarship as positive because they confer the "'psychological blessings' of dignity and self-respect," and the "elimination of inferior grades of citizenship" (4). Widely recognized failures of nationalism are described as situated in countries "unpropitious" to or "not yet ready for freedom" and are explained away as "deviations," "special cases," or necessary side steps on the clearly established path of development. By situating the discussion of nationalism within broader fields of European intellectual history, particularly rationalism and Enlightenment conceptions of citizenship, Chatterjee charges that the very theory of nationalist development must itself be seen as historically and culturally biased. Chatterjee points out that the dominant conception of nationalism is fundamentally contradictory in that nationalism is understood to posit the existence of *independent* cultures but within the same *universal* terms and framework. Chatterjee claims that the failure of Eurocentric views of modernization to recognize social, cultural, political, and ideological difference amounts to an ongoing domination. In his view the effort of nations around the world to approximating similar kinds of Eurocentric "modernity" results in the "continued subjection" of "third-world" nations "under a world order which only sets their tasks for them and over which they have no control" (10).

In order to validate "third-world" nationalist movements, Chatterjee seeks out new and more meaningful ways to understand them. Working from within the discourse of various leaders of, Chatterjee seeks to show how at least one group of "third world" nationalists interrogated not only established institutions of colonial power but forms of perception, cognizance, and ethical evaluation:

Thus nationalist thinking is necessarily a struggle with an entire body of systematic knowledge, a struggle that is political at the same time as it is intellectual. Its politics impels it to open up that framework of knowledge which presumes to dominate it, to displace that framework, to subvert its authority, to challenge its morality. (42)

This does not mean that Chatterjee claims that he himself writes in or from a discursive position outside Western thought but that the discourse of nationalism needs to be investigated at the deeper level of language, assumptions, and cultural structures. Chatterjee does not reject Western theory as much as he seeks to diversify and complicate it. Unlike conventional schemes of historical development as a series of social/political stages generated by a specific economic/historical progression with a homogeneous or universal *telos*, Chatterjee's work sets twentieth-century nationalism in a dynamic context with a complexity of actors leading to a multiplicity of outcomes that are not necessarily more or less "progressive."

Chatterjee's contention that a meaningful examination of nationalist discourse must include an evaluation of how "third-world" nationalisms challenge the assumptions of Enlightenment rationalism and universal modernization is particularly valuable for our investigation of national culture and identity in the "third-world" novels discussed in chapters IV and V. The evolution of a wide variety of resistant national cultures in the areas of European colonization challenge any uniform view of how nations are imagined. Frantz Fanon is exemplary in this respect. As the leading African national theorist his vision of "third-world" nationalism develops resistance to European domination on a broad political, ethical, and epistemological basis. Fanon's position is elaborated in Chapter IV and tied to a discussion of one of the most important African novels of the decolonization struggle, Ousmane Sembène's *Les bouts de bois de Dieu*. Problems of national self-definition are particularly manifest in the postcolonial period where Chatterjee's thought becomes especially relevant. In the analysis of Salman Rushdie's novel *Midnight's Children* in Chapter V, we will see that an awareness of the dilemmas of derivative nationhood is necessary to understand the deployment of "magical realism" as a form of resistance to "first world" rationalism and modernism. It may be possible to affiliate magical realism with a new transglobal "postmodernism"—a possibility that has begun to be explored in studies of Latin American fiction. *Midnight's Children* provides an opportunity to consider new subjectivities and political forms for an increasingly globalized, post-national world.

Although Renaissance and postcolonial texts are not customarily read together, *Making Subject(s)* shows the advantages of doing so. Remarkably both Lope de Vega's and Shakespeare's plays—already at the outset of the sixteenth century—offer a script for native rebellion and national self-assertion. The ways in which this script must be rewritten, even fundamentally rethought, is the project of the "third-world" authors we will examine. As they "write back" to the empire, these authors utilize and transform European languages and literary forms. They draw on and challenge the Manichean distinctions between colonizer and colonized, between Self and Other, narrated by Lope de Vega and Shakespeare. Nearly four hundred years later, they retell the story from their point of view while, like the great canonical figures, they also seek to narrate emerging national histories and bring new national subjectivities into being.

NATIONALISM AND GENDER

The engendering of national subjects in both historical periods is also a gendering, and while the inherited trope posits the colonizer as the masculine/active and the colonized as the feminine/passive, to understand the gendering of the nation we will have to draw on and press the limits of currently available political, literary, and postcolonial theory, refashioning that theory as we go along.

It is disturbing that none of the major theorists of the rise of European national identity including not only Armstrong and Anderson, but also Ernest Gellner, Eric Hobsbaum, and Hugh Seton-Watson, allow the question of gender to enter their analysis. (Nor does it come up in the national allegory debate discussed below.) Fortunately, however, in the 1990s there has been a surge of interest in the relationship of gender and sexuality to national subjectivity. This interest draws particularly on the work of a scholar of German fascism, George Mosse. In his 1985 study *Nationalism and Sexuality: Respectability and Abnormal Sexuality in Modern Europe* Mosse addresses the development of attitudes toward sexuality, manliness, homosexuality, the place of women, and the "code of respectability" that characterized European nationalism and particularly Nazi Germany. Drawing on the scholarship on manners by Norbert Elias and others, Mosse argues that a discourse of "respectability" influenced by evangelical Christianity was utilized by rising bourgeois classes in their social competition both with "undisciplined" lower classes and with an

2 "Third-world" artists retell the story from their point of view while, like the great canonical figures, they also seek to narrate emerging national histories and bring new national subjectivities into being. [*August Visitor (Arrival of White Men in an Ibibio Village)*, Ekog Ekefrey, Nigeria, Acrylic on Canvas, 1991]

"indulgent" aristocracy. If this code of "respectability" was middle class, it was via a modernizing nationalism that it became extended to other sectors of society:

> In order to establish controls, to impose restraint and moderation, society needed to reinforce the practical techniques of physicians, educators, and police. But their methods had to be informed by an ideal if they were to be effective, to support normality and contain sexual passions. In most timely fashion, nationalism came to the rescue. It absorbed and sanctioned middle-class manners and morals and played a crucial part in spreading respectability to all classes of the population, however much these classes hated and despised one another. (9)

A version of manliness that rejected "degeneration" into effeminate practices—for instance uncontrolled passion, masturbation, or a "Jewish" lifestyle—was essential to the respectable "norm" that regulated admittance to the national fraternity. In this way masculinity was established as the foundation of the nation, and women were idealized as a source of morality that simultaneously provided a background for the activity of men who determined the national fate. Indeed,

> Woman as national symbol was the guardian of the continuity of and immutability of the nation, the embodiment of its respectability. (18)

Through "respectability," nineteenth-century nationalism was connected to domesticity, the nuclear family, and informal and formal systems of education emphasizing character building and the inculcation of proper conduct (19). Thus Mosse finds the key to the successful hegemony of nineteenth-century nationalism to be its normalcy, its assertion not only of its universality but its assumption that honorable social existence was only possible inside its discourse.

Although Partha Chatterjee does not take up the question of gender in *Nationalism and the Third World*, in an important subsequent essay, he puts forward a theory of the relationship of women's emancipation struggles and Indian nationalism that significantly ties Mosse's discussion of respectability to "third-world" national struggles. During the nineteenth century, as India struggled for independence, Indian women took part actively in campaigns against widow immolation, remarriage, polygamy, and for a codified age of marital consent, yet

3 The respectable "new woman" drew upon a reformed version of indigenous tradition. (*Bharat Mata*, Mother India as a Bengali lady, Abanindranath Tagore, Watercolor)

later in the struggle for national independence such participation dropped off. In order to explain these developments, Chatterjee argues that the nationalist formulations put forward by the restive Indian middle class had already built the suppression of women into the argument. Against the material superiority of the West, Indian nationalism argued the spiritual and cultural value of its domestic traditions. In this discourse, Chatterjee argues, "The home was the principal site for expressing the spiritual quality of the national culture, and women must take the main responsibility of protecting and nurturing this quality" (243). While the maintenance of the patriarchal domination of home life thus became tied to the struggle for national self-determination, reform of women's roles along the lines of Mosse's respectability became part and parcel of the middle class's acceptance of Western-defined modernization. The "new woman" was defined in comparison to the "common woman" — "coarse, vulgar, loud, quarrelsome, devoid of superior moral sense, sexually promiscuous, subjected to brutal oppression by males" (244). This new woman was subject also to a new patriarchy that contrasted with the manners and superficiality of women in the West and drew upon a reformed version of indigenous tradition. Thus, as Kumari Jayawardena points out (in her introduction to *Feminism and Nationalism in the Third World*), nationalist movements rarely went past granting women legalistic reforms and had little impact upon the patriarchal realities of daily life for the vast majority.

The narrative of national development as an ever-increasing progress in gender equity will be challenged in the chapters to come. As we read the literary texts, we will see how the Malinche myth — tied to the founding of the Spanish empire — functions in Lope de Vega's play to isolate indigenous women from national solidarity while failing to grant them security from the colonizer's overwhelming power (Chapter II). In *The Tempest*, we will explore how European authority is extended over native subjects via a discourse of patriarchal responsibility (Chapter III). Contrasting with this Spanish and English colonial literature, via Ousmane Sembène's widely recognized African feminism we will consider the participation of women in the decolonization struggle and their ongoing efforts to transform oppressive conditions in daily activity (Chapter IV). Finally we turn to Rushdie's *Midnight's Children* to explore how the complex crossing-over, cultural mixture, and class differentiation script the nationalist transformation of family life (Chapter V). Rushdie's fiction, as we shall see, offers a parody of respectability and the heroic male national figure.

NATIONAL ALLEGORIES

As we consider construction of nationalist discourses in literary texts it will be necessary for us to both work with and rethink the concept of "national allegory" that has been extensively debated in postcolonial studies. Instigated in 1986 and 1987 by an exchange of articles in the journal *Social Text* between Fredric Jameson and the Indian scholar Aijaz Ahmad, the controversy has been carried on in a variety of articles, dissertations, and books, most notably a special issue of *Social Text* (1992), Aijaz Ahmad's *In Theory: Classes, Nations, Literatures* (1992), and a special issue of the journal *Public Culture* (Fall 1993). The uproar began over a piece by Jameson extending and modifying his thesis of the influence of the "political unconscious" to encompass "third-world" literature. In this essay Jameson presents a sweeping argument based on the idea that in the "first world," there is "a radical split between private and public . . . Freud versus Marx" that indelibly marks Western literature (69), and in the "third world," on the other hand, the relations between public and private are "wholly different." With this distinction he argues that

> Third-world texts, even those which are seemingly private and invested with a properly libidinal dynamic—necessarily project a political dimension in the form of national allegory: *the story of the private individual destiny is always an allegory of the embattled situation of the public third-world culture and society.* (69) (emphasis in original)

In order to elaborate on why "first-" and "third-world" literature should differ so profoundly, Jameson asserts that "we Americans, we masters of the world" are like the master in Hegel's master/slave dialectic, caught in a "placeless individualism," "psychologism," and "the projections of private subjectivity." In counterpoint, "third-world" writers have a different "cultural logic," that of the slave, who "knows what reality and the resistance of matter really are" and who must be "situational and materialist despite" himself such that "the individual story" inevitably involves the "telling of the experience of the collectivity itself" (85). For Jameson:

the allegorical spirit is profoundly discontinuous, a matter of breaks and heterogeneities, of the multiple polysemia of the dream rather than the homogeneous representation of the symbol. (73)

Jameson's conception of allegory facilitates careful and interesting readings. Specifically, he exemplifies his theory with an insightful discussion of two works, Lu Xun's "Diary of a Madman"—where he argues that the psychological drama of the individual has an "allegorical resonance" for "Chinese society as a whole" (71)—and Ousmane Sembène's *Xala*—where the encroachment of capitalism in Africa is resisted by the strategic presence in the text of the voice of an archaic and utopian communalism based on a collective agrarian relationship to the land.

Jameson's provocative thesis is challenged in a subsequent issue of the same journal by Aijaz Ahmad. Ahmad is particularly disturbed by the all-encompassing nature of Jameson's categories. While he admits that the term "third world" may be useful as part of a polemic to raise the profile of African, Asian, and Latin American literature in the academy, he finds the three-worlds model—which sharply distinguishes capitalist, socialist, and colonized economies—to be woefully imprecise. Ahmad points out that despite several important qualifications Jameson makes, his use of the term "third world" fails to recognize differences within both advanced capitalist countries and the formerly colonized states as well as growing similarities between them. Taking on Jameson's version of "third-world" literature, Ahmad believes that the texts read and valorized in Europe and America are not necessarily representative of the majority of writers in Asia or Africa, especially those who do not write in European languages. Offended by Jameson's "rhetoric of otherness," Ahmad sees his argument as yet another piece of a familiar "monstrous machinery of descriptions" that attempts "to classify and ideologically master the colonial subject" (6).

As subsequent scholars have entered the fray, both the justice of Ahmad's criticism and the resilience of Jameson's concept of allegory continue to emerge. The most important contribution for our current investigation is made by Prasad Madhava whose essay "On the Question of a Theory of (Third World) Literature" offers a well-considered reappraisal of both Jameson and Ahmad. Prasad believes that Ahmad misunderstands Jameson's use of the term "third world," which, rather than referring to "a geography with its millennia of cultural history," ought to be taken to signify "a time-space of subject formation, necessarily determined by imperialism, colonialism, developmentalism, and experimentation with bourgeois democracy and other forms of nationstatehood" (58). Recognizing justice in Ahmad's point that Jameson's radical distinguishing of "first" and "third" worlds—of individual versus collective expression—continues an orientalist paradigm, Prasad argues that "It would be more accurate to reinscribe all literatures in their national context, and *then* begin the analysis of the invisibility of the national framework in the western context and its hyper-visibility in the third world context" (73). In essence Prasad is arguing that the recognition of a national allegory in any given text takes place through a dynamic interaction between the texts themselves and particular institutionalized forms of reading. While it is possible to read a work from a "third-world" country as a "libidinal-private" text, to do so "is only possible from within a nationalist framework, i.e., from a position in which the national framework is invisible as a result of complete assimilation into nationalist ideology" (78). Thus it ought to be possible to grant a similar form of attention to "first-world" texts and recognize national allegories there as well. What would be necessary theoretically is to move beyond transparently established traditions of national literature while still reading with attention to the rise and development of the nation-state.

Thus *Making Subject(s)* follows a careful path through the national allegory debate. I am willing, at times, to use the concept, but we will remove it from its position of putative Otherness in postcolonial studies both by considering its relevance to European texts, and recognizing the profound imprecision the term "third world" (which will be more specifically understood within a colonial and national-state development context). Moreover, rather than seeking to understand nations as homogeneous entities, we will recognize the permeability of national borders as well as the divisive lines of conflict that run vertically, between classes, and horizontally, between ethnic groups. In so doing we will attempt to be precise about what is meant by "national" and to distinguish national allegories from "social," "class," or "communal" ones. Since nations arose in specific historical periods, concomitant national identities may overlap with other forms of group affiliations but are not interchangeable with them. In the course of our analysis, we will see that it is best not to valorize or denounce the national idea *a priori*. Following Lenin, Gramscii, and Fanon, Ahmad points out that nationalism is dependent on the political character of the power bloc which takes hold of it and utilizes it, as a material force, in the process of constituting its own hegemony. (8)

While recognizing the possibility of nationalism to bring repressed voices to the forefront, we must also be conscious that the "strategic use" of any collective national identity may be implicated in the silencing and manipulation of subalterns by elite classes and in the hierarchical gendering of national subjects. In *Making Subject(s)*, we will consider the complexities of national hegemony, its construction as a discourse that both includes and excludes, and its power and legitimacy in particular historic contexts and circumstances.

PART I

Colonizing Nations and the Public Theater in Early Modern Spain and England

·

CHAPTER 2

Other-Fashioning

The Discourse of Empire and Nation in Lope de Vega's *El Nuevo Mundo descubierto por Cristobal Colon*

If, as in the case of the Indians, the entire republic, by common consent of all the subjects, does not wish to hear us, but retain the rituals of their lands, where there had never been Christians, in such a case we cannot wage war against them.

Bartolomé de Las Casas

They were as close to me as a reflection in the mirror; I could touch them, but I could not understand them.

Claude Lévi-Strauss

Once the liminality of the nation-space is established, and its "difference" is turned from the boundary "outside" to its finitude "within", the threat of cultural difference is no longer a problem of "other" people. It becomes a question of the otherness of the people-as-one.

Homi Bhabha

During the sixteenth century, Spain had the largest and most imposing empire of any European power since Rome. From the Philippines to Africa, from Italy to Peru, it was the first imperium on which "the sun never set." Spain was at the forefront of developing and expanding European nations, a model for dominion abroad and absolutism at home. On the peninsula the sixteenth-century agenda included the unification of the Spanish states, the expulsion of the last Moorish rulers, the use of the Inquisition as an instrument of the monarchy, the development of an elaborate system of taxation, and the creation of the most sophisticated state bureaucracy of the age. Nonetheless, absolutism was never complete. Spanish society was conflictive and heterogeneous, with competing centers of economic and political power, and religious, ethnic, class, and gender disparities. The tensions of this age are present in the works of Spain's preeminent dramatist, Lope de Vega (1562-1635). His *comedia, El nuevo mundo descubierto por Cristóbal Colón* (written between 1598 and 1603), exemplary for its diversity and epic proportions, stages the voyage of Columbus and the momentous (so-called) discovery of the (so-called) New World. In addition to Columbus himself, the drama features Ferdinand and Isabella (King and Queen of Spain), the king of Portugal, Spanish dukes, a Moorish king and his court, a group of allegorical figures including Religion, Providence, and Idolatry, the Devil himself, pilots, greedy sailors, a friar, and, most fascinating of all, Lope de Vega's version of native Caribbean islanders. The indigenous "Indians," granted a third of the play's dialogue, include chiefs, princesses, and commoners. Represented as a fully established society in the Caribbean setting, they are accorded a complex social hierarchy and respond both collectively and as individuals to Columbus and his men. Their depiction in *El nuevo mundo* is one of the earliest European literary renditions of a New World nation.

Unlike Shakespeare's *The Tempest, El nuevo mundo* has not received much critical attention.[1] Yet the play, contemporaneous with active Spanish colonization of Meso-America, is relevant to our understanding of Spanish perceptions of Native Americans and of themselves. Since accounts of the first explorers had been available for decades, and fifty years had passed since the famous debate on the justness of war against the Indians between Bartolomé de Las Casas and Ginés de Sepúlveda, Lope's play is useful for investigating the development and reproduction of Spanish attitudes toward its colonized subjects during the formative period of European nations and empires. As J. H. Elliot points out, "If Spain was a pioneer among the bureaucratic states of modern Europe, it was also a pioneer among the European colonial powers, and I believe that the implications of this pioneering role for both Spanish and European history have scarcely begun to be considered" (viii).

Lope's perceptions of Native Americans are drawn from the accounts of explorers and colonists, but we should be wary of accepting his sources as offering transparent truths about the native peoples.

These accounts, like the play itself, are framed in Spanish, European, and Western terms. The portraits of *indios* in *El nuevo mundo* are highly dependent on the complex history of *Spanish* and *European* religious, social, political, and rhetorical practices. It could hardly be otherwise, given the terrible fate of the Caribbean islanders, a case where "making subject(s)" eliminated the subjects themselves. According to Howard Zinn, "In two years [after the Arawak rebellion of 1495] through murder, mutilation, or suicide, half of the 250,000 Indians on Haiti were dead," and by 1650 there simply were no "native informants" still alive in Haiti (4). Accounts by other natives from New Spain were not available at Lope's time. Garcilaso de la Vega, el Inca, did not publish *Commentarios reales* until 1609, and Guamán Poma's *Primer nueva coronica y buen gobierno* was not available until 1920. The very inaccessibility of Amerindian voice gave Lope's representation a greater authority. Michel de Certeau, in his critique of Montaigne's essay, "Of Cannibals," argues that

the discourse that sets off in search of the Other with the impossible task of saying the truth returns from afar with the authority to speak in the name of the Other and command belief. (69)

In this sense, the presence of the Amerindian subjects in *El nuevo mundo* adds authenticity and enhances Columbus' supposed accomplishment.

Still, the established view of Lope de Vega as consistently orthodox and highly nationalistic, has led scholars to miss the conflictive, disruptive, or even subversive ideas found in his writing and to fail to consider the mechanisms by which such ideas are contained, controlled, and framed. In *Drama of a Nation*, Walter Cohen argues that putting the history of the nation on stage with its representations of different and latently conflictive voices establishes the possibility of evaluation and judgment of national action.[2] Cohen, distinguishing Spanish from English historical drama, suggests that for the Spanish external relationships were of critical importance,

In England the enemy is within and the subject is conflict. Spain is the opposite: the English define themselves by what they are, the Spanish by what they are not. All appearances to the contrary, the Hispanic nation is internally harmonious; it has exported its problems. The late-sixteenth-century Golden Age national history play, regardless of its temporal or

geographic setting, tends to emphasize the struggle between Catholic
Spain and its infidel, external foes. (226-7)

In order to create the internally harmonious Spanish nation, differences
within are projected outward onto others, thus the depiction of others
makes possible the recognition of a coherent Spanish national self. At
the same time, the representation in *El nuevo mundo* of another culture
before, during and after Columbus' arrival creates a dialogic situation
with destabilizing, even subversive, possibilities. Native American
difference can suggest the relativism of cultural formations, the
historical and contingent nature of knowledge and power, and, as we
shall see, the complexity of Spanish identity.

Like all great works of art, *El nuevo mundo* is internally
conflictive, intertextually related to other works, and imbedded in
social, historical, and political contexts. In its depiction of Native
Americans the play is an instance of colonial discourse, described by
Homi Bhabha as "an apparatus that turns on the recognition and
disavowal of racial/cultural/historical differences" and "a form of
governmentality that in marking out a 'subject nation,' appropriates,
directs and dominates its various spheres of activity" ("The Other"
154). While the recognition of difference between Spaniard and Indian
in Lope's play tends to highlight Indian inferiority and justify systems
of colonial administration and instruction, there is also a disavowal of
difference, an assertion of likeness. Ironically, however, commonality
between Spaniard and *indio* also becomes part of the "appropriating,
directing, and dominating" of the play's colonial discourse.

GENERIC CONVENTIONS

El nuevo mundo is a *comedia* and the requirements of the genre have an
influence on Lope's making of Native Americans. As a popular form,
the *comedia* tends in the direction of rendering its characters
comprehensible; it naturalizes and "de-exoticizes." The *indio* in *E l
nuevo mundo* speaks Spanish and even refers to Greek mythology. As
the centripetal forces of generic convention pull the Other toward the
Self, the identity of the constructed Native American subject seems
almost to merge with that of the traditional Spanish hero.

Thus the Native American male figures have many of the traits of
the *comedia*'s well-bred *caballero*. Dulcanquellín, the Indian
chief/king, before the arrival of the Spanish is eloquent in his efforts to

persuade a maiden, Tacuana, to love him, and despite having won her in battle, he is respectful of her wishes to postpone their wedding. After a long catalogue of the mineral, fauna, and floral wealth of his kingdom, he tells Tacuana, "Es tierra dichosa y bella, / Y mucho más mi afición,/ Que no hay rica posesión / Que se compare con ella" [It is a fortunate and beautiful land, but so much greater is my affection that there is nothing so rich that can compare with it] (358).[3] Values from the pastoral tradition are attributed to Dulcanquellín: a genteel eloquence, a pride in his country, and respect for wishes of the object of amorous affection.[4] Tacuana's husband, Tapirazu, is every inch the wronged, yet honorable, Spanish nobleman. Valiant, noble, and dedicated to Tacuana, he risks his life by entering Dulcanquellín's court alone, where, ignoring the advice of his frightened warriors, he challenges Dulcanquellín to duel.

The Native American characters in the play are motivated by the classic emotions of the Spanish and European stage. Even the moment that the *indios* are most opposed to the Spanish, their violent rebellion near the end of the play, has its roots in a stereotypically Spanish situation: jealousy and rage over deception by a rival suitor. Dulcanquellín and Tapirazu join forces to seek revenge for what they perceive as chicanery by one of the Spanish colonists, Terrazas, with whom Tacuana has an amorous relationship. These actions construct the *indio* male as a familiar character, one Lope's audience would respect, even admire.

Even in a *comedia* other generic conventions can be influential. The emphasis in *El nuevo mundo* on Christian faith, allegorical character, and miracle echoes the conservative religious form of the *auto sacramental*. Walter Cohen's argument that the secular *comedia* is a national form, containing the (potentially) conflictive voices of different social groups and classes doesn't apply to the *auto*, as he recognizes (379). A vehicle for the teaching of Christian doctrine, the *auto* is thus more monological, less conflictive, than the *comedia*. The situation of the pagan Native American in *El nuevo mundo* can be compared to that of the unconverted Jew in Lope's *El niño inocente*, a *comedia* also thought to be influenced by the *auto sacramental*. Catherine Swietlicki argues against a straightforward reading of that play as anti-Semitic since she believes Lope "authentically" re-creates the language of the Jewish Other. Nonetheless, according to Swietlicki, there is no question that "Within the metatheatrical *auto* the Jew's words are dominated by the monolithic Christian view . . ." (219). Like the *comedia* the *auto* "de-exoticizes," accommodating difference to preexistent patterns. In terms of the *auto*, the Native American is in a well-known category, "non-believer." The intention to convert the non-believer is a conventional generator of plot, and the conversion to Christianity of the Native Americans is a driving mechanism of *El nuevo mundo*.

MOOR AND INDIAN

The making of the Native American subjects in *El nuevo mundo* draws in part on the stereotypical presentation of another "non-believer" and a common figure in Spanish writing, the Moor. In a discussion of the image of the Moor in sixteenth-century Spanish literature, Israel Burshatin observes that

> depictions fall between two extremes. On the "vilifying" side, Moors are hateful dogs, miserly, treacherous, lazy and overreaching. On the "idealizing" side, the men are noble, loyal, heroic, courtly—they even mirror the virtues that Christian knights aspire to—while the women are endowed with singular beauty and discretion. (117)

The duality evident in the treatment of the Moor is also present in the description of the Indians met by Columbus. We have already seen *indios* as "Christian noblemen" within the *comedia*, yet certain aspects of the "vilifying" extreme can also be found in *El nuevo mundo*. Though the Native Americans are never referred to as dogs, they are called "animales rudos" [rude animals] by Friar Buyle when he first sees them looking at the enormous cross the Spaniards erect (366), and referred to as "barbaros bueyes" [barbarous cattle] by the Spaniard Terrazas (369). Nevertheless, the Indians are never presented as "miserly," "overreaching," or particularly "lazy." Although they are seen as "treacherous" in their rebellion at the end of the play, they are also clearly shown to be reacting to a deception practiced by the Spaniards left behind by Columbus when he returns to Spain.

One reason that *El nuevo mundo* itself is such a fascinating textual fragment in the genealogy of Spanish perceptions of the Other is that in one text it juxtaposes scenes with the "traditional Other," the Moorish enemies, and scenes with the "new Other," Native American colonial subjects. The coincidence in 1492 of the expulsion of the Moors from the peninsula and the discovery of the New World links Moor and *indio* together in Spanish national history and consciousness, a point underscored by the presence of Moors in a play about Columbus. Moreover, the well-established traditions of Christian Spain's struggle against the Moors were carried over to the campaigns in the Americas. Criticizing Todorov for failing to consider the influence of Spanish history on contemporary Renaissance views of Native Americans, Roberto González-Echevarría points out that

> the Spaniards had "prepared" themselves for this complex military, political, and social event [the American conquest] in the wars of reconquest against the Arabs. These wars, which lasted for eight centuries and culminated when the Catholic kings took Granada in 1492, had been very much like the campaigns Cortéz waged against Montezuma. . . . The kind of holy war the Spaniards waged against the Indians was a reflection of the holy war the Arabs led against the Spaniards, with Santiago as the counterpart of Mohammed. The polemics of how to treat a different culture that had been defeated did not begin with Montesino's sermon but in recently conquered Granada . . . (285).

The relevance of the experience with the Moors to the conquest, administration, and imaginative projection of Spanish relations with the New World cannot be overemphasized. Edward Said's classic study *Orientalism*, delineating the complex interpenetration of knowledge and practices of colonial domination in European imperialism, does not treat Spain, yet European imagination and domination of others also has deep roots in the history of Spanish/Arab conflict as well as in the Spanish empire.[5]

In *El nuevo mundo* itself, two key aspects of Lope's intriguing portrayal are common to both the Moors and the *indios*: 1) an immoral sensuality, which among the Moors is decadence and among the Indians licentiousness, and 2) a weakness of military tactics: the Moors and the Native Americans are passive until the time for effective action has passed. In the scenes of the Moorish court in the Alhambra, the king of Granada is more interested in amorous dalliance with his courtesan than in preparing for battle against the Spaniards. Both Moorish and Indian women are portrayed as sensuously motivated, full of "el fuego de amor." When it comes to serious conflict, both Indians and Moors are passive until it is too late. The Moors surrender without a fight, and the Indians finally revolt only to give in quickly when the miraculous rising up of a cross convinces them of the truth of

Christianity. Both of these traits, passivity and sensuousness, can be linked not only to racist stereotypes of the Moor but to a feminizing of the Other.

CLASS, LITERACY, AND DOMINATION

Spanish class distinctions are part of Lope's making of the internal order of Native American society in *El nuevo mundo*. The aristocratic class of Dulcanquellín, Tapirazu, and Tacuana is differentiated from that of Palca, Aute, and the "common people." Dulcanquellín explains to the Spaniard Terrazas that even though he himself may be able to understand and even follow the new religion, the masses cannot be expected to go along or even be reasonable: "Que no hay cosa más fiera é indomable / Que el común apellido y voz del vulgo" [There is nothing more fiery and indomitable than the common people and the will of the vulgar] (375). This attitude toward the "masses" was probably familiar to the Spanish audience, although the potential for revolt it implies is distanced by placing it in the mouth of an *indio*. Nonetheless, one effect of casting established class differences into the New World is that these differences are shown to be universalized, and, hence, class differences are naturalized for the peninsular audience.

Class distinctions are transferred to the relationship between Spaniard and *indio* in part through European attitudes toward literacy. There are two "comic" scenes in the Third Act, where Aute, an untrustworthy *indio* commoner, is portrayed as baffled and frightened by the power of writing. Put to work delivering messages for the newly established Spanish settlements, Aute is discovered to have eaten oranges entrusted to him. Aute believes the message paper he was carrying "watched" him and spoke to the friar, revealing his theft. Later, while stealing olives, Aute hides the accompanying written message in a tree so it will not "see" what he does and find him out again. As in Shakespeare's *Romeo and Juliet*, in which Romeo and Mercutio taunt Capulet's illiterate servant, the scene achieves a comic effect by playing on the "lower-class" person's lack of education and ignorance of the written word. In the nascent colonial economy pictured in *El nuevo mundo*, literacy is a powerful weapon of class reproduction and social control. The *indio* is foolish, untrustworthy, a danger to the goods of the European, and needful of a proper education.

At stake in these "speaking paper" or "talking book"[6] scenes is the issue of power arrogated through the ability to write, to dominate a social and a commercial interaction. The indigenous people are portrayed as unable to comprehend an impersonal system; the *indio* needs the Spaniard (as the peasant needs the aristocrat) to bring about "rational" exchange. While the Native American's illiteracy, like that of the Spanish peasant, is taken by the colonizer as an indication of dollardness, the Native Americans' oral culture was, of course, part of a well-defined, highly complex system of signs.[7] European literacy was already part of a prejudicial system and the institutions of literacy facilitated the colonial undertaking in tandem with the missionary project of Christianizing the Indians:

> The Conquest of America was carried out by the first modern state and with the aid of the printing press. Spain's monarchy was a patrimonial bureaucracy that sought to regulate all transactions of power through writing, a symbolic code that replaced the more direct communication of serfs with their lords. A maze of writing mediated the individual and the state, and it was only through writing that the individual attained legitimacy. (González-Echevarría, 289)

René Jara and Nicholas Spadaccini assert that "the domination of the New World was ultimately achieved through writing, which was the primary vehicle for the establishment, rationalization, and control of the overseas institutions of the Empire" (10). The connection between language and imperial domination was already recognized at that time. Antonio de Nebrija, in that same year of 1492, asserted in his dedication to Queen Isabella of the first grammar of a modern European tongue: "Your Majesty, language is the perfect instrument of empire."[8] Armstrong notes that "Castilians claimed that their language would be the successor of the three holy languages, to express the heroic deeds of their kings and their world mission, with barbarians subdued by Isabella learning Castilian just as the Spaniards' barbarian forebears had learned Latin" (266). The privileging of literacy in European society is linked then to advancing capitalism, the development of imperial administration, and the rise of the nation-state.

The *requerimiento* is the prototypical example of *text* justifying conquest. Informing the Indians that their lands were entrusted by Christ to the pope and through him to the kings of Spain, the document offers freedom from slavery for those Indians who accept Spanish rule. Even though it was entirely incomprehensible to a non-Spanish speaker, reading the document aloud to the natives provided sufficient justification for dispossession of land and immediate enslavement of the indigenous people. Las Casas' famous comment on the *requerimiento* was that one does not know "whether to laugh or cry at the absurdity of it" (Todorov, 149). While it may be absurd, the *requerimiento* provides documentary evidence of the simultaneous "recognition and disavowal of racial/cultural/historical differences" that are the basis of colonialist discourse. Indians are different from Spaniards in that they are subjected to the reading of the text; they are presented with a "choice" between slavery and obedience not forced on Spaniards. Yet Indians are assumed to be enough like Spaniards that they can understand the *requerimiento*'s conditions. Thus the text incorporates Native Americans and Spaniards into the same discursive space, "offering" the former the same "choice" as their Spanish counterparts, albeit one couched entirely in a Spanish vocabulary. As Todorov puts it, "it is the Spaniards who determine the rules of the game" (148). The *requerimiento*, although appearing to respect Native American "rights," in fact takes them away. We can see, perhaps more clearly than Lope or his audience, that Aute's sense that the paper has betrayed him is not farcical after all.

"UNDERSTANDING," "SYMPATHY," AND "RESPECT"

Analysis of the belief system and conversion of Lope's *indios* is relevant to an examination of the principal ideological justification for Spanish colonialism, the spread of Catholic Christianity. In *El nuevo mundo*, Lope rejects Columbus' belief that Native Americans have "no religion" and embraces the view that the Christian devil is, in reality, the Indian's God. Thus, even while being "idolatry," Native American religion is actually part of Christianity. The representation of Native Americans as having a "religion" and the representation of that religion as being within the framework of Catholicism establishes a mutual space, creating an important point of similarity between *indio* and Spaniard and making possible what appears to be understanding, sympathy, and respect.

Constructed Native American idolatry is never scathing nor are Indian beliefs ever presented as profoundly strange or foreign. Despite Menéndez y Pelayo's comment (1900) that Lope's portrayal of the Indians "sirven para el contraste entre vida salvaje y la de los aventureros de Europa" [provides a contrast between the savage life and that of the European adventurers] (104), what is most remarkable about Indian religion is its comprehensibility. A conversation that takes place between Dulcanquellín and his god, Ongol, in the pagan temple is reminiscent of a previous conversation of Columbus and the allegorical figures of Idolatry and the Devil that took place in Spain. The customs of Lope's *indios* are not abhorrent to Spaniards. In the Indian worship of Ongol, there are no evil rites, no unspeakable Conradian atrocities, not even the infamous human sacrifice. Although there is cannibalism, it is not associated with Native American religion, nor is it emphasized in the play. Indeed, when Dulcanquellín orders four fat servants cooked to feed the Spanish, the overriding effect is comic, and cultural difference is made a point of light humor.[9]

El nuevo mundo suggests that the *indios* need not so much end pagan practices as merely convert the object of these practices from the Christian devil to the Christian god. Until the climactic scene, the Native Americans are portrayed as "confused." When Dulcanquellín asks Terrazas for an explanation of how it could be that the Caribbean Indian god and "idols" were "thrown out of heaven" by the Spanish god, he receives a lengthy, detailed history of the Christian faith. Dulcanquellín's response elicits sympathy.

Muy largo y intricado y muy difícil
Todo eso me parece; venga el padre
Y trataremos con espacio deso;
Que pues el oro dí, de que habéis hecho
Lo que cáliz llamáis y otras vasijas,
No niego que le soy aficionado . . .

All this seems to me very long and complicated, but the father is coming and we can consider the matter at greater length. Since I have given the gold for what you call your chalice and other vessels I do not deny that I am a lover of your faith . . . (376)

Menéndez y Pelayo, in his introduction to the play, claims Lope would not have read Las Casas, but it is clear that Lope is familiar with the argument that the Indian's spiritual equality requires a more sympathetic conversion than that of the sword and/or the *requerimiento*. Moreover, the Las Casas stance is clearly articulated in the play in a way that appears to be respectful of Indian culture and history while offering the *option* of Christianity. Dulcanquellín, the Indian king, suggests to Columbus' brother that a peaceful promulgation of religion would be the most successful way to win over his people.

Bartolomé, yo creo lo que dices,
Temo tu Dios, y tus razones temo;
Pero esta ley y fe que profesamos,
Como la recibimos, la tenemos.
Nuestros padres, que aquí nos la enseñaron,
Ya de nuestros abuelos la aprendieron . . .
Deja que oigan esa misa, y deja
Que a tu Cristo y sus leyes aficionen . . .
Que de ellos mismos naciera sin duda
Dar por el suelo con los mismos ídolos,
En triunfo y gloria de ese Dios tan alto,
Tan podoroso y fuerte.

Bartolome, I believe what you say; I fear your god and your argument, but this law and this faith my people profess as we received it. Our parents taught it to us and learned it from their grandparents before them. . . . Let the people hear your mass and allow them to love your Christ and his laws . . . so that casting their idols to the ground will come of themselves, and will be to the triumph and glory of your God so high, so powerful, and strong. (375)

While the Las Casas position for the spiritual equality of Indian and Spaniard raises questions about methods of conversion, it does not jeopardize the imperative to convert Native Americans, instruct them in Spanish, and administer them under Spanish law. The development of understanding, sympathy, and respect for the Native Americans in the play is based in large part on their constructed familiarity, the "disavowal of their racial/cultural/historical difference." The limitation of likeness, its implication in the project of colonialism despite its *apparent* subversiveness, is fully evident in the climactic end of *El nuevo mundo*. Despite the persuasive articulateness of Dulcanquellín's address to Bartolomé, the movement of the drama undermines tolerance and supports the position of those who like Ginés de Sepúlveda argued for a holy war against the *indios*.

LIKENESS AND CONTROL

A value system that subordinates all else to the saving of souls is established early in the play during the allegorical tribunal, with its echoes of Inquisition logic. The allegorical character Idolatry who tempts Columbus in the first part of the play seeks to maintain her preexisting claim to the "new" land Columbus intends to "discover" and tries to argue that the Spanish, for all their talk about religious motives are, in fact, only interested in material gain. Idolatry claims that "So color de religión,/ Van a buscar plata y oro" [Under the pretext of religion, they seek silver and gold] (351).[10] But this powerful criticism of the conquest, a critique sustained in the play by the actions of the Spanish sailors and in the court of world opinion by the *leyenda negra*, is contained and controlled by being placed in the mouth of Idolatry. Religion can reject the claims of Idolatry because, "Quien posee con mala fe,/ En ningún tiempo prescribe" [He who possesses with bad faith never prescribes] (351). Religion's argument establishes the basic moral grounds for the rejection of claims made against the Spaniards.

Because both Indian and Spaniard are in peril when confronted by the absolute demands of the true faith, likeness to the Spaniard ceases to work in the Indian's interest. Likeness between *indio* and Spaniard is subversive only insofar as Spanish custom extends protection or rights to the Spanish citizen. Likeness is thus "double-edged," as is manifest in the ending of the play, where it turns on the idea that both Spaniard and Native American possess a "will," in the Christian sense of the term. In the last act, the corruption of the Spanish sailors and the ability of the devil to point this corruption out to Dulcanquellín lead the Indians to what appears to be a rational plan, to rebel against the Spanish and tear down their cross. Yet after being assaulted, in a startling *deus ex machina*, the cross miraculously rises up, and the Indians cease their resistance, proclaiming the truth of Christianity. Dulcanquellín and the *indios* are won over by a dramatic, unexpected miracle, and it is Dulcanquellín, the Native American king and earlier exponent of Las Casas' philosophy, who makes the strongest assertion that any pretense of peaceful, rational conversion is no longer necessary. As a new convert Dulcanquellín declares "Sin duda que es verdadera / La cristiana religión; / Quien dijere que no, muera" [Without doubt, the Christian religion is true; whoever should say "no," let him die] (378). Conversion by miracle moots equality of intellect,

4 The French raise the Christian cross establishing their colony at Maragnan while Tupinambá are depicted as looking on in adoration. (Engraving by L. Gaultier in Claude's *Maragnan*, 1614)

"natural rights," and/or military strength, and *El nuevo mundo* underwrites a providential view of history.

By Inquisition logic, there are no limits on the possessor of the true faith who seeks to reproduce this faith in others. The contradiction between the spiritual equality of the Indians and their subjugation is resolved: their "spiritual equality" is ordained by the Spanish who superimpose their own religious system on the indigenous American. Thus the *deus ex machina* ending, with its echoes of the *auto sacramental*, seals identity between Spaniard and *indio*, between colonizer and colonized. The irrelevance of rationality to a miraculous conversion of the will for both *indio* and Spaniard marks their most essential equality. Ironically, equality itself, the basis for the religious mission, is part of the program of subjugation. Thus, the consequences of making the colonized subject within one's own religious space are devastating to claims against empire. Since the Indian religion is only a reflection of Spanish Catholicism, moral arguments made by the colonized are engulfed by the totalizing framework of the universal faith.[11]

Denying the claims of the colonized subject not only offers a powerful ideological weapon against subversion by contact with otherness but against subversion from "within." It protects against *self-awareness*. For instance, class distinctions are explained by the Indian king, thus diffusing the insulting or subversive effect of such a comment in the mouth of a Spaniard. In the context of early-seventeenth-century Spain, the ideological threat is not the voice of any Native American but the questions raised by Spaniards like Las Casas, who interrogate and attempt to "demystify" the official justification of the colonial mission. The Las Casas position can be clearly and sympathetically articulated in a *comedia* with Native American characters but is nevertheless confined and mastered.

The same play that portrays the Indians as intelligent, with souls worth saving, with traits and customs more like than different from the Spanish, justifies even the most extreme excesses of colonial conquest, as Dulcanquellín pronounces, *quien dijere que no, muera* [whoever should say "no," let him die]. The threat of violence is foreshadowed in the second act when the Indians bow down before the same cross on hearing Spanish gunfire. Since the conversion of the will of the *indio* is so complete that the Native American becomes the spokesperson for the slaughter of non-believers, the crime of the Spanish conquest is thus projected onto its victims. Resistance is reason enough for further victimization. The dramatic structure of the play provides an emotional justification to Lope's audience for accepting Dulcanquellín's conclusion. Whereas up until almost the end violence against the natives would have been unthinkable, the insurrection that culminates in the deadly attack on the Spaniards makes retribution on violent and dangerous pagans seem warranted, not only to Dulcanquellín but to the audience.

The rising up of the cross in the last act establishes for Lope's Native Americans their own sense of guilt for resisting the Spanish and their own recognition of the need for continued subservience to the Spaniard. The *indios* speak as a chorus with one voice, "(Tacuana) Desde hoy comienzo á temblallos. / (Tapirazú) Hoy palo el cetro has de ser / Del Rey de aquestos vasallos, / Danos otra vez perdón" [(Tacuana) From today I begin to tremble. (Tapirazú) Today, pole of wood, you have become the scepter of the King of these vassals. Again, forgive us] (378). The constructed colonial subject asks for forgiveness, accepting guilt in the crucifixion and submitting to the authority of Christ as well as the Spanish king. Individual guilt is connected to the necessity for a hierarchical authority. The reaction to the miracle of the cross posits *a desire to be colonized* in the mind of the Native American. The colonizer's desire to colonize perceives its mate, and the Other is constituted as the projection and reflection of that desire. The powerful sexual language associated with the rising up of the cross/pole/scepter is a striking overlay of religious, patriarchal, feudal, and nationalistic images. Various European discourses of power are brought together to construct the colonized subject's identity, and the represented Native American colonial male subject himself pronounces his inferior, submissive position as penitent, vassal, subject, and "female" within in the language system of the conqueror.

FEMALE DESIRE

Like the photo of the African saluting the French flag, analyzed by Barthes in "Mythologies" (99), the story of Malinche is detached from historical events, from the "signified" and becomes a symbol, a "sign," that can be manipulated by colonizing discourse without pointing to itself as transported or reinvented. A Nahuatl (Aztec) speaker sold as a slave to the Mayas, Malinche, also known as "Malintzin" to the Indians and "Doña Marina" to the Spanish, was given to Cortez and became his translator, mistress, and tactical advisor. Generalized as the representative figure of Native American women under colonialism, the legend of her desire for the European colonizer becomes "natural, eternally true" for women of disparate cultures and historical situations, and what is achieved is what Barthes calls "the elimination" of "the contingent, historical, in one word: fabricated, quality of colonialism" (131).[12]

Demythologizing Malinche has been an important undertaking in the critique of colonial discourse. Mexicans have generally considered Malinche an emblem of the betrayal of indigenous values. Octavio Paz, for example, sees Malinche as representative of the violated and seduced mother of the Mexican national personality. As symbol of the secret conflict of Mexico's past, Paz believes she poses a critical dilemma: she must be, and at the same time cannot be, repudiated (78-9). Todorov makes a rather Eurocentric reading of Malinche by downplaying her role as traitor and celebrating her as "the first example, and thereby the symbol, of the cross-breeding of cultures" (101). Norma Alarcón believes that Paz and others treat Malinche only at the level of the figurative, as a sort of colonizing of female experience by a male discourse. Alarcón argues that the symbolic system that appropriates Malinche must be ruptured by considering the emotional suffering of an historically specific real-life woman (183). Such an approach emphasizes both Malinche as Native American threatened by Spanish colonialism *and* as woman living under indigenous patriarchy. Alarcón's position underscores the heterogeneity of indigenous peoples; at the very least, for instance, we ought to attempt to differentiate the culture of the various Caribbean Islanders Columbus meets from the assorted continental peoples encountered by Cortez. Her attention to the specificity of Malinche's experience urges us to rethink and attempt to contextualize the stories about Indian women told by Columbus and the many European male colonizers who followed him.

In *El nuevo mundo*, we see again that Lope's enormous sensitivity to the currents of his time is evident in his use of the Malinche story, a story which has become by this period what Roland Barthes calls "mythical speech." Although strictly anachronistic to a play about Columbus, Malinche is, nevertheless, the generative model for the development of the three *india* characters met by Columbus and his men in *El nuevo mundo*—Tecue, Palca, and Tacuana.[13] The women in Lope's play reenact the Malinche story but are given other names, and the play incorporates and modifies the Malinche model, projecting it

5 Vespucci awakens an Amerindian and gives her the name of America. (*L'Amérique historique*, Theodor Galle, 1638. After Jan Van der Straet, 1521).

backwards in time to the very earliest encounter of Spaniards and Native Americans and reproducing it as testimony from the mouth of the depicted indigenous female subject.

Throughout the play the *indias* act as mediators between the Spanish conquistadors and Native American males. Tecue is the first to report on seeing the disembarked Spaniards. Palca is the first to meet them and describe the "innocence" of Spanish intentions; her attraction to their bells and mirrors accommodates Dulcanquellín and his court to the Spanish arrival. Palca readily consorts with a Spaniard, Arana.

While each of the minor Indian female characters resembles Malinche, Lope borrows most directly from the Malinche story for the portrayal of Tacuana, the principal *india* character. Like Malinche, Tacuana has been taken from her family by a rival tribe, turns to the Spanish because of divisions among the Native Americans, gives up her *indio* husband in order to become a mistress to a conquistador, and, finally, leaves her own people to join the camp of the invaders. The colonial female in *El nuevo mundo* is represented as unambiguously desiring the Spanish conquistador and Spanish colonialism. Tacuana makes an elaborate speech of welcome to the Spanish soldiers, inviting them to spread their religion from "Haiti to Chile" and requesting them to bring their sons to the "New World" so that they can ". . . casar / Con nuestras hijas, adonde, / Mezclándose nuestra sangre, / Seamos todos españoles" [. . . marry with our daughters, and mix their blood with ours that we may all become Spanish] (371). In this passage nationality is a matter of blood, of race. Spanish blood doesn't mix; it transforms, and the indigenous woman is a willing vessel for the metastasis of racial, cultural, and national identity.

Tacuana's sexual desire is not portrayed as carefree, natural, or unreflective along the lines of Rousseau's noble savage. Nor is it a humble submission before the God-like power of a conquering hero. Instead—and this is what makes it all the more persuasive as justification for Spanish treatment of indigenous women—Tacuana's effort to become Rodrigues' mistress involves a careful ratiocination and an awareness of the appearance of propriety:

Basta, que aqueste español
No es Dios, pues que no conoce
El pensamiento que traigo,
Perdida por sus amores;
Que con aquesta invención

Fingiendo tales razones;
Vengo á sus brazos rendida
Porque así me lleve y robe.
Él piensa que me hace fuerza,
Y amor sin fuerza me pone
Donde descanse mi pena
Que tanto peligro corre.

This Spaniard is not God and does not know what I am thinking: that even with this invented story I am telling (about needing help to escape Dulcanquellín) I am helpless not to love him. I will go to his arms submissively, because if I do so he will do as I wish: abduct me and carry me off. He thinks he will have to use force on me, but I will give my love without being forced. Then I will be able to tell him of the trouble and dangers I risk. (371-2)

The Malinche model depends on the notion of *intelligent* submission: knowing full well who the Spanish are and what they desire, the *india* allies herself with the conquerors, opening soul, heart, and body to their designs. The portrayal of a willed submission of the body by the indigenous female supports the usurpation of the bodies of indigenous men and women into slavery and forced labor in the Spanish New World empire. Tacuana's sexual desire for the Spanish colonizer is linked to Dulcanquellín's desire for Christianity, both legitimate colonial authority. Yet Spanish attitudes toward women express themselves in the differences between Dulcanquellín and Tacuana. The woman's desire is portrayed as guided by her intellect but ruled by her body. As a woman she does not occupy a public political space as do the males. [14] Because she belongs less to the Indian culture and more to her private libido, her desire is traitorous to the colonized nation.

NATIONAL IDENTITY

El nuevo mundo descubierto por Cristóbal Colón celebrates a saintly national hero.[15] Absolutely confident of the existence of the Indies he is driven by divine inspiration. The play follows the early chroniclers, Oviedo and Gómara, and the opinion of Las Casas that "infinitely more than gold, the spread of Christianity is Columbus' heart's desire" (Todorov 10). A comparison with Phaeton, Apollo's overreaching son, by one of Columbus' potential patrons is proved false in the play:

throughout Columbus is upright, confident, and faithful. The carefully made figure of Columbus is metonymic for both the Spanish state and religion, and it is King Ferdinand himself who proclaims that Columbus was predestined by his name, "*Crist*óbal" (378). Spanish national identity is *embodied* in this male hero whose nobility, confidence, and discovery and conquest of the "New World" enact the truth of Christian religion and fulfill national destiny.

El nuevo mundo also provides evidence for Armstrong's argument that religious institution and belief is closely connected to the rise of national identity. According to Menéndez y Pelayo, throughout the diversity of settings and the telescoping of historical events in *El nuevo mundo* there is a "unidad de la grande empresa, interpretada con un sentído religioso y patriótico innegable" [unity of the great enterprise, interpreted with an undeniably religious and patriotic sense] (105). Although Columbus appeals to both the Portuguese and the English monarchies' desire for material gain, Ferdinand and Isabella are appealed to on a specifically religious basis. The Spanish rulers are not only more moral than their European counterparts; their support of Columbus is motivated by divine will.

Pues condoliéndose Cristo
De que entre vosotros reine,
Que le contasteis su sangre
En la cruz, muerta la muerte,
Al rey Fernando de España,
Cristianísimo y prudente,
Manda a Colón envie
Éste que a su fe os convierte.

Then Christ sympathizing with you since he (the devil) ruled among you—Christ who shed his blood on the cross, so that death would die— [inspired] the wise and very Christian Spanish King Ferdinand to send Columbus so that you could be converted to his faith. (376)

The linkages between religious community and nation-state allow the carryover of self-justifying ideology, and the same ideological system that ensures the divine right of kings also protects the colonial enterprise. This is not surprising since in European history nationalism arises simultaneously with imperialism. Justifications of power that flow from religious community to nation and empire can also work in reverse. While a religious nationalism insulates colonialism, colonial domination develops and satisfies national pride. Moreover, the state itself owes some of its ideological and institutional force to the particular history of the colonial relationship. In discussing the development of nationalism, Timothy Brennan argues that

> the markets made possible by European imperial penetration motivated the construction of the nation state at home. European nationalism itself was motivated by what Europe was doing in its far flung dominions. The "national idea," in other words, flourished in the soil of foreign conquest. Imperial conquest created the conditions for the fall of Europe's universal Christian community, but resupplied Europe with a religious sense of mission and self-identity. (1989, 59)

Written at the juncture of imperial power and the coalescing of the modern nation-state, *El nuevo mundo* is an instance of proto-nationalist discourse. In retelling a hundred-year-old story of colonial encounter and Spanish accomplishment, the play unifies present and past in a Christian and national view of history, fashioning Spanish national identity on the world stage.

In *El nuevo mundo*, there are also hints of the development of colonized nations based on European principles. In a fascinating moment a Spaniard advises the Indian ruler on how to govern his own people. When Dulcanquellín prepares to leave to find Tacuana rather than attend Catholic mass, Terrazas tells him: "Allá, en España, decimos / Que son los reyes espejo / Donde se mira el consejo / Que los vasallos seguimos." [There, in Spain, we say that the kings are the mirror reflecting the standard of conduct that we vassals follow] (374). The self-fashioning of the Spanish king in the "mirror" of public opinion is a self-conscious strategy of absolutist politics, something we associate with Charles V (or Louis XIV). Yet Terrazas' expression is double edged, risking subversion in the same way that Machiavelli's *The Prince* does so: the open expression of the modeling of power tends to de-naturalize it.[16] In *El nuevo mundo* the glorified, self-conscious conduct of the king is taught to the would-be colonized ruler, and the nation-state begins its march toward its identification with universal values. Tracing the founding moments of a colonized national identity back to the time of Columbus shows a transposition of European national models, a "marking out of a 'subject nation,'" and it prefigures the difficulties encountered by the anticolonial nationalisms that arise hundreds of years later. In the disappointing postcolonial experience of many "third-world" nations is evident the tainted history of adopted nationalism. The construction of "nationalities" as natural and eternal markers of difference serves the interests of elites in the margins as well as in the center. Yet, progressive possibilities are evident, too, in the interrogation of nationalist structures of identity that cross over and back between colonizer and colonized, between metropole and periphery. Identifying the *indio* through Iberian ethnic, class, and gender differences distills an ever more purified Spanish subjectivity. The analysis of the carefully made colonial subject in *El nuevo mundo*, its breakdown into constituent parts, reveals not so much the eternal nature of Otherness but the conflictive heterogeneity of the constructed and hegemonic Spanish national "Self."

CHAPTER 3

Imagi/Native Nation
The Tempest and the Modernization of Political Authority

Prospero invaded the islands, killed our ancestors, enslaved Caliban, and taught him his language to make himself understood.... I know of no other metaphor more expressive of our cultural situation, of our reality.

Roberto Fernández Retamar

Power is mobilized; it makes itself everywhere present and visible; it invents new mechanisms; it separates, it immobilizes, it partitions; it constructs for a time what is both a counter-city and the perfect society; it imposes an ideal functioning.

Michel Foucault

I am Richard II, know ye not that?

Queen Elizabeth I[1]

As Lope's Spain was celebrating a providential century of world dominion, Shakespeare's England was only embarking on empire. During most of the sixteenth century, England's position was more defensive than offensive. Having lost its French lands and seen its allies in Burgundy and Brittany annexed to the French crown, England found itself the lesser of the great western European powers, with Spain and France clearly predominant and with Scotland and Ireland dangerously close by. Manipulation of the French/Hapsburg rivalry was necessary to ensure English safety and interests. Moreover Tudor title and succession were uncertain, and factions and domestic division occurred. Yet by the end of the sixteenth and the beginning of the seventeenth century many of these factors began to change. Reformation set the stage for the assertion of English nationhood. Social prestige was found under the king; Parliament tended to serve his interests and the suppression of local authorities fostered royal allegiance. There was the growing strength and ability of the Tudor navy including the 1588 victory and the exploits of Drake and his imitators. English sea power led to increasing possibilities for the development of an offensive position. In the expansion of sea power England began the transition from defensive monarchy to church-sanctioned imperial nationhood.

Though in his history plays Shakespeare attempts to narrate a common English national past, it is in the utopian projection of his magnificent New World romance, *The Tempest*, that we find best illuminated the relations of power and subjectivity through which modern nationhood emerges. His ostensible Italian background and banishment not withstanding, Prospero can be seen as a figure of English nationalism—much as Columbus represents Spanish nationalism in Lope's *El nuevo mundo*. While the colonial context is central to both works, the god-directed view of history that justifies authority in the Spanish play gives way in the English drama to Renaissance science, learning, and magic. As Foucault suggests about the development of seventeenth-century state power, Prospero "invents new mechanisms" and "constructs for a time what is both a counter-city and the perfect society." While the incompleteness of English absolutism remains evident in the play, the absolutist desires of the royal imaginary may be more fully realized in the work precisely because of its fictive, fantastical, and otherworldly realm. In a darker vision than Sir Thomas More's *Utopia* (based on reports from the Vespucci expeditions), *The Tempest* provides a New World enactment of the possibilities of European social and political organization.

THE TEMPEST AND THE VIRGINIA COLONY

The numerous links between the *The Tempest* and the first English efforts to colonize the Americas open into broader and more fundamental connections between the work and the contemporary European discourse of empire and nation. Performed in 1611, the play follows closely on the heels of the earliest English settlement in Virginia. Although there had been active English exploration during previous decades, the Virginia company was formed in 1606, and fleets to America were dispatched in 1607 and 1609. Shakespeare was personally associated with several members of the Company, dedicating poetry to two of them, Southampton and Pembroke. A letter by the colonist William Strachey records a hurricane, the landing of the Virginia governor's ship (the *Sea Adventure*) on Bermuda, the wintering over of the passengers on the island, and the settlers' rebellion and is considered a source for *The Tempest*. Other Virginia Company pamphlets have also been associated with *The Tempest*.[2] In the play itself there are numerous allusions to the New World. Ariel refers to "the still-vexed Bermudas" (I, ii, 229). The name of the god worshiped by Caliban is "Setebos," a name that appears in accounts of Magellan's voyages to South America and that is reiterated by Francis Fletcher's account of Sir Francis Drake's voyages.[3] Caliban is called a "Man of Ind" and is compared to Indians "displayed" in London. The speech made by Gonzalo about an island utopia borrows directly from the 1603 English translation of Montaigne's essay about New World peoples, "Of Cannibals." Gonzalo uses the word "plantation" (II, i, 141)—the only time the word appears in Shakespeare—a word that meant, according to the *OED*, "the planting of a colony, colonization," and a word that was current in the discussion of the Virginia settlements.

The derivation of the word "cannibal," its tie to Shakespeare's Caliban, and the ongoing relevance of the Caliban character to English interpretations of its colonized subjects are laced together.[4] Until the sixteenth century, the word for a person who ate the flesh of another is "anthropophagi," a term used by the Greeks to refer to a nation presumed to live beyond the Black Sea. It was on Christopher Columbus' first voyage that the word "cannibal" (or *canibale*) comes into being. While looking for *El gran can* Columbus hears (or imagines he hears) the name "canibale" used by the Arawaks to describe another tribe, the Caribs.[5] Columbus himself refuses to believe the Arawak report that the Caribs eat their enemies. Indeed, the word "cannibal" does not take on a separate meaning in English from "Caribbean islander" until 1796. Thus when Shakespeare derives "Caliban," "cannibal" still refers to a member of the Carib tribe, a tribe reputed to eat human flesh.[6] Since there is no suggestion in the play that Caliban eats human flesh, Caliban's anagramatic name defines him not as *anthropophagi* but, like Dulcanquellín, as the European imaginary of a Caribbean inhabitant.

Unlike the specific verbal references to the New World and texts such as Strachey's letter and Montaigne's essay, the associations with Caliban's name are more "speculative." While it is true that other characters in the play have suggestive names (Miranda, "wonder," and, of course, Prospero), "Caliban" provides not only a locating of the New World inhabitant but, simultaneously and paradoxically as anagram, a scrambling, a *dis*locating. The dislocating of Caliban connects him to a host of other discourses, about European wildmen, about classical beast/humans, about monsters, about Africans, even about the Irish.[7]

As with Lope, Shakespeare's rich absorption of the social universe in which he lived takes the connection between the play and the New World past the merely referential. The very language and imagery of *The Tempest* is tied to the way in which English and New World identities are constructed. John Gillies argues that the play's imagery of temperance and reproductive fruitfulness expresses the English vision of colonization. Gillies shows that the wedding masque staged by Prospero draws on the same language as did settlers' accounts of the relationship between the new English colonials and the fertile discovered land. Thus the emphasis on marriage in the play not only correlates with the play's performance at the wedding of Princess Elizabeth to the Elector Palatine but with the larger metaphor of a marriage between the "virgin" land of Virginia and the masculine English plantation project. The play's view of a nature that is both verdant and wild, parallels reports from the New World, and in this way the beauty and temperance of the land becomes a justification for controlling it, for taking it away from unruly savages. Gillies states that

This use of the temperance *topos* heralds a radical shift in colonial policy. The intemperate Indians ("unnaturall Naturalls") had forfeited their birthright to the temperate land, and were about to be given a dose of their own distemper. (700)

By their supposed savagery the natives lose their claim on the lush, feminized landscape. In the metaphor of marriage between American land and English rule, the native American is a rival suitor debased by his supposed lack of civilization. In *The Tempest*, this discourse has its specific embodiment in Prospero's efforts to protect Miranda from Caliban in order to preserve her virginity for Ferdinand.

NATIVE HOSPITALITY

The role of threatening savage is only one of the guises in which Caliban has appeared. The performance history and interpretation of the play have undergone significant changes, and the Caliban character has served as a screen for the representation of the changing fortunes of the wildman, the savage, the missing link, the rebellious native and the heroic anticolonial freedom fighter (see Cartelli, Griffiths, Nixon, Vaughan, and Vaughan and Vaughan). While *The Tempest* is now frequently read and performed as sympathetic to Caliban (and thus, presumably, interpreted as *anti*colonial), this more favorable depiction of Caliban continues to present a double-edged colonialist viewpoint.

As we saw in *El nuevo mundo*, the depiction of the welcoming native both promoted colonial expansion, and, when that image was shattered by eventual native resistance, native "treachery" was seen to justify harsh retributive measures. Caliban describes himself as initially receptive to Prospero's arrival.

The island's mine by Sycorax my mother,
Which thou tak'st from me. When thou cam'st first,
Thou strok'st me and made much of me; wouldst give me
Water with berries in't, and teach me how
To name the bigger light and how the less,
That burn by day and night; and then I loved thee,
And showed thee all the qualities o'th'isle,
The fresh springs, brine pits, barren place and fertile. (I, ii, 331-339)[8]

Speaking to Prospero, Caliban explains that now you "sty me / In this hard rock, whiles you do keep from me / The rest o'th'island (I, ii, 342-344). Our sympathy for Caliban derives from his self-depiction as a gentle, simple creature at first congenial to Prospero's arrival and only later deceived by him. The motif occurs again in the play when Caliban encounters Stephano. Caliban says "I'll show thee every fertile inch o' th' island—and I will kiss they foot, I prithee be my god . . . I'll swear myself thy subject" (II, ii, 142-6). Stephano is subsequently quick to (falsely) accuse Caliban of "playing the Jack" with him (IV, i, 197).

The image of the welcoming native is a standard feature in the promotion of trade and settlement in the New World, at least as far back as Columbus. Columbus' widely circulated letter about his first voyage tells only of the tractability of Caribbean natives, while his journal, unpublished until 1791, has many examples of native resistance.[9] Early reports from the New World followed a familiar pattern of welcoming natives providing food, the development of increasing misunderstanding, and finally the outbreak of violent conflict. Hulme claims that European settlers were unable to understand their own behavior and thought "initial kindness was a ruse to establish trust before the native's 'natural' violence emerged from behind the mask" (131).

The initially welcoming native that subsequently turns treacherous typified by both Dulcanquellín in *El nuevo mundo* and Caliban in *The Tempest* has become a motif or trope of European colonial discourse. From the Native American perspective the trope is inherently unstable; if Caliban's claim to rule over the island depends on his inherent simplicity and gentleness, then any contrary or resistant behavior justifies European domination. He becomes an 'unnaturall Naturalls,' and Prospero and Miranda must take measures to contain and control him.

In *The Tempest*, as in *El nuevo mundo*, a depiction based on "sympathy" or "respect" for the natives serves to incorporate the Other into the dominant cultural system and naturalize the way that system both re-presents (portrays) and represents (speaks for) the Other whose view is, in fact, neither consulted nor sought. Caliban is not an indigenous person seeking legal standing to adjudicate the rights of property ownership. To mistake his voice for a Native American voice effaces native culture, language, and resistance. What is at stake in *The Tempest* is not that Caliban's "charges" represent "the claims of native populations" (Orgel, 36) but that a carefully made colonized subject ratifies—or challenges—a system of thought which places the Native American under the care and protection of the European.

As the constructed Native American subject recounts the history of encounter, it becomes evident that Prospero's governance over Caliban has been achieved by a certain kind of superior knowledge. Throughout the play, Caliban is shown lacking in sophisticated forms of thought. Though he may be "got by the devil," he has no elaborated religious knowledge or practice. Though Caliban is credited with locating natural phenomena—fresh water and arable land—Prospero still must teach Caliban to identify the sun and the moon. Without Prospero Caliban has no culture or traditions nor even any language. As Native American subject Caliban is presented as a virtual *tabula rasa*—an empty space on which Prospero inscribes the only available way of knowing.

MOONCALF AS MOON ROCK

Scholars have made elaborate examinations of the cultural forebears of Caliban, yet what the characters in *The Tempest* itself remark most about him is his singularity. Despite the Old World genealogy, Prospero gives Caliban (whose mother was Sycorax, a witch from Algiers and whose father was "the devil himself"), Caliban is presented in the play as something "new," as a marvel, a rare foreign monster. Caliban is thus also placed in a familiar discourse of the times, that of the exotic, the creature "discovered" during exploration and brought back for display in the domestic market place. The line between what is discovered and what is manufactured becomes extremely thin.

Freaks and monsters, always objects of interest for the "normal," in seventeenth- and eighteenth-century England apparently held a particular fascination. In 1620 in an effort to dissociate "monstrous births" from the realm of the supernatural, Sir Francis Bacon developed a tripartite schema for the study of natural history that included, along with the "natural" and the "artificial," a third category the "preternatural." Monsters were of considerable interest to such notables as Jonathan Swift, Samuel Pepys, and Sir Hans Sloane (a collector of curiosities and founder of the British Museum). The annual Bartholomew Fair, held over a period of 700 years from the twelfth century to the nineteenth, included displays of freaks. William Wordsworth described the fair as the "Parliament of Monsters." The New World became a source for exotic creatures at the Fair. In "Monsters in the Marketplace: The Exhibition of Human Oddities in Early Modern England," Paul Semonin claims that

from Elizabethan times, when the first inhabitants and specimens of animal life from the new world began to arrive in England, there appeared among the exhibits a startlingly diverse array of monstrous creatures, many of whom were already familiar to their audiences through popular fables, the bestiaries, pictorial prints and biblical lore. (70)

Semonin associates a skeptical attitude toward the monsters with Protestantism and the rise of scientism. He traces the suspicion at least as far back as Shakespeare's time: "From the early days of the English Renaissance, there had been a growing criticism of the gullibility of the penny audience, the 'Mob,' which patronized the monster shows" (71).

In *The Tempest*, Caliban is referred to as "monster" forty times.[10] In keeping with the "lower class" nature of the monster displays, it is perhaps appropriate that it is the clown Trinculo who first articulates the topos. Moreover, as jester to Alonso, Trinculo has a position curiously parallel to that of Caliban in his relationship to Prospero.[11] Trinculo's comments on Caliban deserve careful attention:

> What have we here—a man or a fish?... Were I in England now, as once I was, and had but this fish painted, not a holiday-fool there but would give a piece of silver. There would this monster make a man—any strange beast there makes a man. When they will not give a doit to relieve a lame beggar, they will lay out ten to see a dead Indian. (II, ii, 25-32)

Trinculo's reaction to Caliban is a complex one: he not only identifies Caliban's difference, he also incorporates a self-consciously critical view of the exhibition of curiosities. In suggesting that market-place monsters are fabricated creations, "painted fish"—and that the public that pays to see them are "holiday-fools"—Trinculo's clowning constitutes a double-pronged social comment. His satirical jibes register the insensitivity of his countrymen to suffering and, simultaneously, point to their gullible fascination with the exotic, even when it is false ("painted") in the case of the fish, or in the case of the Indian, when he or she is dead.

Spoken on a far-off, enchanted, even imaginary isle, Trinculo's lines conjure a city of lame beggars and dead Native Americans on display. Indeed this juxtaposition of a lack of charity toward "lame beggars" and a willingness to pay to see dead Native Americans expresses an important relationship between otherness and national identity. At the level of the comic subplot of *The Tempest*, the exotic Native American has no history or culture. Yet, between the "lame beggar" and the "dead Indian" there is a radical division of sympathy along cultural or "national" lines. Trinculo's statement performs the familiar work of colonialist discourse where the recognition of the presumedly radical difference of the Other serves to cohere the Self and diminish *internal* difference. The dead Indian's value as monstrosity and potential display object is recognized and his non-human quality mocked.

Following his reference to "dead Indians" Trinculo appears to offer a possible recognition of Caliban as a human being. Upon discovering that Caliban's flesh is warm, he declares that Caliban "is no fish, but an

6 The first known illustration of Caliban. (*Scene from* The Tempest, William Hogarth, ca. 1736)

islander," and on hearing the sound of thunder, he decides to huddle under Caliban's cloak, saying "Misery acquaints a man with strange bed-fellows" (II, ii, 38-9). Trinculo's crawling under Caliban's cloak may mark them as fellow sufferers in the midst of the tempest, but the comic effect of the scene nonetheless resides in the audience recognizing the inappropriateness, even the horror of bedding down with Caliban.

As the scene continues, a drunken Stephano comes upon Caliban and Trinculo. When Stephano hears Caliban he exclaims, "What's the matter? Have we devils here? Do you put tricks upon's with savages and men of Ind?" (II, ii, 56-7). He then makes the second of the three direct references to Caliban as a curiosity of value: "If I can recover him, and keep him tame, and get to Naples with him, he's a present for any emperor that ever trod on neat's-leather" (II, ii, 67-8). In a discussion of the capture and return of native Americans to Europe by Spanish and English explorers, Stephen Greenblatt states that "Such displays—Columbus' Arawaks or Frobisher's Eskimos—appear to have been immensely popular, and by the early seventeenth century could figure as sources of income" (*Marvelous* 121). Vaughan and Vaughan even suggest that "because kidnapped Indians were London showpieces in the late sixteenth and early seventeenth centuries, Shakespeare may have seen, conceivably have talked with, real Indians" (44). For Stephano, the native provides an opportunity for his personal advancement by constituting an appropriate gift to the emperor. As with Columbus presenting Ferdinand and Isabella with bars of gold and Caribbean islanders in *El nuevo mundo*, the gift of the captured native from the edge of expanding European civilization performs the attainment of empire.[12]

The image of Caliban as display monster comes up for the third time in Act V, and by this point the allusion has become automatic and can be made with an appropriate economy of language. When Antonio first sees Caliban he remarks "One of them / Is a plain fish, and no doubt marketable" (V, i, 265-6). The topos has particular force here because it comes in the final revelation scene, when all identities are made public. The brevity of Antonio's remark and all three allusions to Caliban as display curiosity indicate the familiarity of this depiction to Shakespeare's audience.[13]

What is paradoxical about "exotic" creatures is the way way their very strangeness reinforces the familiar and highlights the authority and credibility of the discoverer just as the Caribbean islanders did for

Columbus when he brought them back to the Spanish court. A contemporary example would be the way in which the fascination of the moon rocks brought back by the Apollo voyages depends not on any essential difference between moon rock and earth rock but on what the very possession of a rock from the moon says about how it was found, and how brought back. The silent moon rock speaks about modern technology and the power of the nation-state, about the ability "to boldly go where no man has gone before."

In a similar way in *The Tempest* the existence of the "mooncalf," as Stephano calls Caliban, demonstrates the power and extension of the emergent English nation. Like the first astronauts to gaze on the moon's surface, the play's European protagonists examine the mooncalf *in situ*, not yet returned to England. Yet, the first thought of those who encounter Caliban is precisely this moon rock syndrome, bringing the rare article home as a profitable curiosity. This scheme is independently hit on by Trinculo, Stephano, and Antonio. Caliban as imperial display object is predicated both on the strangeness of the Other and on the power that—in the name of the sovereign—can stake its claims afar and return with captured exhibits from distant climes. A subject made within a colonial discourse, Caliban's exoticism demonstrates national power and reinforces cultural distinctions.

Displayed as curiosities, New World Indians are observed in their singularity. If Lope's representation of a Native American *society* constructs social difference out of Spanish history, Shakespeare's representation of Native American *individuality* lends itself to the investigation of archetypes, universal truths about colonial/colonizer psychology, "experimental data" about the colonized native. Caliban is a nation of one. As deracinated individuals, kidnapped Native Americans are separated from their communities and trapped in the colonizer's system of signification. Greenblatt shows how Columbus in his diary fits Native Americans into a European image of savage independence: "The Indians have been assimilated to a conception of nomadic barbarism as old as ancient Greece. They are people who live outside of all just condition of the virtuous life" (*Marvelous* 68). As exhibit, they embody—already in the early seventeenth century—a proto-scientific discourse tied to imperial expansionism. The exhibitions of New World natives furnish the collections of natural curiosities and later museums of natural history, familiar institutions which served early American nationalism by occluding the social history of colonization.[14]

Our reading of the function of Caliban as a part of the circulation of native bodies in an emerging imperial economy has resonance throughout Shakespeare's play. In *The Tempest* Caliban identifies Prospero's power as slave master, his ability to extend his domination over the strange and marvelous, his control over nature. It is the presence of Caliban that marks Prospero as Imperial Sovereign. In opposition to Prospero's famous appropriation of Caliban, "this thing of darkness I acknowledge mine," Caliban asserts the profoundly interdependent nature of this relationship: "I am all the subjects that you have" (I, ii, 341).

The formation of Renaissance nationalism drew on imperial models and the expansionist imposition of language and culture. The colonial relationship with Caliban heightens Prospero's stature as a figure of domination. It allows Prospero to serve as representative of England's emerging national authority.

Power, as Prospero presents it in the play, is not inherited but self-created: it is magic, or "art", an extension of mental power and self-knowledge, and the authority legitimizing it derives from heaven—"Fortune" and "Destiny" are the terms used in the play. It is Caliban who derives his claim to the island from inheritance, from his mother. [15]

Just as Prospero and Miranda give Caliban language, so Caliban names Prospero: "I am subject to a tyrant, a sorcerer that by his cunning hath cheated me of the island" (III, ii, 40-41). As with Lope's Indians, the recognition of the justness of European rule must be, in the end, pronounced by the colonized. Caliban's final words are "I'll be wise hereafter, / And seek for grace. What a thrice-double ass / Was I to take this drunkard for a god, / And worship this dull fool [Stephano]!" (V, v, 294-7). As in the Spanish play, where the taming of the Indians takes the form of religious conversion, in *The Tempest*, too, Caliban's transformation to docile native comes as a lesson in a system of colonial education.

Ruling the distant native is increasingly part of European absolutism, that period in the history of Europe that precedes full-fledged nationalism. Prospero tells Alonso "This cell's my court. Here have I few attendants, / And subjects none abroad" (V, i, 166-7). The return of Prospero to Milan at the end of the narrative heralds the beginning of a new imperial reign. When Gonzalo learns that Miranda and Ferdinand will marry, he thanks the gods and credits them—

significantly bypassing Prospero—with having "chalked forth the way which brought us hither" (V, i, 203-4). Imperial authority meets with spiritual approval. The blessings of the state and religion coincide as King Alonso chimes, "I say 'amen', Gonzalo," (V, i, 205). Gonzalo proclaims that Prospero's new glory should be set "down / With gold on lasting pillars!" (V, i, 207-8). As Dennis Kay argues these pillars are an important imperial reference:

From the time when Charles V had adopted the device of the pillars of Hercules with the motto *plus ultra*, they had become a standard feature of imperial iconography. As such they were employed by most monarchs who entertained imperial ambition, including Elizabeth. In the "Sieve" portrait, for example, the Queen appears next to a column decorated with medallions telling the story of Dido and Aeneas: the imperial column thus participates in a triumphant assertion of British history and its providential movement, and, takes alongside the globe on the right of the portrait (which implies an empire stretching out to the West), presents Elizabeth as "the Virgin of the expanded empire, using the echo of the device of Charles V for her own ends." (322)

From Charles V to Elizabeth, from Lope to Shakespeare, from Columbus to Prospero, the representations of European imperial nationalism are generalized. Already by 1611, twenty-three years after the Armada, British imperialism is incipient in an "exotic" play ostensibly about Italian nobility.[16]

SLAVE ECONOMIES

With the foregoing discussion of Caliban as New World native and imperial subject in mind, we may consider the relationship of the Caliban character to New World slavery. Shakespeare could not have known, of course, that the first slave ship would arrive in Jamestown a mere eight years after the writing of *The Tempest* or that by the time of the French and Indian wars, fully as much as two-fifths (40%) of the population of Virginia would be black slaves.[17] Yet he was obviously aware of the slave trade and the presence of slaves, both Africans and Native Americans, in the Caribbean plantations. By 1611 the African slave trade was 170 years old; a million Africans had already been brought to the New World by the Spanish and Portuguese. In *The Tempest*, Caliban is specifically referred to by Prospero as his "slave" on four occasions. Miranda calls him "abhorred slave." Caliban's mother is from Africa, and Caliban is born on the island. Thus a case could be made, one supposes, that the representation of Caliban in *The Tempest* is the earliest depiction in English of African Americans. That there should be confusion over Caliban's identity—as to whether or not Caliban is a Native American or African American slave—is not surprising. Elizabethans tended to lump together Africans and North American "Indians." Indeed, escaped African slaves frequently joined Indian bands in the Caribbean forming important rebel groups of "maroons."[18] Similar relationships obtained between European and Native American and between European and slave. In both there was the necessity to subdue, appropriate, discipline, and educate in the ways of civilization. As we have seen, kidnapping of Native Americans was a figure in the English imagination. As is the case with Caliban as Native American subject, Caliban as slave recognizes Prospero's authority.[19]

SOVEREIGN'S POWER AND MAGIC BOOK

Despite the fact that Alonso is the King of Naples, it is Prospero who is the central figure in the play's construction of a Renaissance sovereignty. Prospero's authority on the island depends on the use of magic and spectacle. The wedding masque, the elaborate manipulation of illusion, the disappearing feast, the invisible noises and music, the familiarity with spirits and quasi-humans—all these identify Prospero as a ruler patterned on the magus. In *The Tempest*, magic is the instrumental technology of political authority and social control.[20] Moreover, Renaissance magic is the active expression of formal knowledge and the precursor to empirical science.[21] The command of formal knowledge—eventually associated with Bacon's conception of enlightenment reason—is critical to the administration and rationalization of the imperial nation-state. Stephen Orgel writes, "Prospero's art is Baconian science and Neoplatonic philosophy, the empirical study of nature leading to the understanding and control of all its forces" (20). The instrument of Prospero's domination of nature and the society of the island is magic, and his magical powers are tied to his book learning and library. Benedict Anderson points out the role of books in the consolidation of national identity, and we may also note the same kind of significance for the role of book knowledge in relation to nation-state legitimation and administration.[22] In the case of England Christopher Hill argues that

> In the early seventeenth century the king ceased to exhibit himself to his subjects . . . and royal propagandists began deliberately to use control of pulpit and printing press to project a new image of monarchy. (41)

Books are properly related to knowledge, magic and authority in *The Tempest*.[23] Prospero, moreover, is both scholar/teacher and Renaissance prince, yet in his narration of his life he poses a contradiction between the study of the liberal arts and effective management of the state. The love of books, he says, distracts him from attention to governance:

> And Prospero the prime duke, being so reputed
> In dignity, and for the liberal arts
> Without a parallel; those being all my study,
> The government I cast upon my brother,
> And to my state grew stranger, being transported
> And rapt in secret studies. (I, ii, 72-77)
>> Me, poor man, my library
> Was dukedom large enough; Of temporal royalties
> He thinks me now incapable . . . (I, ii, 109-11)
> Knowing I loved my books, he furnished me
> From mine own library with volumes that
> I prize above my dukedom. (I, ii, 166-9)

Notwithstanding Prospero's analysis of his own fall from power *in Milan*, it may be useful, in order to understand the play's construction of princely authority, to examine more closely the practice of Prospero's rule *on the island*.[24] Rather than revealing an incompatibility between liberal arts and public administration, *The Tempest* may be said to enact the marriage of knowledge and power. It is from his books that Prospero learns the magic that he will use to master Caliban and Ariel and control the island and its visitors. Prospero's use of spectacle intimidates his enemies and allows him to enforce his will. It is only close to the end of the play, when his authority has already been assured by their use, that Prospero abjures his magic and "drowns" his books. Indeed, Prospero's abjuration of magic appeals to pre-scientific personal and aristocratic notions of governance and is symptomatic, as

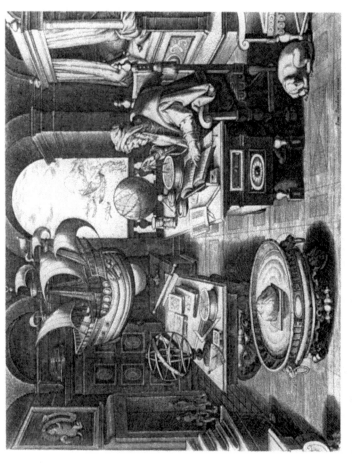

7 Prospero's authority derives from an interaction of learned traditions and the exploration and control of nature. (*Lapis polaris, magnes*, Theodor Galle after Johannes Stradanus, seventeenth century)

we shall see, of the social crisis brought about with the imposition of an increasingly absolutist authority.

The relationship between Prospero's tokens of knowledge and his magical power is clearly identified by Caliban. "I am subject to a tyrant, a sorcerer that by his cunning hath cheated me of the island" (III, ii, 40-2), Caliban tells Stephano and Trinculo. Since the contradictions of absolutist rule are sharpest in the relationship of Caliban as slave and as colonized subject, it is he who is best positioned to identify the functioning of Prospero's imperial power. Caliban's animosity toward the book is paradigmatic of the relationship between colonial subject and colonizing nation. When Caliban plans revolt as the first priority, he advises Stephano and Trinculo to capture Prospero's books,

> Remember
> First to possess his books; for without them
> He's but a sot, as I am, nor hath not
> One spirit to command—they all do hate him
> As rootedly as I. Burn but his books.
> He has brave utensils, for so he calls them,
> Which when he has a house, he'll deck withal. (III, ii, 90-5)

Caliban emphasizes that without possession of the book Prospero will be "as I am." For Caliban, the book is not the vehicle to knowledge but the tool of the magician that makes possible the performance of authority. Books are "utensils," magical instruments of power, and they are also, in themselves, the legitimation of the right to authority, commodities on display in the aristocratic household. At stake in the struggle between Caliban and Prospero is ownership of the technology of power/magic.

This notion, that the secret of the book's power is in the possession of the object rather than a knowledge of its contents, is not only Caliban's. Prospero, too, speaks of his books in this way when he abjures his magic, for his expressed intention is not to forget what he has learned or to put the knowledge away from him but to "break my staff, / Bury it certain fathoms in the earth, / And deeper than did ever plummet sound / I'll drown my book" (V, i, 54-6). In this passage books and staffs are equated, and repudiation of magic is achieved by casting away the physical implements of its power.

In *The Tempest*, the book motif arises during the first moments of Caliban's meeting with Trinculo and Stephano. When Caliban tells Stephano that he adores him, Stephano holds up a cup of wine and replies, "Come, swear to that: kiss the book, I will furnish it anon with new contents. Swear" (II, ii, 136-7). The drunken Stephano's play on words, using "book" to mean "cup," humorously conflates the familiar expression "kiss the cup" and the tradition of kissing the Bible to confirm an oath. As discussed in the last chapter, the encounter between native and book is a familiar trope in colonial discourse. The book is the central religious icon, the quintessential national commodity, and the legitimating tool of colonial rule. Whether it is the holy book of Christianity or the proto-scientific book of Prospero's magic, literacy establishes imperial and national authority. Caliban may be taught to speak, but to teach him to read is beyond the pale of consideration.

In the scene with Trinculo and Stephano, there is a carnivalesque mockery of English social relations. While Caliban is clearly subservient to the Englishmen, there is also a grouping together of native, clown, and drunken servant in an effective humorous moment. When Trinculo and Caliban are asked to "kiss the book" by Stephano, the play appears to be toying with the icon of English religious and secular authority. Stephano is a comic figure precisely because he imitates the conduct of the noblemen. The inversion of class roles in this scene is funny rather then threatening because it stages potentially disruptive actions within the contained sphere of Prospero's island and under the jurisdiction of Prospero's vigilant eye.

SURVEILLANCE AND THE NATION

In *Discipline and Punish* Michel Foucault examines the layout of the Panopticon, the building designed by Jeremy Bentham at the end of the eighteenth century for the surveillance and reform of prisoners. In Bentham's plan the prisoners can be viewed from a centrally situated tower. "Each individual, in his place, is securely confined to a cell from which he is seen from the front by the supervisor; but the side walls prevent him from coming into contact with his companions" (200). For Foucault, the Panopticon is not only a method of prison incarceration but a model of institutional discipline relevant to the history of mental institutions, hospitals, schools, and work places. Using the Panopticon as a metaphor for society, Foucault traces an evolution away from medieval and feudal notions of power to Enlightenment and statist notions of centralized and anonymous control. As "a figure of political technology" (205), the Panopticon serves as a model for the nation-state itself.

Though written some two hundred years before Bentham's Panopticon, *The Tempest*, in its depiction of Prospero's rule over the island, suggests some of the Panopticon's most essential features.[25] Magic and his all-seeing, ubiquitous servant Ariel allow Prospero to observe and manipulate the activities of his captives. Prospero is either physically present or secretly monitoring (through Ariel) every action in the play. He is on stage but invisible to the other characters in many scenes he closely "directs," including the courtship of Ferdinand and Miranda, the disappearing banquet, and the final monologue in front of the "charmed" Alonso, Sebastian, Antonio, and Gonzalo. Like the Panopticon's prisoners, the shipwrecked passengers are forced to the island, separated, kept ignorant of one another's activities and constantly watched by their attentive warden.

It is Prospero's surveillance that constructs the imagined community of the island/nation, and his all-seeing eye that unifies the diverse actions of the play. While Elizabethan spying was less systematic, perhaps, than the modern version, John Archer has recently argued that in Shakespeare's day "sovereignty and intelligence were united in a culture of surveillance that was chiefly defined by life at court" (3). Like an expanding capitalist economy, Prospero's attention in *The Tempest* is all-pervasive. Spreading over theater and world, it reaches the "whole surface of the globe. It must nestle everywhere, settle everywhere, establish connections everywhere" (Marx and Engels 476). Prospero's simultaneous staging of events orchestrates synchronous time from the center, the hallmark of the absolutist nation.

Foucault argues that a crucial feature of the eighteenth-century Panopticon is the way that an awareness of surveillance leads to the internalization of the larger disciplinary system within each individual. Social control is exercised through *self*-control.

He who is subjected to a field of visibility, and who knows it, assumes responsibility for the constraints of power; he makes them play spontaneously upon himself; he inscribes the power relation in which he simultaneously plays both roles; he becomes the principle of his own subjection. (202-3)

In the proto-Panopticon of Shakespeare's seventeenth-century drama, Prospero's subjects are themselves only imperfectly aware of Prospero's gaze. As police force, Ariel is mysterious and invisible. The characters are seen by Prospero, but during most of the play, they do not recognize him in return. Prospero's rule is more personal than systematic. In this sense the model of ruler and citizen inscribed by *The Tempest* should be read only as a precursor to more fully modern national subjectivity developed in the ensuing centuries. The play allows us to consider the complexities of the making of national identity.

NATIONAL AND COLONIAL PEDAGOGY

Contemporary scholars of nationalism such as Gellner and Anderson insist on the importance of national systems of education to the formation of national identity in the modern period. As we shall discuss more fully in the next chapter, Homi Bhabha describes the making of national subjectivity as a "pedagogical" process. Studies of colonialism refer to the formation of colonial systems of instruction in order to understand "third-world" nationalism. In examining the history of Early Modern national consciousness, then, it is critical to look at the development of education and pedagogy in England and trace the rise of national or proto-national sentiments. *The Tempest* offers a site for such a project. Given England's precocious national consciousness and the country's influence, through colonial rule, on educational institutions and nationalist movements in the Americas, Africa, and Asia, the rise of English educational systems and the conflictive nature of English absolutism assume a particular significance to the development of nations and citizenship.

The late sixteenth and early seventeenth centuries saw the development of educational systemization under the impetus of the Reformation and, concomitantly, a movement toward national consolidation. Christopher Hill claims that

The whole trend of educational advance during the century before the Reformation had been towards a more secular, lay-controlled education in the vernacular. The dissolution of the monasteries and chantries gave an opportunity for creating a national educational system. (39)

In Tudor and Stuart England the state functions of education were increasingly recognized: "The Reformation made education an especially critical and politically sensitive area."[26] Standardized school books were first imposed in the 1540s.[27] In 1559 the Protestant reformer Thomas Becon advocated the importance of Christian education as a means for forging an obedient citizenry:

Through the schoolmaster the youth of the Christian commonwealth is brought up in the knowledge of God and of his holy word, and also in the science of good letters and virtuous manners; and so trained up in them from their very cradles that as they grow in age so likewise they increase in godliness, virtue, learning, knowledge, good manners and innocency of of life, and afterward become the faithful servants of God and profitable members of the commonweal, yea, and good citizens of the country where they inhabit. (Cressy 21)

Successfully confronting, on the one side, aristocratic and eclesiastical anxieties that schooling might be heretical, seditious, or educate people above their "station," sixteenth-century education advocates drew on the Reformation to found new schools, unify instruction in Latin grammar, and create a new orthodoxy in education. A firm link between established systems of education and allegiance to the developing state appears to emerge clearly in the seventeenth century. An Oxford beadle writes in 1678,

Miserable is the face of any nation where neither schools nor universities be frequented: no law, no safe commerce, a general ignorance and a neglect of duty both to God and man. Now that universities flourish and schools are in many populous towns erected, from those places of public education especially, persons are sent into all parts of the land, engaged in the strictest bonds of allegiance. (Cressy 19)

While home schooling in the courts of kings and individual noblemen was common throughout the medieval and Renaissance periods, during Shakespeare's time education was increasingly systematic and nationalized. The home instruction of an aristocratic young woman, such as Miranda, was still the custom in the period,[28] as was the inclusion of non-family members as pupils in the courtly context. Caliban's education in Prospero's household is thus not unusual. The seventeenth century also included an increasing

awareness of the relationship between education and the maintenance
of social order. The development of specific training and instruction for
all classes of society, for aristocrats (such as Ferdinand) as well as for
commoners (such as Trinculo) was of ever-increasing importance in the
development of a national economy. A connection between national
identity and national education was becoming evident in the Early
Modern period. Reading *The Tempest* as a study in proto-national
instruction allows the investigation of incipient links between state
power and educational authority, links that played a decisive role in the
consolidation of national and imperial rule.

Artist, magician, patriarch, sovereign, colonial administrator—
Prospero is also an eminent scholar, intellectual, and pedagogue.[29] In
fact, Prospero might be better described as "teacher"—rather than the
familiar "playwright"—since he does not so much script characters as
instruct them. Yet, ever scholar/teacher, Prospero does more than
manipulate the activity of others. He trains, disciplines, and informs his
"students," bringing their disparate spaces and times into one spatial
and temporal dimension. Homi Bhabha describes the political unity of
the nation in this way: "Quite simply, the difference of space returns as
the Sameness of time, turning Territory into Tradition, turning the
People into One" (300). Prospero's role as teacher is central to the
development of the play's actions and shapes the identity of its
characters. While the characters in *The Tempest* are unaware that they
are under surveillance, they are each in some sense "educated" or
"trained" to incorporate the sovereign's eye. Prospero's national
pedagogy resituates individuated subjects in a reinforced social order.
Even Prospero's acknowledgment of difference is thus also a testimony
of ownership and replication; recall "this thing of darkness I /
Acknowledge mine" (V, i, 275-6).

Prospero has prepared a "lesson plan" appropriate to each social
class on the island. The nobles Alonzo, Sebastian, and Antonio must
learn that their crimes against Prospero cannot be forgotten, and they
must be made ready to reinstate Prospero in his position as rightful
Duke of Milan. Prospero prepares his "pupils" to gain this knowledge
by separating them from the others, who need to learn different lessons.
The "shipwreck," the "loss" of Ferdinand, and the confused magic of
the island are the "anticipatory set" for Prospero's instruction of
Alonso, Sebastian, and Antonio. Dislodged from the certainties of
social position, uncertain of their grasp of reality, they are ready to be
"reeducated." Ariel's appearance to them as a harpy after the

disappearance of the banquet is the critical scene of Prospero's instruction. Ariel begins by redefining their identity, challenging their self-understanding:

You are three men of sin. . . . I have made you mad; And even with such-like valour men hang and drown / Their proper selves. (III, iii, 53-8)

Using Prospero's words, Ariel informs them that the storm and the current disruption of their peace is the work of supernatural powers "incensed" over Prospero's "supplanting." Thus when Alonso finally "discovers" Prospero in the final scene, he pronounces "on his own" the words Prospero wants to hear, "Thy dukedom I resign, and do entreat / Thou pardon me my wrongs" (V, i, 117-8). The "three men of sin" learn that their actions are observed by a "natural" authority to which they must ultimately pay obeisance.

Prospero's power appears to derive from magical spectacles, enchanting music, and entertaining masques. In twentieth-century terms, we might say that the consent to Prospero's authority is manufactured through technological effect and mass media. "Scientific management" is brought about by Prospero's book-learned magic, his command over Ariel, the knowledge of human society necessary to its manipulation, and his position as behind-the-scenes coordinator of activity. Alonso's recognition of Prospero entails the restoration of Prospero's dukedom and the entreating of pardon. What the nobles experience is the power of Prospero's "scientific" organization and administration. In a sense, the most fundamental lesson the aristocrats learn is that of the power of the rising national administrative class exemplified by Prospero. They come to recognize a new kind of political power, one based not so much on inheritance but on the well-schooled manipulation of perception. [30]

Since Ferdinand is the next in line to the throne, it is important that he be Prospero's student before he become his son-in-law. Though his magic will allow Prospero to control Ferdinand directly (he causes him to drop his sword on their first meeting), Prospero develops instead a relationship with Ferdinand that depends upon the latter's recognition of Prospero's superior abilities. In the beginning, Prospero orchestrates his influence over Ferdinand through Miranda. Ferdinand's first words to Miranda invoke an educational relationship.

> Most sure, the goddess
> On whom these airs attend. Vouchsafe my prayer
> May know if you remain upon this island,
> And that you will some good instruction give
> How I may bear me here. (I, ii, 422-6)

Prospero contends that the labor that he requires of Ferdinand is to make him value Miranda all the more ("too light winning / make the prize light" (I, ii, 452-3)). Yet it is evident that taking Caliban's job of hauling wood also serves to establish Prospero's authority over Ferdinand. From the outset this authority is tied to discourses of pedagogy. When Ferdinand first attempts to resist Prospero's with his sword, Prospero responds, "My foot my tutor?" (I, ii, 470). The mixed metaphor of the school/body is used to establish the proper hierarchy between Prospero and Ferdinand. Drawing on the image of the king's two bodies, Prospero identifies himself as both "head of state" and tutor to Ferdinand, and, by extension, to the rest of the nation.

Prospero is insistent, to the point of disconcerting harshness, with both Miranda and Ferdinand about the importance of sexual purity and the dangers of unrestrained desire. In this, of course, there are present the psycho-sexual tensions of the father/daughter relationship including the patriarchal domination of Miranda. Throughout, Miranda's education is closely attended to by Prospero, who regards it as valuable and serious: "Here / Have I, thy schoolmaster, made thee more profit / Than other princes can that have more time / For vainer hours, and tutors not so careful" (I, ii, 171-4). The inscription of a code of propriety both identifies the social body and insures its orderly continuation. In the sexual passion for Miranda, Ferdinand and Caliban are linked; in the restraint of passion they are distinguished. Prospero's inculcation of propriety develops the "internal" policing that locates subjection within the individual and within the nation.[31] His domination of Miranda can be contrasted with Caliban's attempt to gain power over her; Prospero's pedagogical efforts are both more effective and more lasting.

Because Caliban's treatment by Prospero and Miranda cannot be separated from the larger English discourse on education, an analysis of the training Caliban receives on the island is relevant to the practices and assumptions that will come to underlie European/Native encounters, most particularly European efforts to educate the "savages" in the ensuing centuries of British and European colonialism. In this sense if *El nuevo mundo* demonstrates the efforts of the Spanish to educate Caribbean islanders from the time of Columbus, *The Tempest* offers one of the earliest representations of British colonial education. In a remarkably paradoxical way, both the successes and failures of Caliban's education serve to legitimate European cultural domination and ratify assumptions about "barbarian" others.

It is significant that the portrait of Caliban as student conforms clearly to images *already established* in English educational discourse. The depiction of Caliban can be tied to existing descriptions of the reluctant student. Compare, for instance, Shakespeare's Caliban with Thomas Nash's 1600 portrait of Will Summers.

Who would be a Scholler? Not I, I promise you: my minde alwayes gaue me this learning were such a filthy thing, which made me hate it so as I did: when I should have beene at schoole construing *Bate, mi fili, mi fili, mi Batte* I was close vnder a hedge or vnder a barne wall playing at spane Counter or Iacke in the boxe: my master beat me, my father beat me, my mother gaue me bread and butter, yet all this would not make me a squitter-booke. It was my destinie, I thanke her as a most courteous goddesse, that she hath not cast me away vpon gibridge. Oh, in what a mightie veine am I now against Horne-bookes! Here before all this companie I profess myself an open enemy to Inke and paper. . . . Nownes and Pronounes, I pronounce you as traitors to boyes buttockes. . . .[32]

Both Summers and Caliban are professed enemies of books, which they both personify as figures of evil and the source of their punishment. Like Caliban, Summers' education is focused on the acquisition of language (for Caliban, English; for Summer, Latin). Like Caliban, Summer would prefer to be out-of-doors, "under a hedge," close to nature. There is a similar patriarchal pattern in the enforcement of learning. As Summers is beaten by his master and father, so Caliban is beaten by Prospero. Both Caliban and Summers appeal to female goddesses for protection: Summers personifies his "destiny." Caliban worships the god of his witch mother, Setebos. While both Caliban and Summers are figures from a comic tradition, their outrage against a disciplinary pedagogy is understandable, even convincing.

Significantly, in Nash's satirical play Will Summers is Henry VIII's jester. The juxtaposition between Prospero and Caliban is anticipated in Nash's play by the pairing of the Renaissance absolutist monarch—and Henry was one of the most extensively educated

monarchs of the period—with the reluctant Will Summers. The tension between a nationalizing absolutist pedagogy and a defiant rejection of literacy should be seen as one of the key motifs of the period in both the New World *and* theOld.
The portrait of Caliban in *The Tempest* illustrates European assumptions about the natives, assumptions still in operation in subsequent educational schemes in the colonies. The linkage of the colonial relationship to the pedagogical was contemporary to the play.

In 1609, the Revered William Crashaw, who "was serving as a sort of director of publicity for the company," imagined "Virginea" as a young woman being schooled by an older and male "England" in the course of a scriptural dialogue appended to the published version of an important sermon to the Counsel.[33]

The fundamental assumption of a colonial education is that the educator knows the native better than the native knows himself. Drawing on European traditions of the "wild man," medieval travelogues, and the reports of European contact with the New World, Shakespeare creates a character whose difference is already familiar within European discourse. As we have seen in *El nuevo mundo*, Europeans considered Native American religion to be based on worship of the Christian devil. Prospero describes Caliban as "Got by the devil himself" (I, ii, 319). Even Caliban's eloquence about the magic of the island, for instance, can be read as part of a European view of the relationship of the "wild man" to nature. The space of Caliban's supposed difference, cast in the form of pastiche, is quite familiar.[34] In thinking of Caliban as a New World figure, it is important to connect with the European discourse about the savage other, a discourse already of tremendous importance in "the violent encounter of civilizations, the missionary enterprise, mass enslavement and death, the immense project of colonization" (Greenblatt, *Marvelous* 52). Prospero's attitude is typical of the colonizer who sets himself up to educate the native, the teacher who already knows the native without even learning his speech.

Indeed, before Miranda teaches him to speak Caliban is said to "gabble like a thing most brutish." The task, then, is to make Caliban's speech comprehensible, i.e., to give him a "civilized" tongue. The ability to enforce the learning of one's language onto others always marks imperial rule. The link between language and domination had already been implicit in the central role of Roman Latin as a requirement for the educated classes of Europe. While the educated in Renaissance Europe had to learn Latin, the colonized had to learn the language of the colonizers. In the context of the play, the teaching of language to Caliban holds up to the audience a mirror in which they can recognize their own vernacular English as "national" (in the sense that, unlike Caliban, they understand the language "naturally") and "imperial" (in the sense that Caliban must learn [London] English just as the English learn Latin). In the *Globe* Theater, the audience can see itself as a nation united on linguistic lines, with English raised to both "national" and imperial standards.[35]

Once the master's language is learned by Caliban, it becomes evident that his "failure" to be educated stems from even "deeper" gaps. There is that in Caliban's nature which no amount of nurture can cure.

> Abhorred slave,
> Which any print of goodness wilt not take,
> Being capable of all ill! I pitied thee,
> Took pains to make thee speak, taught thee each hour
> One thing or other. When thou didst not, savage,
> Know thine own meaning, but wouldst gabble like
> A thing most brutish, I endowed thy purposes
> With words that made them known. But thy vile race—
> Though thou didst learn—had that in't which good natures
> Could not abide to be with; therefore wast thou
> Deservedly confined into this rock,
> Who hadst deserved more than a prison. (I, ii, 357-9)

Miranda admits that Caliban did learn, but that his brutishness stemmed from his belonging to a "vile race," one that "good natures could not abide to be with." Described by Prospero as "hag-born," "savage," "brutish," Caliban is accused of seeking "to violate the honor of my child" (I, ii, 347-8). Here are invoked fears of racial mixture and savage sexuality that neither end nor begin with Shakespeare. Miranda's suggestion that Caliban's race deserves "more than prison," begins to sound like a racist justification for genocide.[36]

"As well as grammatical and religious instruction no Tudor or Stuart schoolboy's experience was complete without a measure of corporal punishment" (Cressy 90). Efforts to constrain or restrict overly violent schoolmasters were common in Shakespeare's time. Roger

Ascham wrote his important essay *The Scholemaster* (1563) after participating in a discussion about scholars of Eton who ran away from the school for fear of beating. The record of efforts to limit corporal punishment are indicative of the perception of its excess. Consider one headmaster's ordinance for his teachers (written in 1629), which tells us about *acceptable* corporal punishment:

I constitute and ordain that schoolmasters do not exceed in their corrections above the number of three stripes with the rod at any one time, that they strike not any scholar upon the head or the cheek with their fist or the palms of their hands or with any other thing . . . that for speaking English in the Latin school the scholar be corrected with the *ferula*, and for swearing with the rod.[37]

There is extensive corporal punishment meted out to Caliban. In response to Caliban's cursing, Prospero administers "cramps" and "pinches:"

For this be sure tonight thou shalt have cramps,
Side-stitches that shall pen thy breath up. Urchins
Shall, for that vast of night that they may work,
All exercise on thee. Thou shalt be pinched
As thick as honeycomb, each pinch more stinging
Than bees that made 'em. (I, ii, 325-30)

Prospero's infliction of pain on Caliban is intended as a form of discipline rather than torture. The pain is not administered in order to extract truth or knowledge from Caliban but rather to subject him to Prospero's rule, to insure his cooperation and development within the master/slave relationship. Pain is only administered after demonstrations of disobedience or obstinacy. This "exercise" of pain is continuously applied over an interval of time. It is sharp, frequently and lastingly given but not disfiguring (beyond "leopard spots") or life threatening.

That such violence was (and is) seen as proper and necessary relates to the role of punishment within the pedagogical structure of Prospero's and English power. In seeking to tame Caliban's "nature," Prospero's disciplining must not interfere with Caliban's usefulness as a servant. Through his knowledge of character and his power/magic, Prospero fulfils the fantasy of the slave master/colonial administrator who, through physical force and intimidation, can subjugate his charges without diminishing labor power. Prospero's methods of discipline threaten to make Caliban "roar" so loud as to frighten animals.

> If thou neglect'st, or dost unwillingly
> What I command, I'll rack thee with old cramps,
> Fill all thy bones with aches, make thee roar,
> That beasts shall tremble at they din. (I, ii, 367-70)

The spirits Prospero sends to torture Caliban are, apparently, animals themselves, whose purpose is to fill Caliban's head with animal images, sounds, and fears.

> For every trifle are they set upon me,
> Sometime like apes that mow and chatter at me,
> And after bite me; then like hedgehogs, which
> Lie tumbling in my barefoot way, and mount
> Their pricks at my footfall; sometime am I
> All would with adders, who with cloven tongues
> Do hiss me into madness. (II, ii, 7-14)

Caliban fears that he may lose his intelligence and that he may turn into a beast. The suggestion, voiced in a warning to Trinculo and Stephano about what may happen if their plot is found out, is that Prospero will transform them into creatures farther down on the evolutionary scale: "We shall loose our time, / And be turned to barnacles, or to apes / With foreheads villainous low" (IV, i, 248-250). Prospero's discipline produces brutish behavior, and Caliban's fear of being reduced to bestiality is justified. When Prospero and Ariel catch Caliban, Stephano, and Trinculo they are hunted down like animals. Prospero's spirits become the hunter's ravenous dogs chasing the rebellious slave:

> Fury, Fury! There Tyrant, there! Hark, hark!
> Go charge my goblins that they grind their joints
> With dry convulsions, shorten up their sinews
> With aged cramps, and more pinch-spotted make them
> Than pard of cat o' mountain.
> [Ariel]   Hark, they roar.
> Let them be hunted soundly. (IV, i, 257-264)

The final lesson of Caliban's education is an acceptance of the inevitable failure of revolt. In his last act, Caliban appears in scraping submission to Prospero's authority. Encountering Prospero again after being hounded by the spirits, Caliban exclaims, "I shall be pinched to death!" (V, i, 276). Yet Prospero does not punish him and, as he does with the Neopolitans, offers rather his pardon. The "generosity" of the disciplinarian in refraining from torture, thus, as with a trained dog, inspires Caliban's obedience. Told to go quickly to Prospero's cell, Caliban now responds without the foot-dragging resistance he customarily displays: "Ay, that I will; and I'll be wise hereafter, / And seek for grace" (V, i, 294-5).

As so many of his plays attest, Shakespeare was intensely interested in and had great insight into the functioning of regal authority. If Columbus is for Lope the image of Spanish religious conviction and national allegiance, Prospero is Shakespeare's representation of English nationalism in its (unfulfilled) aspiration to pass from monarchical rule to an imperial absolutism. Absolutism calls for the administrative organization of national rule rather than the personal, idiosyncratic and incomplete subjection of monarchy. It engages the discourses of formal knowledge in its production of public spectacle and private surveillance. Included in absolutism is the domination of subjects beyond the nation itself. Thus Prospero's rule is ubiquitous and omnipresent. Essential to his rule is a form of surveillance that educates a national subject that knows it is being watched.

According to Foucault, the system of knowledge that establishes the relationship between individual and nation is revealed in the way society houses prisoners, investigates and manipulates human behavior, and educates its children. What is significant about the Panopticon is not simply its effectiveness as a prison but its implications as a model of pedagogy for the social order.

> The Panopticon was also a laboratory; it could be used as a machine to carry out experiments, to alter behavior, to train, or correct individuals. . . . To try out different punishments on prisoners, according to their crimes and character, and to seek out the most effective ones. . . . To try out pedagogical experiments—and in particular to take up once again the well-debated problem of secluded education, by using orphans. (203-4)

Prospero's island is indeed a sort of laboratory, where the isolation and manipulation of characters allows Prospero to "carry out experiments," "alter behavior," "train" and "correct" individuals. Unlike Lope's Caribbean islanders, Caliban is the sole representative sample, the test subject for the scientific cultural experiment of the island laboratory. As author of the island's "national curriculum," Prospero not only observes the inmates of the island; he also forms them. The basic activities of the play are those of correction, discipline, and reeducation, the essential technologies of Early Modern national authority.

Colonial education is doomed to failure. From Prospero's view Caliban is congenitally recalcitrant, and his education thus wasted. And, indeed, racism and colonial exploitation make more likely the native's rejection of colonial education. Acquiring language is not sufficient to alter their supposedly unregenerate nature. At what point, then, will the native turn the colonizer's language against him and adopt Caliban's stance? "You taught me language, and my profit on't / Is I know how to curse. The red plague rid you / For learning me your language!" (I, ii, 362-4). Even Caliban's awareness of Prospero's presence does not inhibit his rebellious actions. Though he has been schooled to know that Prospero's tortures are waiting for him, he is undaunted, "His spirits hear me, / And yet I needs must curse" (II, i, 4-5).

TREASON AND UTOPIA

Prospero's authority crosses over and back between the "New World" of the island and the "Old World" of Europe and the Europeans. Prospero first exercises his power/magic over Ariel, Caliban, and the natural elements. With this new world under his control he is ready to work his magic on the denizens of the old, on Ferdinand, Alonso, and the rest. Hulme notes a certain historical congruency in the progression of Prospero's use of magic, or in broader terms, in the way European technology takes on the aura of magic in the colonial context:

Prospero's magic is at his disposal on the island but not off of it; it can do anything at all except what is most necessary to survive. In other words there is a precise match with the situation of Europeans in America during the seventeenth century, whose technology (especially of firearms) suddenly *became* magical when introduced into a less technologically developed society, but who were incapable (for a variety of reason) of feeding themselves. (128)

Stephen Greenblatt argues that the orchestration of "wondrous" actions and spectacles was a conscious strategy on the part of Europeans to impress and manipulate New World peoples.[38] But this ability to impress is wielded not only in foreign lands. Knowledge of social control gained in the colonial contact can be recycled into tactics to control the citizens on the home front. As *The Tempest* indicates, the relationships between national sovereignty and colonial domination, between colonial native and domestic citizen, are complex and mutually constituted.[39]

Increasing national and colonial control assumes an expanding threat of disruption, treason, and rebellion. Using an image appropriate to *The Tempest*, Karl Marx describes bourgeois society as a "sorcerer, who is no longer able to control the powers of the nether world whom he has called up by his spells" (478). The same might be said of absolutism—the English revolution, however partial and incomplete, was a mere generation away. Nowhere is this image of power run wild more apparent than in the utopian dream of freedom that runs throughout the play. This dream is present in Gonzalo's imaginative utopia, in Ariel's reiterated requests for freedom, in Miranda's and Ferdinand's desire for each other, in the natural beauty of the island, in the relationship of Caliban to nature and in his recollection of pre-Prospero independence (when he was "mine own king"), and, above all, in Stephano's, Trinculo's and Caliban's treasonous rebellion.[40] Their plans to kill Prospero, marry Miranda, take over the island and insure that "thought is free" (III, ii, 121) lead to the interruption of the wedding masque and render Prospero more "distempered" and "angry" than Miranda has ever seen him. Though in *The Tempest* events take on mock seriousness, as in *El nuevo mundo*, the activity of colonial revolt and its suppression shape the plot of the drama.

Prospero's surveillance—his use of magical technology and disciplinary pedagogy to establish a monarchical, nearly absolutist rule on the island—is contrary to the utopian imagination so markedly present in the play. That this imagination has a treasonous component is recognized by Curt Breight's work on rebellion in Shakespeare's England. Breight documents an extensive "discourse of treason" in late sixteenth-century England. He argues that

Renaissance London was filled with representations of treason in the form of sermons, proclamations, cheap pamphlets, chronicles, drama, public trials, body parts, and the manufacture of such parts through public executions. (3)

Public torture and execution of possible "conspirators" took place on a regular basis. Addressing *The Tempest*, Breight emphasizes that the enactment of authority on the stage presupposes the judgment of the people on the conduct of the ruler:

Shakespeare casts Prospero as stage manager of conspiracy in episodes that directly resemble contemporary treason cases and documents. Nearly all the characters *inside* the play are physically and psychologically subjected by Prospero in his bid for political rehabilitation through mystification of his power as a divinely protected figure. But the audience exists *outside* Prospero's manipulation of characters and situations and is thereby enabled to perceive Shakespeare's clever demystification of various official strategies within the discourse of treason. (1)[41]

While not dismissing those that read Shakespeare as making a conservative intervention in English colonial discourse, Breight describes Shakespeare's position *vis-à-vis* the national sovereign as either "clever radicalism, subversion, or irreverence."[42] Breight sees the Caliban-led attack on Prospero as class associated: "Caliban's conspiracy appears to present a précis of Elizabethan fears regarding masterless men, and the drunkenness of the conspirators enforces the specific official beliefs that subversion sprang from the local alehouse" (17). Breight notes our distance in history from the spectacle of Elizabethan punishment and thus explains the failure to recognize the severity of Caliban's various punishments. Breight's lengthy quotations from contemporary witnesses as to the use of heated iron pincers to "pinch" chunks of flesh from the bodies of state prisoners compellingly make his point.

Breight identifies a national discourse of treason in *The Tempest*, yet this discourse cannot be separated from the imperial imagination. While serving as a training ground for European practices of authority, the New World is also the site of the imaginative projection of prelapsarian paradise. Gonzalo's Montaigne-inspired fantasy of an egalitarian, undisciplined society draws on the marvelous

representations in medieval and Renaissance travel literature that while
stereotyping the Other also offer utopian dreams of freedom:

Had I plantation of this isle, my lord . . .
And were the king on't, what would I do? . . .
I'th'commonwealth I would by contraries
Exercise all things, for no kind of traffic
Would I admit; no name of magistrate;
Letters should not be known; riches, poverty,
And use of service, none; contract, succession,
Bourn, bound of land, tilth, vineyard, none;
No use of metal, corn, or wine, or oil;
No occupation, all men idle, all,
And women too, but innocent and pure; . . .
All things in common should produce
Without sweat or endeavour. Treason, felony,
Sword, pike, knife, gun, or need of any engine
Would I not have, but nature should bring forth
Of it own kind all foison, all abundance
To feed my innocent people. (II, i, 140-62)

Gonzalo's vision of a commonwealth is immensely appealing not only
in light of contemporary European society but in terms of what
Prospero's island is not. Gonzalo's vision is contrary to the experience
of Prospero's power/magic, surveillance, disciplinary pedagogy,
manipulation, and control. Leaving the hierarchy of Renaissance
society behind the settler can in the "New World" create a better, more
just nation.[43] The failure of this possibility is what drives the ending of
the play, Prospero's abjuration of his magical powers and his all-seeing
rule.

     Despite its liberating possibilities in the English or European
context, the discourse of utopia serves to encourage New World
colonization and exploitation. As advertising propaganda for settlement
the utopian myth is effective in recruiting "your tired, your poor, your
huddled masses yearning to breathe free." Simultaneously, the fantasy
of New World utopia contains within it the inspiration for colonial
domination. While the attractive possibility of the utopia depends, in
part, on the imagined life style of the Native American, the reality of
New World colonization increasingly demands the reorganization of
Native American society in an acceptable, subordinate role. The

disappointing discovery that native life does not conform to European notions of utopia provides an insidious justification for European governance of native society. The surprising difficulty of survival in the New World leads to desperate conscription of the Native American into forced labor. Prospero instructs Miranda that Caliban's services are necessary:

> [Miranda]   'Tis a villain, sir,
> I do not love to look on.
> [Prospero]   But as 'tis,
> We cannot miss him, He does make our fire,
> Fetch in our wood, and serves in offices
> That profit us. What ho, slave! Caliban!
> (I, ii, 308-13)

The "failure" of the native to welcome the settlement of the European with open arms leads to the European's vengeful use of force.

The celebrated abjuration of magic at the end of the play manifests a nostalgic return to pre-scientific personal and aristocratic notions of governance. This return is necessitated by the fearful aspect of enthroned absolutist domination and serves as an ideological containment of the representation of tyrannical power. The attraction of this scene, its "humanizing" of Prospero, is both compelling and propagandizing. The compulsion the audience feels to have Prospero forswear his magic emanates from the democratic impulse to reject his overweening, autocratic rule and all-powerful use of magic.[44] The moral unregeneracy of Sebastian and Antonio, however, portends the resumption of political intrigue and princely manipulation on the return to Italy. The epilogue of the play is part of the process of satisfying the audience's democratic impulses and gives us clues as to how the abjuration of magic works as apology. Prospero posits that the power to release him is in his audience:

> Now 'tis true
> I must be here confined by you,
> Or sent to Naples. Let me not,
> Since I have my dukedom got,
> And pardoned the deceiver, dwell
> In this bare island by your spell,
> But release me from my bands

With the help of your good hands. (V, i, 321-8)

Lacking "spirits to enforce, art to enchant" (V, i, 332) Prospero is no
longer the sovereign but now poses as the prisoner requesting—as have
all the other characters in the play—freedom from bondage. In
addressing the audience directly, Prospero, the humbled sovereign,
seeks legitimation from "the people." Thus, in the simultaneous
recognition of the operation of absolutist authority, there is the promise
of democratic rule.

In this sense the ending of the play is both promise made and
promise broken. The enactment of national authority on the stage
presupposes the judgment of the people on the conduct of the ruler.
This is the public theater's threat to authority. Yet, the theater also
offers a mechanism of public control; in Brechtian terms, the catharsis
of pity and fear has a politically pacifying effect. By describing the play
simply as "clever radicalism," Breight doesn't take adequate
consideration of the mechanisms of ideological containment. As Orgel
points out in the preface to the Oxford edition,

> Prospero's epilogue is unique in the Shakespeare canon in that its speaker
> declares himself not an actor in a play but a character in a fiction. The
> release he craves of the audience is the freedom to continue his history
> beyond the limits of the text. (204)

In going beyond the limits of the text, one must also inquire about the
audience's freedom. In *The Tempest*, the abjuration of magic and this
final positing of power in the hands of the audience mystifies the
relations of power, and allows the powerful position of judgment to
take its realization only in the imaginative realm of the theater.

CONCLUSION

Lope and Shakespeare are monumental figures in their respective
national cultures and in the narration of their respective national
histories. Their *œuvre* consolidates disparate social and political
elements into common national subjectivities and reflects the Early
Modern transition from idiosyncratic monarchy to emerging nation-
state. *El nuevo mundo* and *The Tempest*, in particular, correctly help us
to situate European nationhood in an imperial relationship to the rest of
the world. The plays we have examined form part of a colonial

discourse that constructs identities not only for Spaniards and Englishmen but for dominated non-European subjects as well. While this European discourse scripts unsuccessful native resistance and rebellion, the second half of *Making Subject(s)* draws our attention to presumedly successful native rebellions that forged the emergence of "third-world" nations in another great period of national emergence, the later half of the twentieth century.

PART II

Anticolonial Nationalism and the Postcolonial Novel

Pedagogical and Performative Nationalism in Ousmane Sembène's *Les bouts de bois de Dieu*

The mobilization of the masses, when it arises out of the war of liberation, introduces into each man's consciousness the ideas of a common cause, of a national identity and of a collective history.

Frantz Fanon

We then have a contested cultural territory where the people must be thought in a double-time; the people are the historical "objects" of a nationalist pedagogy, giving the discourse an authority that is based on the pre-given or constituted historical origin or event; the people are also the "subjects" of a process of signification that must erase any prior or originary presence of the nation-people to demonstrate the prodigious, living principle of the people as that continual process by which national life is redeemed and signified as a repeating and reproductive process.

Homi Bhabha

In the second section of this book we will consider the ways that postcolonial writers rework and redefine colonial relationships in order—like Lope and Shakespeare—to formulate national identities and establish national histories. Rather than a dialectical process of action, reaction, and synthesis, we will see that anti- and postcolonial nation building is better understood as what Homi Bhabha calls "mimicry"—a complex, shifting, and uncontainable series of actions that undo, play with, and write back to the scripts first established by a

Eurocentric colonial discourse. To understand "third-world" nationhood requires a knowledge of national emergence in the European past, of colonialism, of the anticolonial struggle, and of the simultaneous and ongoing process Ngugi has called "the decolonization of the mind." From the making of national subjects in Renaissance Europe, we thus turn in this chapter to the narration of resistant national consciousness in the "third world."

Incorporating social, cultural, and historical diversity, the nation-state has become by our own time the universal political structure for a presumably global modernity. In much of the "third world," and in Africa particularly, European systems of administration and models of individualistic citizenship were imposed on heterogeneous populations and traditions. Anticolonial struggles led to the establishment of nation-states that, ironically, have perpetuated underdevelopment and neocolonial exploitation. Accepting the Western-defined nation-state as an inevitable stage of political, social, and cultural modernization, "third-world" nations continue, as Partha Chatterjee puts it, to be subject to "a world order which only sets their tasks for them and over which they have no control" (10).

Frantz Fanon's conception of the creation of national culture in the struggle for liberation from colonialism provides a starting point for the consideration of nationhood in the African context. Abdul JanMohamed, Neil Lazarus, and Ngugi wa Thiong'o bring Fanon's thought to the politics and language of the European-language African novel, and Homi Bhabha extends Fanon's consideration of national culture into a discussion of identity formation. Bhabha's distinction between the pedagogical and the performative aspects of national identity (suggested in the above citation, and spelled out below) allows us to explore more carefully Ousmane Sembène's construction of a revolutionary African national culture. In twentieth-century Africa as well as in Renaissance Spain and England, pedagogical relationships and systems of education are important to the formation of national identities. By comparing *Les bouts de bois de Dieu* to two other exemplary texts that treat education under colonialism, Ngugi's *Petals of Blood* and Rigoberta Menchú's *testimonio*, we will see how the pedagogical and the performative are constructed in Sembène's novel. Recognizing the cross-over and complexities of national culture in the anticolonial *Les bouts de bois de Dieu* opens into the issues of postcolonial identity, treated in the next chapter. The complexity of these founding discourses is nowhere more evident than in the representations of the anticolonial movement by Africa's creative writers. Produced in the same overdetermined space as the nation, caught between inherited European forms and non-European identities, the first generation of African postcolonial novels can be read as an active attempt to re-create a collective national history.[1]

In returning in the 1990s to the discourses of African anticolonial struggle, my purpose differs significantly from readings that seek more simply to legitimate African nationhood—an effort that repeatedly falls back on those cultural grounds set out by nineteenth-century European nationalism: common heritage, tradition, language, and shared enemies or outsiders. Instead, as when we examined European national emergence in the Renaissance, we must consider the overdeterminations, deviances, and differentiations in the imagining of African nationhoods. It is this complexity that will enable us to understand the relationship of the founding "third-world" national discourses to the present postcolonial/global situation.

FANON AND THE AFRICAN NOVEL

While independent nationhood was the rallying cry in anticolonial movements, "independent" is a misleading way to view polities modeled on previously existing states and situated within borders inscribed by European colonizers. This contradiction is critical today as economic and cultural globalism operates to complicate rather than eliminate marginalization and oppression within African nations. Yet, the most perspicacious nationalists of the anticolonial era were aware of the potential pitfalls of nationhood even as they strived to achieve it.

Frantz Fanon's now-classic essays in *Wretched of the Earth* (1961) are salient to any reading of the African novel that seeks to examine the relationship between revolutionary literature and the emergence of national identity. In "On National Culture," Fanon proposes a definition of national culture relevant to Africa during its struggle for independence from Europe. Fanon's notion depends on the active efforts of intellectuals to achieve a just social order. Given the power of colonial authority to write the history of the people they conquer, African historical narratives that describe a dignified cultural past are a necessary part of all anticolonial resistance:

The claim to a national culture in the past does not only rehabilitate that nation and serve as a justification for the hope of a future national culture.

In the sphere of psycho-affective equilibrium it is responsible for an important change in the native. Perhaps we have not sufficiently demonstrated that colonialism is not simply content to impose its rule upon the present and the future of a dominated country. Colonialism is not satisfied merely with holding a people in its grip and emptying the native's brain of all form and content. By a kind of perverted logic, it turns to the past of the oppressed people, and distorts, disfigures and destroys it. (170)

Arguing that a discourse on African culture counter to the colonialist one is necessary, Fanon also warns that a resistant discourse is vulnerable to the terms and strategies it seeks to reverse. Any attempt to assert African cultural values is necessarily conditioned by European racist denigration:

The Negro, never so much a Negro as since he has been dominated by the whites, when he decides to prove that he has a culture and to behave like a cultured person, comes to realize that history points out a well-defined path to him: he must demonstrate that a Negro culture exists. (171)

Fanon believes that nativist movements such as those organized around Cesaire's and Senghor's concept of *nègritude*, rather than throwing off colonial domination, tend to be defined by it: "The unconditional affirmation of African culture has succeeded the unconditional affirmation of European culture" (172). Fanon is concerned lest intellectuals in marking a reversal of colonialist attitudes toward the "savages," develop an uncritical stance toward the traditions of their society. Against a nativism which leads "up a blind alley," Fanon proposes a more comprehensive notion of national culture offering not a folkloristic repetition of past practices but a conscious present-oriented activity intimately connected to the effort to achieve liberation and justice.

A national culture is not a folklore, nor an abstract populism that believes it can discover the people's true nature. It is not made up of the inert dregs of gratuitous actions, that is to say actions which are less and less attached to the ever-present reality of the people. A national culture is the whole body of efforts made by a people in the sphere of thought to describe, justify and praise the action through which that people has created itself and keeps itself in existence. A national culture in the under-developed countries should therefore take its place at the very heart of the struggle for freedom these countries are carrying on. (188)[2]

Rather than following nineteenth-century European nationalists, such as Herder, who look for (and, indeed construct) an ethnic, racial, or spiritual unity in the ancient past, however, Fanon derives his nationhood from within the existing (if currently unjust) juridical and economic structures that govern colonial society. Fanon's view of national culture thus takes the term "national" in its most "present oriented" sense. For him, any movement directed beyond colonialism and toward national independence must take account of present realities and not allow itself to be determined by mythical racial thinking or backward-looking sentimentality. Thus, in its attention to present *and* future, Fanon's conception of national culture is both historical and utopian. It is based on a dynamic interpretation of culture that looks to the struggle of the national people rather than to contrived "traditions":

> The desire to attach oneself to tradition or bring abandoned traditions to life again does not only mean going against the current of history but also opposing one's own people. (180)

Drawing on marxism, existentialism, and the imperatives of the colonial situation, Fanon thus offers a conception of national culture which is contingent and participatory.[3]

Fanon was aware of the potential problems of nationhood even as he strove to achieve it. As the first epigram to this chapter suggests, Fanon was convinced that the nation-state offered a crucial pathway for colonized people to free themselves of the subservient mentality inculcated by European rule, to reconstruct their identity and their sense of "collective history." Simultaneously, as he explains in the essay "The Pitfall of National Consciousness" (from *Wretched of the Earth*) he recognized that a mere accommodation of African social and cultural practices to a borrowed nation-state political structure served the interests of an already Europeanized class, "the bourgeois leaders of under-developed countries [who] imprison national consciousness in sterile formalism" (163). In "Pitfall," Fanon argues that the African bourgeoisie acts as "the transmission line between the nation and a capitalism, rampant though camouflaged, which today puts on the masque of neocolonialism" (124). Thus Fanon argued that a meaningful nationalism was possible but had to be grounded in the ongoing efforts of all sectors of the population to overthrow domination and exploitation.

It is no wonder that Fanon's thought has had such a powerful impact on both African writers and critics or that it continues to play a touchstone role in contemporary postcolonial theory (consider Said's *Culture and Imperialism* as a case in point). Biodun Jeyifo emphasizes the critical opening provided by Fanon's notion of culture:

> If culture is not merely the distinctiveness of a certain way of life, if it is not only a domain of beliefs, practices and institutions which retains an "essence" while other domains like the economic and political change, if indeed the analytically isolable cultural sphere changes, complexly and dialectally, with all other spheres of human action, then we are prepared to see "culture" in the same non-reified and dynamic sense in which we are prepared to see, say, the economic and political spheres. (4-5)

In *Manichean Aesthetics: The Politics of Literature in Colonial Africa* (1983), Abdul R. JanMohamed brings Fanon's thought on colonial domination to an examination of the English African novel as produced by both whites and blacks during the colonial period. JanMohamed analyzes the way in which the Manichean divisions between colonizer and colonized identified by Fanon (in *Wretched of the Earth*) tend to dominate fiction about Africa. While nationalism or the nation is not JanMohamed's primary emphasis, his work may be said to extend Fanon's thought on the relationship of African art to African national identity. JanMohamed emphasizes that the narratives of African writers are strongly influenced by European paradigms for African modernization. Bearing both economic and social imperatives, modernization theory entails not only the capitalist development of the continent and the incorporation of Africa into the Western-dominated world market but also the transformation of "primitive" and "tribal" notions of social and individual order into "nationalist" and "individualist" ones.   .

JanMohamed elaborates his argument about modernization in a discussion of the Nigerian writer Chinua Achebe. In Achebe's use of a realist narrative of Ibo history to confront the colonialist version of the African past he incorporates a view of the individual that is inevitably modernist.[4] As a way of showing the nefarious effect of colonialism on the colonized, Achebe's fiction focuses on those moments of greatest personal alienation in his tragic heroes, Okonkwo in *Things Fall Apart* and Obi in *No Longer at Ease*.

> The most important internal contradiction, the social estrangement of Achebe's heroes due to their tenacious adherence to values cherished by society, depends for its success on the fact that from the beginning of the narratives the heroes are *potentially* alienated. Each narrative then gradually develops this potential until the protagonists experience the final calamities that result in their absolute alienation. (162)

While these instances of individual alienation are profoundly related to the encounter with the new colonial order, they do not lead to community or collective resistance. JanMohamed's examination of Achebe's work within the context of modernization theory reveals how realist modes of narration foreground a colonist alienation between individual and society rather than narrating collective action. Achebe's novels may be seen as "national" in the sense that they "correct" colonialist discourse on African primitivism and portray the dilemmas of emerging African nations, but they fall short of Fanon's notion of national culture in that they fail to portray resistant national culture as *in the making*.

That the making of national culture should not be confused with formal national independence is a point emphasized by Neil Lazarus, another scholar of the African novel who derives his categories and critical insight from Fanon. In *Resistance in Postcolonial African Fiction* (1990). Lazarus argues that Fanon's thought has "an extraordinary explanatory power" but that at times it conflates the struggle for national independence with full-scale African revolution. Lazarus calls this tendency in Fanon his "messianism."[5] Lazarus contends that the radical intellectuals and writers who were influenced by Fanon's work overvalued the independence struggle and were consequently unable to explain the cooptation of nationalism in the post-independence era. Though the urgency of the struggle in Algeria inspired Fanon's messianic aspirations for national independence, Lazarus points to Fanon's "Pitfall" essay as a warning against the appropriation of the nationalist cause by the national bourgeoisie. While focusing his critique on the novels of Ayi Kwei Armah, Lazarus argues that messianic expectations of independence led many African writers to disappointment and disillusion in the postcolonial era. Lazarus argues instead that even in the postcolonial period, African intellectuals must continue to address "questions of national culture and political justice" (214).[6]

The problem of how to reconcile Fanon's conception of the engaged and ongoing construction of national culture with current deconstructionist thinking on the formation of identity is addressed by Homi Bhabha in his essay "DissemiNation: Time, narrative, and the margins of the modern nation" (in *Nation and Narration*, 1990). In Fanon's writing, Bhabha finds a productive tension between historical materialism and the poststructuralist emphasis on the instability of representation. Bhabha says that he "starts with" Fanon's essay because Fanon warns against the appropriation of culture by intellectuals who claim to represent the people and focuses instead on the moment that national culture is performed. Bhahha marks in Fanon's thinking a separation between the intellectual's description of a fixed national culture and the performance of national culture "that cannot be a knowledge that is stabilized in its enunciation." (303) It is from this separation that Bhabha develops a distinction between "pedagogical" and "performative" nationalism. Bhabha identifies the pedagogical with the stereotype, that which is institutionalized as reproducible knowledge. In the colonial context, the attempt to assimilate "the natives" to European culture and citizenship offers an instance of a pedagogical expression of national identity. Yet the effort by resistance nationalists to locate and fix a national identity in a folkloric, nativist, or *nègritude* past is no less pedagogical.

The "performative" as Bhabha uses the term refers on the other hand to Fanon's conception of national culture, to a conscious present-oriented activity intimately connected to the struggle for liberation and justice. To elaborate what he means by the performative Bhabha borrows from Fanon the phrase "the fluctuating movement that the people are *just* giving shape to" (303). Thus the concept of performance focuses on the ever-changing moment of resistance. Bhabha identifies the performative with instability, that which, through struggle, seeks to alter the terms of identity. He writes,

The present of the people's history, then, is a practice that destroys the constant principles of the national culture that attempt to hark back to a "true" national past, which is often represented in the reified forms of realism and stereotype. Such pedagogical knowledges and continuist national narratives miss the "zone of occult instability where the people dwell" (Fanon's phrase). (303)

This tension between the repetition of stereotype and the formulation of a Fanonian national culture, between a colonial discourse and an anticolonial resistance provides a powerful framework for reading "third-world" literature. Our examination of *The Tempest* has emphasized the pedagogical formation of national identity, the construction of increasingly isolated subjects in an ever more codified social order through various processes of surveillance, discipline and education. This chapter proposes a closer look at the other side of the picture, the activity of anticolonial resistance and the production of subjects through the performance of national culture.

THE PROBLEM OF LANGUAGE

As we have seen in Lope's and Shakespeare's plays, in the colonial context, language is critical to establishing the status of colonizer and colonized. Thus, anticolonial writers who take up their pens to write in English or French or Spanish raise the question of the appropriateness of the performance of "third world" national culture in a European tongue. Can a text written in the language of the European masters completely resist colonial domination? Can, for instance, a francophone novel perform the national culture of Senegal? Does the depiction of national struggle by African and "third world" authors who write in European languages inevitably stereotype national culture and remain unalterably pedagogical?

There are multiple reasons for the existence of an extensive African anticolonial literature written in European languages. The educated classes, although a relatively small proportion of the population, are usually literate in a European language. Indeed, a European language is the first or only language for some Africans, and many Africans are multilingual.[7] Given the enormous language diversity within many African countries, a European language *makes possible* communication between citizens of the same country or between Africans in different nation-states. A European language allows the African writer to address an international audience, including readers in the metropole. Moreover, a European language may offer the only way for African writers to get into print.

Many prominent African writers believe they can use European languages and literary forms, developing African national culture by preserving African linguistic flavor. To this end these writers modify

European languages and genres. Gabriel Okara describes the effort to accommodate English to African perspectives:

> As a writer who believed in the utilization of African ideas, African philosophy and African folklore and imagery to the fullest extent possible, I am of the opinion the only way to use them effectively is to translate them almost literally from the African native language into whatever European language he is using as a medium of expression.[8]

Chinua Achebe speaks in a similar vein:

> I feel that the English language will be able to carry the weight of my African experience. But it will have to be a new English, still in full communion with its ancestral home but altered to suit new African surroundings.[9]

The syncretic combining of European and African languages subverts one of the most powerful weapons of colonial domination. In *Things Fall Apart*, for instance, Chinua Achebe describes the plan of the district commissioner to inscribe the complex, painful events of the destruction of the Ibo people in a mere paragraph of his book, *The Pacification of the Primitive Tribes of the Lower Niger*. This title, with its mix of academic anthropology, pseudo-scientific objectivity, and militaristic euphemism, is appropriated by Achebe ironically undercutting colonialist discourse. The title is "double voiced," in Bakhtin's sense of belonging to two different language contexts.[10] In speaking of national culture, Fanon emphasizes not a return to "pure" or "pre-contact" traditions but the dynamic nature of all cultural formations and the importance of making national culture in the contested struggle for liberation. Accepting Fanon's definition of national culture allows one to argue that even a syncretic expression, if forged in the process of resistance, should be considered a manifestation of African national culture.

However, Fanon's thinking on the question of language and national culture is complex and not always consistent. In his essay "The Negro and Language" (in *Black Skin, White Masks*) Fanon emphasizes both the dilemma of language in the colonial situation and the power that the colonized takes on when he masters the colonizer's idiom. While it is essential that the intellectual know the people of his or her nation, the role in Fanonian thought of European languages in the formation of national culture could at best be described as ambiguous. In the colonial context "an inferiority complex has been created by the death and burial of local cultural originality." He notes with a certain irony that "The colonized is elevated above his jungle status in proportion to his adoption of the mother country's cultural standards"(18). In the struggle against European colonialism, Fanon viewed the adoption of European languages as a necessary step:

A man who has a language consequently possesses the world expressed
and implied by that language. What we are getting at becomes plain:
Mastery of language affords remarkable power. (18)

While Fanon recognizes that the native's use of European languages plays a role in the struggle against colonial rule, there are moments in Fanon's thinking when it appears that African literature written in European languages should not be considered as "national" in the future-directed sense to which his theory aspires. In "Reciprocal Bases of National Culture and the Fight for Freedom" (in *The Wretched of the Earth*), Fanon charts a course away from expression in European languages, a direction radical African writers are increasingly deciding to follow.

While at the beginning the native intellectual used to produce his work to
be read exclusively by the oppressor, whether with the intention of
charming him or denouncing him through ethical or subjectivist means,
now the native writer progressively takes on the habit of addressing his
own people. It is only from that moment that we can speak of a national
literature. Here there is, at the level of literary creation, the taking up and
clarification of themes which are typically nationalist. This may be
properly called a literature of combat, in the sense that it calls upon the
whole people to fight for their existence as a nation. (193)

Fanon, writing in French, is intensely aware that European languages continue to be part of the colonialist and the neocolonialist project. Literature written in a European language presents significant problems for the writer who wants to communicate with his or her own population who not only do not read French (or any other European language) but may be illiterate in their own tongue as well.

After a careful study of the thought of Frantz Fanon the Kenyan writer Ngugi wa Thiong'o made a decision to write in his native

Gikuyu rather than in English. The most complete statement of his decision is found in *Decolonizing the Mind* (1986), an essay in which he describes African literature written in European languages as inextricably tied to colonial educational systems and the rise of an African bourgeoisie critical of colonialism. This class, anxious to establish its national authority and international respectability, found that literature in European languages was appropriate to their purpose.

Right from its conception it [Afro-European literature] was the literature of the petty-bourgeoisie born of the colonial schools and universities. It could not be otherwise, given the linguistic medium of its message. . . . This literature by Africans in European languages was specifically that of the nationalistic bourgeoisie in its creators, its thematic concerns and its consumption. Internationally the literature helped this class, which in politics, business, and education, was assuming leadership of the countries newly emergent from colonialism, or of those struggling to so emerge, to explain Africa to the world: Africa has a past and a culture of dignity and human complexity. (20)

Ngugi argues that, from its inception, "Afro-European" literature played a role in anti-imperialist struggles, but that, after independence, as the nation-state became controlled by a *comprador* bourgeoisie, this literature became cynical and disillusioned. Ngugi blames the post-colonial failure of Afro-European literature on its reliance on European languages. As writers attempted to examine neocolonial societies and internal exploitation, they found themselves increasingly cut off from the peasants and working class of their own countries. Ngugi's solution was to write in Gikuyu, which meant attempting to forge drama and novels in a language without a literary history. He describes how his Gikuyu novel (translated into English as *Devil on the Cross*) became part of the oral traditions of the largely illiterate Gikuyu population:

A family would get together every evening and one of their literate members would read it for them. Workers would also gather in groups, particularly during the lunch break, and they would get one of them to read the book. It was read in buses; it was read in taxis; it was read in public bars. (83)

By writing in an African language and by promoting African theater and oral culture, Ngugi's work in the late 1970s and 1980s sought to create the kind of engaged and dynamic African national culture aspired to by Fanon.

As African writers committed to the struggle against colonialism and for social justice, Ngugi and Ousmane Sembène are frequently compared. Both are leading figures in examining the role of language in the construction of African national culture. Sembène, even more than Ngugi, is associated with the peasants and working class. One of the few African writers without a university education, he is an experienced fisherman and dockworker.

Cet homme du peuple y est profondément resté enraciné, et son "populisme" ne provient pas d'un choix d'intellectuel en crise de conscience, mais d'une expérience vécue qui lui fait trouver immédiatement le ton et les sentiments justes quand il parle des ouvriers ou des paysans. (Kesteloot, 225)

This man of the people remains profoundly rooted in them, and his populism is not the choice of an intellectual in a crisis of conscience, but a lived experience that immediately finds the right pitch and feeling when speaking of the workers or of the peasants. [11]

Given his working-class background and the history of France's extensive efforts at assimilation in Senegal, the question of language is especially critical for Sembène.

Like Ngugi, Sembène has made significant efforts to valorize the use of African languages for the expression of African culture. The trajectory of Sembène's work is increasingly toward Wolof as the language for the expression of Senegalese culture. [12] Sembène is unequivocal about the importance of Wolof:

Je pense que la langue ouolof devrait être la langue nationale du Sénégal à la place du français. N'est-elle pas parlé au moins par 80% de la population? (Sembène, "Interview," 121)

I think that the Wolof language should be the national language of Senegal instead of French. Isn't it spoken by more than 80% of the population?

Along with the linguist Pathé Diagne, Sembène founded *Kaddu*, the first journal in the Wolof language.

While Ngugi turned·to theater and writing in Gikuyu, Sembène combined his writing with film making.[13] The leading Senegalese movie maker, Sembène was one of the first to produce full-length films in Africa. Sembène believes film serves a particularly important educational function.

De toutes les écoles la meilleure c'est le cinéma qui réunit plus d'adeptes que n'importe quelle mosqué, église, ou parti politique. (Tire, 45)

Of all the schools the best is the cinema which gathers together more followers than any mosque, church, or political party.

Sembène's cinematographic career began in 1962 with *Borom Sarret* and has continued up to the present with a series of films based on his own writing. His films have won awards at festivals in Africa, Europe, and the Soviet Union. Sembène has also begun to write both fiction and film scripts in Wolof (e.g., *Ceddo* in 1977). He believes that film is taking the place of the oral tradition of the African village or, in his own words, that "cinema replaces the palaver tree" (Schipper, 568).

While decrying the rise of an African bourgeoisie and challenging the uncritical use of European languages to express African culture, Fanon, Ngugi, and Sembène nonetheless emphasize the revolutionary role of African writing in European languages at particular moments in the history of anticolonial struggle. Unlike Ngugi, however, Sembène continues to write in French. In 1981 he published the two-volume novel *Le Dernier de l'empire*. In his postcolonial writing, Sembène's use of French is increasingly ironic, directing acerbic attacks against the nationalist bourgeoisie. *Xala*, for instance, would appear to turn the French language against the very Senegalese who use it. The transition to new forms that are more closely tied to African languages—such as film and theater—raises questions about Ngugi and Sembène's European language writing, yet neither writer has repudiated his earlier work. Sembène claims that "I work with the material of everyday life of ordinary people. They recognize themselves in my works and identify with my characters."[14] Moreover, both colonial educational systems and European languages and literatures continue to have an important place in African nations more than a generation after independence, a point both Ngugi and Sembène recognize.[15] While the expression of a national culture in languages not spoken by all or even a majority of the residents of a newly independent state is one of the contradictory legacies of African nationhood, it is important to recognize that the struggle for the supremacy of one language or dialect over another has been part of nearly all national histories in the "first" as well as the "third-world."

LES BOUTS DE BOIS DE DIEU

Written in the year of Senegalese independence (1960), Ousmane Sembène's now-classic *Les bouts de bois de Dieu* is an exemplary text for reviewing the postcolonial nation-state against anticolonial nationalist discourse. In *Les bouts de bois de Dieu*, Sembène narrates the history of the Dakar-Niger railway strike that occurred in French West Africa between October 1947 and March 1948 and in which Sembène personally participated as a labor organizer. A hard-fought struggle and, in the end, a victory for African workers, this strike enhanced the power of trade unions and proved an exemplary instance of coordination between the peoples of Senegal and Soudan some thirteen years before independence and the formation of the Mali Federation.[16] The 380-page novel alternates scenes from three towns at different points along the rail line: Dakar, on the Western Coast (now capital of Senegal); Thiès, a rail junction point for the Northern line to Saint-Louis; and, Bamako on the Niger River at the eastern terminus of the rail line (now capital of Mali). Through the novel we learn of the building of the railway, the appropriation of African lands, the abuse of African workers, the transformation of African society by the expansion of the colonial economy, and the violent crushing of an earlier strike by the French authorities.

By juxtaposing individuals and scenes from diverse social, economic, cultural, and generational perspectives, the imaginative community of the novel seemingly encompasses the whole of the French West African Colony. Indeed, *Les bouts de bois de Dieu* is remarkable for the variety and vividness of its depictions. There are African railway workers with diverse occupations and personalities, as well as religious leaders, shop keepers, students, political prisoners, and villagers including mothers, grandparents, relatives, adolescents, and children. There are French railroad supervisors, clerks, colonial administrators and their families, soldiers, a prison camp commandant.

The proliferation of individuals in the novel is at first confusing, but through Sembène's deft characterizations and the return of narrative attention to particular figures, individual voices and personalities eventually emerge. Among the most prominent characters are: Bakayoko, a railway worker who is a key organizer of the strike—a character we finally meet half-way through the novel; Penda, a strong-willed prostitute who leads the women's march and is shot when the women enter Dakar; N Dye Touti, an educated young woman who must choose between French and African allegiances; and Fa Keita, a spiritual patriarch taken to a colonial prison camp. There are unforgettable scenes of public confrontation: the attack by the soldiers in the marketplace; the night-time defense of the workers compound led by women bearing flaming straw against mounted soldiers; the shooting of two African children by a railroad supervisor; the wresting of a microphone from the French-speaking dignitaries by Bakayoko to call, in Wolof, for a general strike; and the surrounding of the homes of the colonial administrators by the families of the strikers.

The characters of *Les bouts de bois de Dieu* perform precisely the kind of dynamic and engaged resistance that Frantz Fanon identifies as national culture. The novel begins with a meeting of workers who convince each other that their starvation wages and humiliating treatment justify resistance and a strike. This popular organization of the workers is met by a violent crackdown by the government forces and a life-and-death struggle ensues. The hunger and desperation of the families of the strikers spreads throughout the community, and yet by standing together to demand more equitable treatment, a powerful collective determination is forged. Unanticipated forms of resistance emerge that transform the culture of the Africans. The wives of strikers determine that they will leave their families and march from Thiès to Dakar to demand national attention to the cause of the striking workers. As they pass through villages, they draw the support of the countryside, and their final triumphant arrival at Dakar brings the whole city into the streets. Through the struggle and self-confident negotiations with the colonial administrators, the workers recognize the authority of their own voices and their ability to rule themselves.

Even though the novel is composed in French, *Les bouts de bois de Dieu* is by no means an endorsement of that or any other European language as the only or even the most significant expression of African national culture. While all of the educated Africans portrayed are able to speak French and most of the other African characters know some

French words, French is clearly identified throughout the novel as the language of the colonial domination. When Africans speak French to each other, it usually indicates the adoption of a false and artificial sense of superiority. The older generation admonish the young to cherish their African language. For instance in the first chapter Niakoro objects to Ad'jibid'ji's use of French words:

Dans ma ligné qui est aussi celle de ton père, personne ne parle le toubabou et personee n'en est mort! Depuis ma naissance—et Dieu sait qu'il y a longtemps—je n'ai jamis entendu dire qu'un toubabou ait appris le bambara ou une autre language de ce pays. Mais vous autres, les déracinés, vous ne pensez qu'á ça. A croire que notre langue est tombée en décadence! (18)

Among my people, who are your father's people, too, no one speaks the white man's language, and no one has died of it! Ever since I was born—and God knows that was a long time ago—I have never heard of a white man who had learned to speak Bambara, or any other language of this country. But you rootless people think only of learning his, while our language dies. (4)[17]

Although the younger, Western-educated generation is shown to be familiar with French, those Africans that speak French exclusively are almost always portrayed as co-opted by the French colonial system. The complicitous Imams, governor-general, and mayor-deputy all speak in French. The strikers put the colonizer's privileged language in question in negotiations with the railway management.

. . . étant donné que votre ignorance d'au moins une de nos languages est un handicap pour vous, nous emploierons le français, c'est une question de politesse. Mais c'est une politesse qui n'aura qu'un temps. (277)

. . . since your ignorance of any of our languages is a handicap for you, we will use French as a matter of courtesy. But it is a courtesy that will not last forever. (179-80)

In the race track meeting in Dakar at the end of the strike, these corrupt officials (installed by the colonizer) speak exclusively in French even though their words are understood by only half their audience, and when Bakayoko seizes the microphone he speaks in Wolof. At this point in the novel, Bakayoko's challenge to the use of French by the elite Africans is telling, "Personne ne peut mettre en doute les paroles de ces personnes, mais que vous ont-elles dit, à qui ont-elles parlé dans une langue que la plupart d'entre vous ne comprennent pas?" (336) [No one is questioning the words of these men, but what *did* they tell you, and to who were they talking, in a language most of you do not understand (217)]. Bakayoko's use of Wolof asserts the importance of the language of the majority of the people and challenges the privilege accorded to French and the French nation. The claim for an independent nationhood made in the anticolonial struggle is a claim of equality, a demand for political, economic, social, and cultural rights.

Appropriating the novel and using a European language, the text is part of the emergent tradition that writes into being the perspective of an anticolonial Other. The novel's relationship to French can be examined not only thematically but in terms of its use of language. To borrow Henry Louis Gates Jr.'s term, there are moments when *Les bouts de bois de Dieu* "signifies on" colonialist and Orientalist assumptions about Africans. In *Signifying Monkey* Gates traces the politically informed use of word play and irony to the West African (Yoruba) trickster figure of Esu-Elegbara. A figure closely tied to the act of signification in itself, Esu represents the multiplicity of meaning:

As figures of the duality of the voice within the tradition, Esu and his friend the Monkey manifest themselves in the search for a voice that is depicted in so very many black texts. The tension between them surfaces in the double-voiced discourse so commonly found here. (21)

Sembène playfully and subtly manipulates metaphors, reversing their polarity. Beatrice, the wife of Isnard, is described in the novel's last pages as "allait et venait d'une pièce à l'autre comme une panthère en cage" (378) ["pacing back and forth, from one room to another, like a panther in a cage" (244)]. Here the image of the dangerous, unpredictable African animal, often applied to the African by the colonizer, is reversed, attached to the colonizer in order to suggest the entrapment, frustration, and futility of colonial rule.

Written in French, *Les bouts de bois de Dieu* utilizes double-voicing in order to undercut the racist discourse of the Europeans. The language of the Frenchmen, Dejean in particular, is given an ironic cast. It articulates the most vicious racism and yet serves the novel's anticolonial message. Dejean imagines that

... il exerçait une fonction qui reposait sur des bases naturelles, le droit à l'autorité absolue sur des êtres dont la copuleur de leur peau faisait non des subordonnées avec qui l'on peut discuter, mais des hommes d'une autre condition, inférieure, vouée a l'obéissance sans conditions. (274-5)

... he was simply exercising a function which rested on the most natural of all bases—the right to an absolute authority over beings whose color made of them not subordinates with whom one could discuss anything, but men of another, inferior condition, fit only for unqualified obedience. (177-8)

Here there is an iteration of the colonial attitude toward the colonized that is immediately undercut by the events of meeting with the strike leaders. Because it is written in French, the novel appropriates the colonial language in order to parody and "speak back" to European discourse. Moreover, *Les bouts*, as a French-language African novel, deconstructs its own authority, refusing to be taken as the singular expression of Senegalese nationalism.

CLASS AND NATION

The French language is not the only ambiguous European legacy for emerging African nations. The inherited colonial economic system is also fraught with inconsistency and unevenness. Economic development under colonial rule is, on the one hand, premised on the strategy of dividing the natives in order to facilitate colonial authority and, on the other, on the attempt to unite the colonial territory with coherent infrastructures and communication systems so as to achieve more efficient exploitation. In "Imperialism: The Highest Stage of Capitalism" Lenin identifies the importance of railways in the colonies to capitalist penetration and exploitation:

Railways ... (serve as) capitalist threads which in thousands of different intercrossings bind enterprises with private property in the means of production in general, (they) have converted this work of construction into an instrument of oppressing a thousand million people in the colonies and semi-colonies. (in Ojo, 62)

The Dakar-Niger line, site of the rail strike in *Les bouts de bois de Dieu*, was built during the heyday of French colonial rule in Africa. Begun in 1882 and not finally completed until 1924, the line was constructed under the *corvée* system, that is by forced African labor. The railroad led to a rapid increase in the population of the principal towns through which it passed, towns which invariably contained both a poor and sprawling African slum and a wealthy French district.

While the colonial infrastructure divided the French from the African, it simultaneously led to increasing communication and solidarity among Africans themselves. Sembène's portrayal of the Dakar-Niger railway strike traces the significance of this contradiction to the development of resistance consciousness. Indeed, *Les bout de bois de Dieu* underscores the importance of the railroad to the development of anticolonial national identity in Africa. Accounts of African nation building point especially to the Dakar-Niger line:

A railroad bound the hinterland to the coast, and it set up internal lines of circulation for people as well as goods. . . . Partly as a result, the internal lines of communication ran inward from the port towns to the local hinterland, and, in time, each rail terminus became the capital of an independent republic. Even the efforts to join together some of these states, such as the brief Mali Federation linking Senegal and Mali, were based on the economic and political realities that grew up around the rail line—in this case, the railroad from Dakar east to Bamako on the Niger. (Bohannan and Curtin 340)

The focus of action in *Les bouts de bois de Dieu* on the Dakar-Niger rail line reflects the historical relationship of colonial infrastructure to the emergence of African national identities.[18] European economic infrastructures in Africa not only facilitated the exploitation of the natural and human resources, but they ironically helped map the geography of African resistance to colonialism, linking together people of diverse cultural, social, and linguistic backgrounds and mapping the geography of African resistance to colonialism. Exploitation increased its penetration and efficiency, worker class solidarity developed:

As colonial frontiers created new barriers, colonial transportation and communication networks erased some of the old ones. In time, this opened the possibility of colony-wide political organization which could give effective voice to a new demand for independence. (Bohannan and Curtin 343)

Along the Dakar-Niger line, there was active resistance to the colonial system, particularly during the 1930s and 40s. After the Second World War and with the return of conscripted African troops, the discontent began to be mobilized in independence movements. At the Brazzaville Conference of 1944, demands that workers in the colonies be given the same rights as French workers were recognized, but the failure of the French government to adopt or implement the Overseas Labor Code it had drafted touched off the 1947-8 strike that Sembène participated in. Written in 1960, the year of independence, *Les bouts de bois de Dieu* looks back to this period as critical to the formation of African anticolonial and national consciousness.

Through the activities of the colonial economy differences of custom and local language are overcome and the affiliations of Africans to one another are strengthened. In *Les bouts de bois de Dieu*, frequent expressions of mistrust and hatred between the Bambaras (in the East) and the Wolof (in the West) are set against homogenizing social change brought about by the railroad.[19] In the first pages of the novel, this animosity is explicit in the mind of Niakoro.

Lui avait-on assez rebattu les oreilles avec ce Sénégal, le travail qu'on y trouvait, les fortunes qu'on pouvait y faire. Elle n'en avait rapporté que deuil et douleur. Depuis lors, elle appelait les Sénégalais "les esclaves" et lorsqu'elle parlait de son cadet, elle disait: "Il ressemble à un Oulofou, il en a la démarche et les maniè polies."

"Mais, pensait Niakoro-la-vieille en suçant ses joues, qu'on ne me parle plus de tous ces gens-là. Est-ce que les Bambaras ne comprendront jamais que ces esclaves, fils d'esclaves, ne sont que des menteurs? Nous autres, Bambaras, n'avons jamais cédé devant un ennemi, nous n'avons qu'une parole, nous, et nous allons jusqu'au bout. Et voilà maintenant que ces cheminots sans cervelle veulent une autre grève et comme la dernière fois, ce soront les Soudanais qui se feront tuer." (15)

She had been told often enough about this Senegal, about the work to be found there, the fortunes to be made, but she had brought back only mourning and sorrow. Since then she had called the Senegalese "the slave," and when she spoke of her younger son she said, He seems like one of the Wolof people, one of the westerners; he has the bearing, and the manners."

"But now," Niakoro thought, sucking at her cheeks, "I want to hear no more of those people. Slaves, and sons of slaves, they are nothing but liars—will the Bambaras never learn that? The Bambaras have never run before an enemy; we speak honestly, and we do as we say we will do. And now these brainless workers on the trains want another strike, and it will be the Sudanese who are killed, just as it was the last time." (2)

Because the relations of production are exploitative and under the control of a powerful colonial elite, resistance requires new kinds of solidarity. Early in *Les bouts de bois de Dieu* two workers discuss how their attitudes toward their neighbors have changed as they have developed awareness of the common cause of all workers:

—Avant, les Dahoméens, je les chinais, et tu sais pourquoi?

—Non, répondit Arona en ouvrant de grands yeux où ne se reflétait qu'un esprit simple et sans malice.

—Parce que je les considérais comme mes inférieurs. Tu te souviens de la causerie de Bakayoko sur "les méfaits de la citoyenneté"? Et bien maintenant, j'ai compris et j'ai honte. Oui, Bakayoko a raison, cette grève nous apprend beaucoup de choses. (74)

"I used to make fun of people from Dahomey before—and do you know why?"

Arona opened his eyes wide, seemingly in perfect candor. "No," he said, "why?"

"Because I thought I was better than they are, that's why. Do you remember the talk Bakayoko gave, on 'the pitfalls of citizenship'? Well, now I understand what he was talking about, and I'm ashamed of myself. Bakayoko is right—this strike has taught us a lot of things." (38-9)

In *Les bouts de bois de Dieu*, we see how the system of economic production instituted by the colonial power to exploit African labor and extract natural resources also unified new and potentially rebellious social classes. In the novel this emergent proletariat class begins to reject the intertribal prejudices, and the affiliations of traditional African society begin to lose their meaning. The railroad is a metonym for the technology brought by European colonialism; the railroad is frequently referred to simply as "la machine." Fa Keita describes the effect of "la machine" on African society and African modes of production:

—Il y a bien longtemps, dit Keïta, bien avant votre naissance, les choses se passaient dans un ordre qui était le nôtre, et cet ordre avait une grande importance pour la vie de chacun. Aujourd'hui, tout est mélangé. Il n'y a plus de castes, plus de griots, plus de forgerons, plus de cordonniers, plus de tisserands. Je pense que c'est l'œuvre de la machine qui brasse tout ainsi. (153-4)

"A long time ago," Fa Keita said, "before any of you were born, everything that happened happened within a framework, an order that was our own, and the existence of that order was of great importance in our lives. Today, no such framework exists. There are no castes among people, no difference in the quality of grain or of the bread that is made from the grain; there are no weavers, no artisans in metal, no makers of fine shoes. I think it is the machine which has ground everything together this way and brought everything to a single level." (94)

As the capitalist mode of production undermined feudal relations in Europe, so "la machine" transfigures African society, producing "new men" and a new, revolutionary class:

C'etait la machine qui maintenant régnait sur leur pays. En arrêtant sa marche sur plus de quinze cents kilomètres, ils prirent conscience de leur force, mais aussi conscience de leur dépendance. En vérité, la machine était en train de faire d'eux des hommes nouveaux. (63)

Now the machine ruled over their lands, and when they forced every
machine within a thousand miles to halt they became conscious of their
strength, but conscious also of their dependence. They began to
understand that the machine was making of them a whole new breed of
men. (32)

The novel asserts international affiliations for the working class,
even as it speaks of the specificity of African colonial exploitation. Not
only do the strikers get support from other African workers, but from
French workers, and, indeed, from the sympathetic colonial, LeBlanc.[20]
Bakayoko tells the striking workers and their families, "Vous savez que
vous êtes soutenus, de Kaolack à Saint-Louis, de la Guinée au
Dahomey, et même en France, les secours s'organisent" (288) ["You
know there is support for you everywhere—from Kaolack to Saint-
Louis, from Guinea to Dahomey, and even in France itself" (184)].
    While there can be international solidarity, Sembène also shows
that resistance by African workers threatens French national pride. The
demand to be treated as employees rather than as "Negroes" leads the
French director to imagine that there has been an insult to the French
nation itself. Lahbib, one of the strike leaders, explicitly rejects a
national interpretation in favor of one based on class.

—[Dejean] Vous êtes menés par des bolcheviques et vous insultez
une nation, une race qui vaut cent fois la vôtre!

—Monsieur le directeur, vous ne représentez ici ni une nation, ni une
race: une classe. Et nous aussi nous représentons une classe dont les
intérêts sont différents de ceux de la vôtre. Nous cherchons un terrain
d'entente et c'est tout! (280-1)

[Dejean] "You are led by a bunch of Bolsheviks, and you are sitting
there insulting a great nation and a great people!"

"Monsieur le directeur," Lahbib said, "you do not represent a nation
or a people here, but simply a class. We represent another class, whose
interests are not the same as yours. We are trying to find a common
meeting ground, and that is all." (182)

In Sembène's insistence that the strike is based on class differences there is already in place a critique of the incipient national bourgeoisie that was coming into power at the time of the novel's writing. The strike reveals that the small African middle class allied its interests more closely with the colonizer than with the African people. As with Dulcan-Quellin in *El nuevo mundo*, the new leadership is versed in European forms of authority, and the co-optation of African leadership by the colonial power is a repeated theme in the novel breaking up any monolithic identity between Africans. The proto-national administration put in place by the French in pre-independence Senegal is corrupt from the beginning. Bakayoko describes the attitude of the strikers toward their "deputies,"

—Nos députés, dit-il avec un sourire ironique qui tira sa bouche jusqu'à la grande balafre qui lui fendait le visage, nos députés, savez-vous ce que nous en penson? Pour nous, leur mandat est une patente de profiteur. Voilà ce que nous en pensons. Nous les connaissons. Il en est parmi eux qui, avant de se faire élire, ne possedaient même pas un deuxième pantalon. Maintenant, ils ont appartement, villa, auto, compte en banque, ils son actionnaires dans des sociétes. Qu'ont-ils de commun avec le peupple ignorant qui les a élus sans savoir ce qu'il faisait? Ils sont devenus des alliés du patronant . . . (281)

"Our deputies. Do you know what we think of them? To us their mandate is simply a license to profiteer. We know them, and that is what we think of them. There are some of them who, before their election, did not even own a second pair of pants. Now they have apartments, villas, automobiles, bank accounts, and they own stock in companies like this one. What do they have in common with the ignorant people who elected them without knowing what they were doing? They have become your allies . . ." (182)

This analysis of the colonial period extends into the neocolonial one. Sembène uses other examples to further his point about the separation of African politicians from the working people and peasants. The African deputy mayor, supporting the French, argues against the strike. His use of the collective pronoun, emphasized by Sembène's italicization, suggests the way in which a nationalist discourse can be perverted to serve the interests of colonialism.

8 The new African leadership is versed in European forms of authority. (*Motorcade with Mitterand and Mobutu,* Moke Zairian, Zaire, Paint on flour sack, 1990)

—Il n'y a plus d'eau et plus rien à manger dans *nos* maisons, les boutiquiers ne veulent plus *nous* faire crédit. Cette grève est l'œuvre de quelques brebis galeuses conseillées par des éléments étrangers, care une telle manière d'agir n'est conforme ni à *nos* mœurs, ni à *nos* coutumes. (334)

"There is no water and no food in *our* homes, and the shopkeepers refuse to give *us* credit. And yet, this strike is the work of a few black sheep, acting on the advice of foreigners, because such a way of acting in not in keeping with *our* habits and *our* customs." (215)

Indeed, the final chapter of the novel sets the striking workers of the railway strike against the rising colonial elites who cooperate with the colonizer. In this squaring-off is the tension between two forms of national culture, the one seeking to transform the nation by a pedagogical imitation of the French, the other a dynamic and engaged performance of a different future.

To the extent that Sembène's novel emphasizes class as an organizing principle of colonial resistance, it presents history as a dialectic of progress where European technological superiority drives African social change. While there is increasing colonial domination, there is also the possibility of resistance and independence. Of course, in classical marxist thought, the rise of the bourgeoisie is a progressive development preparing the way for the proletarian revolution. For Marx, even though feudalism is replaced by "wage slavery," the economic energy unleashed by the rising bourgeoisie is essential to the development of the truly revolutionary class, the proletariat. In utilizing this teleological model of modernization and development, *Les bouts de bois de Dieu* emphasizes the transformative effects of capitalist development in the context of mid-twentieth-century colonized French Africa. While dividing Africans among themselves, creating classes with different interests, the changes brought by the colonial economy are also seen to instill new forms of community consciousness. Class identification has a place in the formation of a Fanonian national conscious in the novel. In *Les bouts de bois de Dieu*, there is an emphasis on class relationships and the active struggle of the people rather than on an artificial or essentialized national unity.

Les bouts de bois de Dieu does not take a strictly orthodox approach to historical change, however. The specificity of African culture—evidenced in the role of women, the experience of colonial education, and the resistance to European domination—elaborates, extends and complicates a purely class-based analysis of national development.

Sembène's decision to portray Senegal's national railway strike years later, at the moment of national independence, is critical in this regard. Sembène does not portray the nation in nativist fashion as a "pure" or "uncontaminated" context that is easily exoticized. Whereas the majority of the narration of Achebe's *Things Fall Apart*, for instance, is concentrated on the precontact tribal life of the Ibos, in Sembène's novel, the identity of the people is not to be found in a return to their tribal past but instead in active resistance to domination and exploitation in the present. The choice of the strike rather than the anticolonial struggle itself is also significant. The outcome of the strike is the formation of a collective consciousness based on an accumulation of local resistances coordinated along the rail line. Thus Sembène is not subject to the messianistic aspirations of a novel that focuses strictly on the independence struggle itself.[21] The emphasis on the strike as opposed to the independence struggle marks precisely the distinction Lazarus maintains must be made in his discussion of Fanon's messianism. Achieving the ends of the strike is not a messianic aspiration. In the light of ongoing colonial rule and the continued exploitation of other workers, the railway strike is only a partial victory, yet the spontaneity of the strike serves as warning to the new national leadership: unless the African workers are treated justly, there is every reason to believe revolt will occur again, even if the administration of the railroad (or the state) is in African hands.

WOMEN AND THE NATION

Read in the postcolonial period, *Les bouts'* complex linkage of class and nation facilitates an ongoing interrogation of African social differences within claims of unified nationhood. In a similar fashion, Sembène implicitly explores the displacement of women in Eurocentric nationalist rhetoric (foreshadowed by works such as *El nuevo mundo* and *The Tempest*). The "radical" theories of national culture of Fanon, Anderson, and Chatterjee contain no analysis of the role of women or of family life in the development of national identity. Though the relationship of women to emergent national culture is an under-theorized area, there is important work already done. Jayawardena (*Feminism and Nationalism in the Third World*, 1986) argues that in Asia and Africa "struggles for women's emancipation were an essential and integral part of national resistance movements." She also points out that these struggles, often dominated by the concerns of bourgeois women,

> did not move beyond the sphere of limited and selected reforms: equality for women within the legal process, the removal of obviously discriminatory practices, the right to vote, education and property, and the right of women to enter the professions and politics, etc. These were reforms which had little effect on the daily lives of the masses of women; neither did they address the basic question of women's subordination within the family and society. (9)

When nationalist movements turn nostalgically to the past in search of cultural roots, the roles for women are even more limited. Mina Davis Caufield expresses the concern that nationalist movements "may perpetuate the oppression of women in the name of tradition and in opposition to Western influence" (70). George Mosse describes a similar phenomenon in connection with the position of women in the discourse of nineteenth-century European nationalism:

> Woman was the embodiment of respectability; even as defender and protector of the people she was assimilated to her traditional role as woman and mother, the custodian of tradition, who kept nostalgia alive in the active world of men. (97)[2]

According to Jean Franco's study of women's writing in Mexico, the limited roles available to women in nationalist discourse restrict imaginative possibilities for women:

> A bleak wind seems to have shriveled up nineteenth-century women's writing—the bleak wind of nationalism. In order to account for this we have to look at woman's place within the signifying system of nationalism that came to be imbedded in discursive formations in educational and judicial institution, in the spatialization and conduct of everyday life. (xvii-iii)

In the writers she studies, Franco finds that nationalist narratives with women as protagonists were rare. As she puts it, "rewriting master narratives around a heroine is fraught with difficulty" (133) and "women's attempts to plot themselves as protagonists in the national novel become a recognition of the fact that they are not in the plot at all but definitely somewhere else" (146).

In light of these concerns about the restrictions nationalist movements may place on women and given the paucity of woman-centered narratives of national revolution, Sembène's accomplishment in *Les bouts de bois de Dieu* is unusual and remarkable. In discussions of African writers, Sembène is often singled out for his sophisticated depictions of women. Karen Smyley Wallace writes:

Ousmane Sembène, a contemporary Senegalese novelist and film maker, is noted for his finely chiseled portraits of females as real, palpable individuals. By creating women figures who do not merely represent shadows of the male figure, nor echoes of the male voice, Sembène's works reflect the complexities of a changing Africa. He . . . renders the female character a dynamic being, who must constantly struggle to redefine her perception of self in the developing African continent and in the world. (65)

Brenda Berrian comments:

He [Sembène] is one of the first African writers to move his female characters from a secondary role, in which they complement their men, to a primary one in which they express their feelings, hurts, joys, and think and react to pressing situations. (196)

In analyzing a series of Sembène short stories, Berrian concludes:

Sembène does not hesitate to take to task such explosive topics as child paternity, adultery, arranged polygamous marriages, tyrannical men, divorce, child custody, and the imposition of double moral standards upon women. . . . Sembène is committed to defending the rights of African women by insisting that they need to reclaim the economic, political, and social positions that they had held in the past. He is not afraid to expose the contradictions that control people's actions, and the collision with their menfolk that occurs when women assert themselves. (203)

In *Les bouts de bois de Dieu,* women have an active and shaping role in the struggle against colonial exploitation, in the transformation and reformulation of social, political and economic structures, and in the perpetuation of meaningful and viable African traditions and culture. The machine and the experience of the strike bring about critical changes for the African women in the novel. These new roles are recognized by the men: "Et les hommes comprirent que ce temps, s'il enfantait d'autres hommes, enfantait aussi d'autres femmes" (65) ["And the men began to understand that if the times were bringing forth a new breed of men, they were also bringing forth a new breed of women" (34)]. From the fire that interrupts the invading militia, to the protest at the police station, the march and the triumphant entry into Dakar, the actions of the women in the novel are spontaneous, collective, and in defense of family life and family systems. The proposal by the women to march to Dakar in support of the strike challenges traditional notions about their place.

De mémoire d'homme c'était la première fois qu'une femme avait pris la parole en public à Thiès et les discussions allaient bon train. (289)

It was the first time in living memory that a woman had spoken up in public in Theis, and even the onslaught of night could not still the arguments. (185)

Penda as a leader of the women equals in significance Bakayoko as a leader of the men. The consequences of the participation of the women in the strike, and thus in the struggle for national independence, is far reaching.

Le retour des marcheuses a été bien accueilli, mais les hommes ont du mal à les dompter. Moi-même au début, elles venaient m'assaillir comme des lionnes, elles voulaient tout commander! Enfin, tout est rentré dans l'ordre. . . . Mais à l'avenir il faudra compter avec elles. (348)

The women got a big welcome when they came back, of course, but now the men are having all sorts of trouble with them. At first they even pounced on me like tigresses—they wanted to start running everything! But things are a little calmer now. . . . In future, though we will have to reckon with them in whatever we do. (225-6)

The women expect leadership positions in all aspects of the struggle, and *Les bouts de bois de Dieu* portrays women as performers of a national culture evolving from existing African cultural and social practices.

Sembène's women are a constitutive element in the development of a collective, anticolonial identity. The nationalist subject constructed by the text, both male and female, places community, family responsibility, and the assertion of basic needs at the center of the political agenda. Moreover, the declaration of African family identity is directly tied to the principal objective of the railway strikers. While the demand for family allowances is based on an internationalist claim (all workers in France receive these allowances, so African workers should receive them as well), the struggle is over a question of cultural recognition and respect: polygamous African families must not be judged on the European model; second wives are not concubines. While the colonizer finds evidence of his own humanity in the claims of the accomplishments of his nation, his national culture, and national language, the humanity of the colonized is undermined by the assault on non-Western values and practices, such as polygamy.[23] One of the essential effects of the strike is to require the French to recognize Africans as human beings with a culture and family life worthwhile on its merit. The family allowances demanded by the workers are a key issue in the strike negotiations precisely for this reason. Despite the fact that white employees of the company receive family allowances, family allowances for African workers are simply not negotiable according to the director of the railway company:

Mais céder sur la question des allocations familiales, c'était beaucoup plus que d'agréer un compromis avec des ouvriers en gréve, c'était reconnaître pour valable une manifestation raciale, entériner les coutumes d'êtres inférieurs, céder non à des travailleurs mais à des Nègres et cela Dejean ne le pouvet pas. (280)

To give in on the question of family allowances was much more than a matter of agreeing to a compromise with striking workers; it would amount to recognition of a racial aberrance, a ratification of the customs of inferior beings. It would be giving in, not to workers but to Negroes, and that Dejean could not do. (181)

9 As in Sembène's text, women and family are at the center of the armed struggle. (Woman with child supported by armed men, Yoruba, Nigeria, 1920)

Sembène's distinctive African feminism recognizes the political and economic importance of women in tribal society, and the emphasis on family allowances and the participation of the women in the strike takes place in an African cultural context.[24] In the performance of a Fanonian engaged national culture, Sembène's portrayal of women draws on the daily life of village women to explore and transform gender roles in a distinctly African way. In effect, Sembène's women challenge bourgeois notions of equality often predominant in nationalist movements and, by contrast, point to the limited political participation of women and the marginalization of family life in Western politics.

COLONIAL EDUCATION AND PEDAGOGICAL NATIONALISM

Although as we have seen in *El nuevo mundo* and *The Tempest* colonizers have attemped to educate the natives from the beginning, systems of state-sponsored colonial education in the language of the European power were instituted in the European empires in Africa and Asia in the nineteenth century. Though they were never attended by a large percentage of the population,[25] colonial schools were eventually instrumental in the creation of a class of educated natives, fluent in the colonizer's language, and capable of serving as intermediaries between the colonial rulers and their subjects. In the history of European colonial rule in Africa, Senegal in particular stands out as the most sustained attempt to institute the French policy of assimilation.[26] In Senegal and throughout the "third world," the class of European-educated colonial subjects played a leading role in independence movements and in the administration of newly emerged nation-states.[27] Furthermore, as discussed in the last chapter, the establishment of educational systems in the colonies provided a model for the extension and standardization of national educational systems in the metropole. Thus colonial education and national education are historically related and can be seen to perform somewhat similar social functions. In terms of the construction of national identity, modern state-sponsored educational systems are often explicit in their mission to eliminate local differences and unify populations, thus ensuring "social order" and national allegiance.

Educational content and institutions are frequently the subject of "third-world" authors writing in European languages. For these writers there are sharp contradictions between the practices, beliefs, and values of their home or community and those of their schooling, a schooling that takes place in a system established by a colonizing European power. It is thus not surprising that many anticolonial writers turn to an examination of their own identity in order to consider the dominations of colonialism. The emphasis on autobiographical elements in "third-world" writing can be viewed not as a solipsistic exercise but as part of a politicized project of reevaluating metropolitan culture. The "distress and difficulty" (Fanon's expression) of the "third world" intellectual's contradictory experience can result in a literature of paralysis and frustration as evidenced in such African writing as Kane's *Ambiguous Adventure*, Emecheta's *The Joys of Motherhood*, or Dangarembga's *Nervous Conditions* — all texts which foreground colonial or neocolonial schooling.

Other "third-world" writers focus rather on the anticolonial struggle itself, emphasizing engaged resistance and the utopian possibilities of social change. These writers are more likely to see national culture in the way Fanon describes it and to project a subversion or transformation of education as central to the aspirations of an oppressed people. We can consider the depiction of colonial education and its role in national struggle by comparing *Les bouts de bois de Dieu* with two complementary texts, Ngugi wa Thiong'o's 1977 novel *Petals of Blood* and Rigoberta Menchú's 1985 *testimonio Me llamo Rigoberta Menchú y así me nació la conciencia*. These comparisons of education under colonialism will allow us to further elaborate the distinction between pedagogical and performative nationalism in the construction of national identities.

Ngugi presents the oppression of the colonial school and looks to ways that the educational system can be transformed. *Petals of Blood* articulates the theme that the principles of the colonial school are established by the colonizer and designed to maintain the legitimacy of the colonial system. At the Siriani Preparatory School described in the novel there is a strict hierarchy between teachers and students and among the students themselves. Lessons are conducted in English and the texts are written by and largely about Englishmen. The African experience is not considered a worthy field of study, and a Siriani education serves to justify the status quo.

Ngugi emphasizes that real decolonization is not a superficial exchange of foreign elite control for domestic elite control but a thoroughgoing social transformation. When student revolts at Siriani lead the authorities to replace the British headmaster with a native

Kenyan, Chui, the colonial education, despite student demands, continues unchanged. Chui requires the European teachers to instruct their students in "good idiomatic English," and he quotes Shakespeare (173) to justify discipline and the maintenance of the prefect system. Chui's behavior is no better than that of the former British headmaster; indeed, it is worse: when the students demand a curriculum with emphasis on African culture, he calls in the riot squad. Chui's complicity with the exploitative system left intact by the British extends to his involvement on the board of English corporations that continue to do business in Kenya. Ngugi's postcolonial text emphasizes that the "third-world" intellectual must not simply step into the shoes of the colonizer or facilitate the collaboration of the educational system with ongoing international capitalist exploitation.

Petals of Blood thus develops in fictional form the theoretical issues laid out in *Decolonizing the Mind*. For Ngugi decolonizing education means revision of content, methods and organizational structure. During one of the rebellions at Siriani, students seek,

... to be taught African literature, African history, for we wanted to know ourselves better. Why should ourselves be reflected in white snows, spring flowers fluttering on icy lakes? ... We wanted an African headmaster and African teachers. We denounced the prefect system, the knightly order of masters and menials. (170)

Petals of Blood calls for more than isolated student revolts. It attempts to point the way for a national revolutionary movement in Kenya and suggests directions for a meaningful Africanization of the educational system.

A colonial education is an important influence on several of the characters in Sembène's novel (published eighteen years before *Petals of Blood*). We learn of the contradictions of colonial education in *Les bouts de bois de Dieu*, not through direct narration of the struggle of students to transform the curriculum but through the consciousness of several characters who are constantly reevaluating African society through the prism of their experience in the French school. N'Deye Touti is the pivotal figure in the novel's treatment of colonial education. When she looks at the way the Africans live, she superimposes the images of France from her school books.

N'Deye Touti avait grandi ici-même, elle avait joué dans ces cavernes sombres, dans ces ruelles étrangleés, ces courettes empestées. Ces souvenirs étaient vifs comme une blessure. Elle en était presque a bénir l'incendie qui venait de détruire ces témoins de son enfance et de sa honte. Elle imaginait des maisons peintes de couleurs claires, des jardins pleins maisons peintes de couleurs claires, des jardens pleins de fleurs, des enfants vêtus à l'européenne jouant dans des cours propres. (184)

N'Deye Touti had grown up in this very spot; she had played in these tortuous alleyways, these vermin ridden courtyards and gloomy cabins. The memory was as sharp as the pain of an open wound, and she was almost ready to bless the fire which had destroyed the witnesses to her childhood and her shame. She had a vision of houses painted in clear, fresh colors, of gardens filled with flowers, and children in European clothes playing in tidy courtyards. (115)

This denigration of African life is countered early in the novel by Bakayoko, who asserts *nègritude* values:

—Il y a tant de belles choses chez nous, qu'il n'est pas nécessaire d'en introduire d'étrangères. Surtout que de là où viennent ces gestes, nous pouvons en apprendre bien d'autres, beaucoup plus fructueux pour notre pays. (108)

There are so many beautiful customs right here that there is no reason to bring in foreign ones—especially when there is still so much we have to learn, about things that can be useful to our country. (63)

While N'Deye Touti has learned to read and write at the colonial school, she has also become alienated from the society in which she lives:

Avant la grève, elle fréquentait l'école normale de jeunes filles, ce qui lui donnait une nette supériorité sur les garçons mais en même temps faisait d'elle l'écrivain public du quartier. En écrivant leurs lettres d'amour ou leurs requêtes, en remplissant leurs feuilles d'impôts, elle se sentait de plus en plus éloignée de tous ceux qui formaient son entourage. Elle vivait comme en marge d'eux; ses lectures, les films qu'elle voyait, la maintenaient dans un univers où les siens n'avaient plus de place, de même qu'elle n'avait plus de place dans le leur. (100)

Before the strike she had gone to the teacher's training school, which gave her a considerable advantage over the boys, but at the same time made her the public scribe for the whole neighborhood. And it was hard to fill out tax forms, and write letters applying for jobs, and even love letters, for all of your family and friends without beginning to feel more and more remote from them. She lived in a kind of separate world; the reading she did, the films she saw, made her part of a universe in which her own people had no place, and by the same token she no longer had a place in theirs. (57)

N'Deye Touti's education is separated from the experience and needs of her people; it has in fact kept her ignorant of the relations of power in the colony. Several of the older women expect that because N'Deye Touti has attended school she will be able help the women decide what to do during the strike.

—[Mame Sofi] Tu dois avoir une idée sur la grève, toi qui vas à l'école?
—[N'Deyue Touti] Tu sais bien que non, tante, c'est trop dur pour moi.
—Qu'est-ce qu'on vous apprend à l'école, alors?
—Tout, tout de la vie. . . .
—Eh bien, la gréve, ça ne fait pas partie de la vie? Fermer les boutiques et l'eau, ce n'est pas la vie? (87)
[Mame Sofi] "You go to school—you must have some ideas about the strike?"
[N'Deyue Touti] "You know I don't Aunt. It's too complicated for me."
"Well, what do they teach you in school then?"
"Everything—everything about life."
"And the strike is not part of life? Closing the shops and turning off the water—that is not part of life." (47)

Far from preparing Africans to understand the colonial system, the school alienates Africans from one another and trains them to accept the boundaries and inequalities of colonial society. N'Deye Touti is very concerned with following the law, even when it is patently unjust.

On lui avait appris à l'ecole qui y avait des lois et que nul n'avait le droit de se faire justice lui-même. Pour elle, tout ce qui venait de l'école ne pouvait être mis en question. (177-8)

She had learned at school about the workings of the law, and she had been taught that no one had the right to take the law into his own hands. And for N'Deye there was no questioning the truth of anything she learned at school. (111)

In order to perpetuate colonial domination the French school, to use Homi Bhabha's terms, treats culture "pedagogically," as something to be given to students, rather than "performatively," as something the students must make for themselves.

N'Deye Touti's conflict is incarnated in her attraction to both the fancy-dressing Beaugosse (his name means "good looking kid") and the strike leader Bakayoko. Both men are educated, but Bakayoko is committed to the community while Beaugosse forswears working with the strikers in order to follow his individualistic ambitions and find favor with the colonial administration. Though N'Deye Touti finally rejects Beaugosse, the novel eschews any simplistic romantic ending. N'Deye Touti must come to terms with the fact that her attraction to Bakayoko has been superficial. When last seen, she is undertaking the hard physical labor of fetching water for the family—an action it would have earlier been impossible to imagine her performing. N'Deye Touti's last scene is thus profoundly hopeful as she has apparently learned the value of helping others. Her former personality is not lost; rather it becomes acceptable, "on l'appelait toujours 'Mad'mizelle', mais on mettait dans le mot de l'admiration et de l'affection" (347) ["Everyone still called her 'mad'mizelle,' but now there was admiration and affection in their use of the word" (225)]. In the context of the novel N'Deye Touti's reintegration into the work life of the community is not a defeat of her individuality but a personal and communal triumph.[28]

RESISTANCE EDUCATION AND PERFORMATIVE NATIONALISM

The portrait of N'Deye Touti highlights the way in which a formal education facilitates the administration of colonial rule; however, informal, participatory, oral, and tribal educational practices are utilized by resistant nationalism in its "performative" aspect. In the last section we drew on *Petals of Blood* in order to examine the treatment of formal colonial educational systems in *Les bouts de bois de Dieu*. In this section the *testimonio* of Rigoberta Menchú, a Guatemalan Indian peasant woman, will allow us to identify a revolutionary education that is outside the colonial school system in order to examine the prospects for revolutionary education in *Les bout de bois de Dieu*.

Me llamo Rigoberta Menchú depicts Guatemalan Indians under harsh oppression educating themselves *outside* a colonial school system and through their participation in the struggle to maintain their lives and identity in a context of extraordinary oppression and violence. At the time her story was recorded, Menchú neither read nor wrote. The importance of her *testimonio* is that it can offer perspectives less influenced by the colonial school and the traditional genres of Western imaginative literature. The narrator of *testimonio* doesn't undergo—at least not to the same degree—the "third-world" intellectual's "dilemma," and the text, though not completely free of the problematics of biography, autobiography, or ethnography, speaks from the experience of an oppressed people more directly than any of these forms. Menchú identifies in concentric circles with her family, village, Guatemalan Indians of different cultures and languages and with the poor and working class. As John Beverley says of all testimonial,

> [It] represents an affirmation of the individual subject, even of individual growth and transformation, but in connection with a group or class situation marked by marginalization, oppression, and struggle. (23)

Because of his limited formal schooling and his background as a fisherman, soldier, and dockworker, Sembène's social position is closer to that of Menchú than to the other African writers with which he is usually grouped. *Les bouts de bois de Dieu* is not a *testimonio*. Indeed, it is Sembène's third novel and a self-consciously imaginative work of fiction with a freedom in characterization and narration that is not possible in the *testimonio* form. Further, unlike *testimonio* or autobiography, the shifting narrative attention in *Les bouts de bois de Dieu* keeps any one character from being at the center of attention. Still *Les bouts de bois de Dieu* resembles *testimonio* because it speaks of a communal struggle in a specific historic context. Some critics find in the style and language of the novel the kind of directness and honesty that characterize *testimonio* writing. A.C. Brench says of Sembène that dealing with African workers and their problems, he never attempts to force sophistication on them. The workers are concerned with their basic needs. He treats these in terms they use and understand. As he makes clear from the beginning, *Les bouts de bois de Dieu* is the story of their struggle; he is in this respect a chronicler, not a writer of fiction. . . . The simplicity of his vocabulary and sentence structure, the direct, uncompromising descriptions are those the workers would recognize as their own. Ousmane, as one of them and as a novelist, has been able to re-create the effect of this simplicity and directness. (117)

Thus, despite the differences between the texts, the ways in which *Les bouts de bois de Dieu* suggests *testimonio* make a comparison with Menchú's work appropriate.

The process of education as it is described in *Me llamo Rigoberta Menchú* is along Freirian lines; the focus is less on a specific educational content than on the relationship of learning and participation, on praxis. In *Pedagogy of the Oppressed* Paulo Freire describes the importance of escaping "the duality in which *to be* is *to be like*, and to be like is to be like the oppressor" (33). The Menchú family attempts to circumvent this duality by refusing to send their children to the national school where they would lose their Indian culture and become "ladinoized." Rigoberta Menchú learns about history through her grandparents and parents as well as her own observation and experience. Her father's efforts to secure land rights for the people of his village land him in prison. Barbara Harlow has pointed out that jails themselves can, ironically, be sites of education in resistance movements, in part because they are outside the control of the national educational system. It is while in prison that Rigoberta's father learns about the relationship of the peasants' struggle for land in the countryside with the workers' struggle for rights in the city.

Colonial oppression involves the pedagogical imposition of language and culture via educational and religious institutions. The resistance to colonialism learns from the oppressor, appropriating tactics, altering and converting them to new ends. Education in Spanish and inculcation of Catholic belief have been key parts of the dominant culture's deprivation of language and culture of the oppressed in Guatemala, yet Rigoberta Menchú learns to speak Spanish as a way to communicate with other Indians and so forge a common resistance. Her training as a Catholic catechist is put to use as she organizes different Indian villages, teaching self-defense tactics against military raids. The testimonial itself may be described as an appropriation of the written word by an oral culture. Resistance to colonialism necessarily involves contact with *ladinos*, but as resistance takes place in and through the community, it leads not to a loss of Indian culture but rather to its expression and development.

In the testimonial, the education that takes place during anticolonial resistance is a "national" education which proposes a common resistance against a totalitarian nation-state. As a performative rather than pedagogical construction of national identity, a resistance education is based on the scattered centers of diverse villages and communities. It is often controlled by women. Rigoberta's mother travels to villages where she doesn't speak the language but is able to communicate with the women as she participates with them in daily tasks. When one of the government soldiers is captured, it is the women of the village who, by telling stories of their own experience, manage to reeducate him. [29]

Menchú's testimonial draws our attention to the ways in which resistance education is performed in Sembène's novel. Instead of focusing on the formal colonial school system instituted by the French and its pedagogical inculcation of culture, it points toward the evolution of communities in their struggle for justice and independence.

Most of the African characters in *Les bouts de bois de Dieu* have not received formal educations in the elitist colonial system; the strike itself provides an education in authority and resistance to a wide spectrum of the population. Tiémoko points out that "cette grève est une école" (140) ["This strike is like a school" (85)]. Among the Africans leadership emerges from characters who might otherwise have remained insignificant. Samba, Tiémoko, and Lahbib are all laborers who end up taking responsible positions in the course of the strike. Mame Sofi, Houdia M'Baye, and Bineta enlarge the scope of action for women and become active agents in the struggle for African rights. Ramatoulaye and Penda emerge as powerful public figures, leaders of the women's resistance to French authority. Unlike the colonial school that distances its pupils from their families, the strike furthers the relationship between individual and community. The strike serves as a ritual of passage into adult participation in the tribe, "cette épreuve devenait pour certains plus significative que les épreuves d'initiation du temps de leur adolescence" (317) ["the ordeal they were passing through was taking on an even greater significance than the rites of initiation to manhood that they had undergone in youth" (203)].

Through personal relationships and oral traditions, there is an interactive transfer of knowledge within African communities. Throughout *Les bouts de bois de Dieu*, there are scenes of the older wiser characters giving instruction to younger ones, who, in turn, counsel their elders, Fa Keita speaking at the meeting in the first chapter of the novel and in his home to the assembled strike leaders in the last chapter, Bakayoko guiding Tiémoko and N'Deye Touti, Maimouna's counsel to Penda, etc. The same thing occurs at a metatextual level: through the reminiscences of the ancient watchman, the reader learns of the story of Mour Dial and the history of the French appropriation of African lands.

Though his haunting absence in much of the novel renders Bakayoko an all-the-more compelling representation for postcolonial African social justice, the text complicates African nationalism still further, deviating from a strictly European-defined call for proletarian utopia. While some readings of the novel stress the omniscience of Bakayoko,[30] close attention to the text indicates a plurality of authoritative voices. In the process of community self-education, the perspective of the heroic leader of the strike, Bakayoko, is not presented as a monological or pedagogical voice of "truth." Bakayoko's judgement is challenged at several key moments and in ways that assert the difficulty of choosing between African traditions and the revolutionary changes sweeping the colony, i.e., the complex overdetermination of African traditions. Bakayoko, who consistently refers to the class interests of the railroad workers, is implicitly contrasted with Fa Keita, who espouses love and mutual respect based on his deeply held religious convictions. Fa Keita's beliefs are grounded differently from those of some of the more radical strikers. Fa Keita emphasizes that violence against the French is not what is important.

Mais faire qu'un homme n'ose pas vous gifler parce que de votre bouche sort la vérité, faire que vous ne puissiez plus être arrêté parce que vous demandez à vivre, faire que tout cela cesse ici ou ailleurs, voilà quelle doit être votre occupation, voilà ce que vous devez expliquer aux autres afin que vous n'ayez plus à plier devant quelqu'un, mais aussi que personne n'ait à plier devant vous. (367)

But to act so that no man dares to strike you because he knows you are speaking the truth, to act so that you can no longer be arrested because you are asking for the right to live, to act so that all of this will end, both here and elsewhere: that is what should be in your thoughts. That is what you must explain to others, so that you will never again be forced to bow down before anyone, but also so that no one shall be forced to bow down before you. (237)

Fa Keita's philosophy cannot be dismissed as religious cant because it comes after his bitter experience in the colonial concentration camp and is clearly distinguished from the hypocritical, self-interested beliefs and traitorous actions of the Imams.[31] While Bakayoko cannot understand Fa Keita's refusal to hate the unjust, the tremendous respect and authority Fa Keita has among the strikers indicates the power of his personal example and his beliefs within the African community. Lahbib, a key intellectual leader of the strike, expresses views that echo Fa Keita and anger Bakayoko, who dismisses them as " tendre l'autre joue" (295) ["turning the other cheek" (189)]. Another example of a challenge to Bakayoko's authority occurs when he learns of the death of his mother and the kidnapping of his father by the military authorities. His uncle urges him to return home: "Fils, il n'y a plus d'homme à la maison là-bas, tu l'as lu dans la lettre, ta famille a besoin de toi" (293) ["My son, there is no longer a man in your house. You have read the letter—your family needs you" (188)]. But Bakayoko determines that his commitment to the strike is more important than his responsibility to his family, a sentiment not all participants in the strike would share. Maïmouna, the blind woman who seems to have special insight into people, makes this judgement of Bakayoko: "Dans le cœur de Bakayoko il n'y a place pour personne. Pour son prochain, il est plus aveugle que moi . . ." (304) ["In Bakayoko's heart there is no room for anyone. He is blinder to his neighbor than I am . . ." (196)].

This expression of a diversity of perspectives leads to a multiple and dialogic rendering of culture in *Les bouts de bois de Dieu*, and Bakayoko becomes just one point of reference in a complex community discussion. Paulo Freire describes the importance of such a dialogue for the pedagogy of the oppressed:

But to substitute monologue, slogans, and communiques for dialogue is to attempt to liberate the oppressed with the instruments of domestication. Attempting to liberate the oppressed without their reflective participation in the act of liberation is to treat them as objects which must be saved from a burning building; it is to lead them into the populist pitfall and transform them into masses which can be manipulated. (52)

In the praxis of the strike, the Africans confront the way in which their society is changing. The debate over the role of books in the colonial context is particularly significant as books involve not only the imposition of colonial authority, but, as we have seen in both *El nuevo mundo* and *The Tempest*, literacy and a written culture are used to dominate oral societies. In *Les bouts de bois de Dieu*, there is an argument about the role of European books that takes place between Tiémoko and Niakoro (wife of Fa Keita). Tiémoko seeks to replace the method of beating strike breakers with a version of the European public trial that he has learned about in a French book. Niakoro is opposed:

—Tiémoko, continua la vieille femme, réfléchissez? Vous n'êtes pas des toubabous [Europeans]. Comment voulez-vous juger cet homme respectable et respecté!

—Tout ce qu'il faut est dans ce livre, dit Tiémoko.

—Ce livre a été écrit par des toubabous, dit l'ancien.

—Les machines aussi sont aux toubabous! Ce livre est la propriété d'Ibrahima Bakayoko et lui-même a dit un jour devant toi que ni les lois ni les machines n'appartiennent à une seule race!

—Les toubabous font des choses qui nous humlient et maintenant, vous voulez faire comme eux. [32] (143-4)

"Tiémoko," the old woman said, "have you thought about this? You are not *toubabs*! How can you judge a man who is respected by everyone."

"Everything we need is in this book," Tiémoko said.

"That book was written by the *toubabs*! the book belongs in Ibrahim Bakayoko, and right here, in front of you, I have heard him say that neither the laws nor the machines belong to any one race!"

"The *toubabs* do all kinds of things that humiliate and debase us, and now you want to do the same." (87)

Though the Africans decide to hold the trial according to French legal traditions, there is an awareness that the community is faced with difficult choices. Despite the fact that the trial has followed French procedures, it is Fa Keita's intervention at the conclusion of the trial that preserves African customs in the midst of a French proceeding. Fa Keita argues that the humiliation of the strike breaker in front of the community will be a more just punishment than anything the European book might suggest. His view is accepted and the strike breaker released.

Whereas the pedagogical takes as its starting point "the people" (what Freire calls "the masses"), a performative national culture manifests divisions, splits within the national Self and between "Self" and "Others." Bhabha put it this way:

> The performative intervenes in the sovereignty of the nation's self-generation by casting a shadow between the people as 'image' and its signification as a differentiating sign of Self, distinct from the Other or the Outside. . . . [The nation becomes] a space that is internally marked by cultural difference and the heterogeneous histories of contending peoples, antagonistic authorities, and tense cultural locations. (299)

A Fanon/Bhabha national culture forged in the struggle for justice and liberation eschews the (re)construction of any "pure" or homogeneous "Africanness." European practices, such as railroads, books, or trials, may become part of a dynamic African national culture.

POSTCOLONIAL IDENTITY AND AFRICAN NATIONALISM

Instead of constructing a monolithic national identity, *Les bouts de bois de Dieu*, depicts moments in the lives of a diverse group of Africans, many of whom decide to demand less exploitative working conditions by holding out in a protracted strike despite colonial authority and violence. The cinematographic structure of Sembène's novel, with its rapid cuts from locale to locale, emphasizes connections between the experience of different groups of people up and down the rail line.[33] Abdul JanMohamed describes Ngugi's *A Grain of Wheat* in a similar way:

These retrospections and the multiplicity of points of view through which we come to understand the characters create the experience of an organic community which can only be known through its historical and interpersonal interactions; in the novel there is no omniscient, privileged view of these interactions that constantly reshape the past, present, and future. (210)

By capturing a multiplicity of perspectives the novel operates in the way that Benedict Anderson describes the national newspaper: by linking events of disparate locations in a simultaneous presentation, it facilitates the imagination of the national community. In the triumphal conclusion of the novel, there is a joining together of the resistances of women, railway workers, families, villages, and dispersed regions—a coming together of a national community.

Anthony Appiah distinguishes two stages of African writing.[34] The first stage embraces nationalism; the second stage recognizes it as coopted by a nationalist bourgeoisie. In an important sense Sembène's novel bridges the gap between the first and second generations of the African novel. In its depiction of a performance of a Fanonian struggle the novel constructs a dynamic and engaged national culture. In its refusal to fetishize "traditional Africa," in its recognition of the power of the *comprador* bourgeoisie to appropriate "national culture" to their own interests, in its portrayal of the diversity of struggle and its on-going nature *Les bouts de bois de Dieu* eschews any fixation on an "essence" for African nationalism.

By examining the figure of El Hadj in *Xala*, Jameson sees the individual as an allegory for the national, the social quality of "libidinal dynamics" that he believes characterize the "third world" (82). Yet the power of *Les bouts de bois de Dieu* lies precisely in its insistence that no one individual can represent the entire "national people." The plurality, divergence, and complexity of characters in *Les bouts de bois de Dieu* resist the suturing of allegory. Reading *Les bouts de bois de Dieu* in the light of a Fanon/Bhabha version of national culture, one where the immediacy and complexity of performance replace the hierarchy and reification of pedagogy, is to identify an alternative to the compromised nationalism of many postcolonial states.

CHAPTER 5

(Dis)Integrating Nation and Self
Midnight's Children and Postcolonial Autobiography

The government of independent India in 1947, even after the amputation of the north-west and most of Bengal, found itself responsible for most of a subcontinent. India was a historical and a religious concept, but there was no Indian nation.

Hugh Seton-Watson

There was an extra festival on the calendar, a new myth to celebrate, because a nation which had never previously existed was about to win its freedom, catapulting us into a world which, although it had five thousand years of history, although it had invented the game of chess and traded with Middle Kingdom Egypt, was nevertheless quite imaginary, into a mythical land, a country which would never exist except by the efforts of a phenomenal collective will—except in a dream we all agreed to dream; it was a mass fantasy shared in varying degrees by Bengali and Punjabi, Madrasi and Jat, and would periodically need the sanctification and renewal which can only be provided by ritual of blood. India, the new myth—a collective fiction in which anything was possible, a fable rivalled only by the two other mighty fantasies: money and God.

Salman Rushdie

The tension between the high hopes of national liberation and the stark reality of economic underdevelopment, political corruption, factionalism and neocolonialism is repeatedly thematized in postcolonial writing. Before independence, in the era of colonial rule and mounting anticolonial struggle, Fanon described the "passionate search" by "native intellectuals" for "national culture" that was not "distorted, disfigured, or destroyed" by the European versions of native history (*Wretched* 169-70). By writing into being a "national people" with implicit rights to autonomous self-rule, anticolonial writers used European languages in order to formulate a cultural basis for the ideological and political struggle against European domination. Ironically, however, in constructing national cultures, conflictive divisions, such as those of ethnicity, tribe, religion, caste, and language were down-played, just at they were in the colonialist narratives of Shakespeare and Lope that we have examined. In postcolonial nations, these differences assume enormous importance. Given the disappointing history of post-independence nations, it is not surprising that postcolonial writers question monolithic state authority and challenge representations of unified national identity and narratives of coherent national development. Thus, as embodiment of both possibility and frustration the nation itself has come to have a complex position in postcolonial writing and thought.

Salman Rushdie's *Midnight's Children* is one of the most important extended examinations of the dilemmas of emerging nationhood. Like the other literary works we have examined, *Midnight's Children* incorporates a diversity of classes and social groups within a national framework. The novel has been called "glittering," "dazzling," "a *tour de force*." Frequently compared to *One Hundred Years of Solitude*, its five-hundred-plus pages combine magical realist and metafictive techniques with Indian story-telling and mythology. Utilizing a novel to narrate Indian national history, *Midnight's Children* makes European forms its own by running together otherwise incompatible genres including the epic and the mock epic, the tragic and the comic, the testimonial and the parodic, the *bildungsroman* and the picaresque. Indeed, the novel's organization could be said to follow that of Indian oral narrative, described elsewhere by Rushdie himself as having a "looping and digressing and swirling shape" ("*Midnight's Children* and *Shame*" 8). As "Indian" as *Midnight's Children* may be, it is written in English, and it makes an attempt to represent a national, postcolonial history to an international audience steeped in Orientalist ways of knowing about "the East."[1] While no brief analysis of *Midnight's Children* can capture the scope or complexity of Rushdie's writing or its reception, a central problematic of postcolonial literature can be explored in an investigation of *Midnight's Children*.

ANTICOLONIAL AUTOBIOGRAPHY AND THE FORMATION OF THE NATIONAL SUBJECT

Using the form of a fictionalized autobiography, *Midnight's Children* narrates Indian national history. The novel may be read both in and against an emerging tradition of anticolonial autobiography. Works as various as Kane's *Ambiguous Adventure* and Mahatma Gandhi's *The Story of My Experiments with Truth* or more overtly fictionalized accounts such as Camara Laye's *Enfant noir*, José María Arguedas's *Los Rios Profundos*, or even Premchand's short story "Resignation," are part of this tradition and display a recurrent pattern.[2] In its prototypical form, the anticolonial autobiography narrates a subject from childhood, through a colonial education, to an awareness of colonial oppression and a decision to resist this oppression in the interest of a nation or group of people. The recurrence of this narrative as a generator of colonized subjectivity is suggested by the figures of Dulcanquellín and Caliban—though they are characters on the European stage, in highly compacted form their lives more or less follow this pattern. In addition to their place in colonial discourse, anticolonial autobiographies develop in certain respects from the nineteenth-century "novel of education," such as *David Copperfield*, *Great Expectations*, or *Jane Eyre*, which describe the upwardly mobile trajectory of an individual subject and his or her sympathy with the class they leave behind. Yet, the anticolonial autobiography is narrated in the culturally conflictive colonized zone where individual identity is consistently subsumed within that of an oppressed group, despite other social, class or ethnic distinctions. Thus it is most appropriate to view anticolonial autobiographies not only from the perspective of the novel of education but in the framework of "third-world" history and theory.

Frantz Fanon's analysis of the "evolution" of the "native intellectual" provides a relevant starting point for the consideration of anticolonial autobiography. In the last chapter we saw the importance of Fanon's dynamic notion of national culture to the African novel. In the same classic essay, Fanon identifies three phases in the development of "third-world" writers: first, an unqualified assimilation of European thought and trends; second, a disturbed period where there is a questioning of this assimilation and an attempt, in Fanon's words, to "recall" "the life of the people"; and, third, a "fighting" phase, where "the native, after having tried to lose himself in the people and with the people, will on the contrary shake the people" (179). When fully rendered, anticolonial autobiographies narrate the "evolution" of the "native intellectual" through Fanon's progression, usually adding an initial childhood period, so that in their complete form there are four distinguishable stages: (1) a traditionally ordered and usually harmonious childhood and family life; (2) a separation from the family, often through a colonial school system, and the development of an awareness of contradictions caused by colonial or racial oppression; (3) a rejection of assimilation and a "return to the people"; and (4) a participation in a social struggle directed toward national liberation or independence. The anticolonial autobiography thus differs markedly from *Les bouts de bois de Dieu*, which has a multiplicity of vision, a consciously dynamic and present-oriented view of the making of culture, and a recognition of the possible appropriation of the national cause by particular classes.

For the "native intellectual" seeking to resist colonial domination, the nation appears as an attractive and "natural" compromise between the apparently irreconcilable poles of West and non-West. The nation appeals precisely because of its blending of the utopian possibility of community solidarity ("recalled" from childhood) and the aspiration for individual freedom from domination (stressed in the European thought and literature that are part of the colonial education). For the intellectual, national independence is associated with both modernization and the return to tradition: membership in the world community and re-creation of a "passionately sought" cultural identity. Embodiments of this interplay of modernization and tradition are everywhere to be found, from the iteration of folkloric "traditions" at the highest moments of state ritual to the complex and hybridized narration of postcolonial writers.

Paradoxically, then, emerging nations assert their difference within a form of social, cultural, and political organization and governance developed in *Europe's* relatively recent past. Partha Chatterjee argues precisely that the central problem of "third-world" nationalist thought is the paradoxical existence of *independent* national cultures always within a *universal* framework of nation-states:

Nationalist thought, in agreeing to become "modern," accepts the claim to universality of this "modern" framework of knowledge. Yet it also asserts the autonomous identity of a national culture. It thus simultaneously rejects and accepts the dominance, both epistemic, and moral, of an alien culture. (11)

As restoration of the ancient traditions of the people, then, the nation is always fictive. Moreover, the administrative districts of European imperialism that become the new national boundaries often do not correlate even with precolonial or even colonial cultural, linguistic or ethnic divisions. The hybrid nation-state can be directly associated with cultural identity only for a minority of colonial subjects, primarily the cosmopolitan, Western-educated elites. This is not to say that nationalist struggles do not intend to alter oppressive relations for the "masses" of the colonized peoples. It is instead to follow Fanon in recognizing that "national culture" can be co-opted by the European-educated bourgeoisie so that in the former colonies

national consciousness, instead of being the all-embracing crystallization of the innermost hopes of the whole people, instead of being the immediate and most obvious result of the mobilization of the people, will be in any case only an empty shell, a crude and fragile travesty of what it might have been. (121)

The anticolonial "nationalist" autobiography, like the nation-state itself, is also caught up in the paradox of non-western/western nationalism. Despite its apparent claim to "indigenous authenticity," the anticolonial autobiography is inescapably hybrid. It narrates into being a cross-cultural and incipient national subject whose full realization is deferred or postponed to the moment of "independence." The postcolonial subject is thus tied to the narratives of anticolonial resistance and national independence which literally call him (and less often, her) into existence. The narrator of *Midnight's Children* describes what it means to be born into a postcolonial identity: "I had been mysteriously handcuffed to history, my destinies indissolubly chained to those of my country" (3). While anticolonial thought and resistance identify the nation, the frustrations of post-independence national history break it apart. In postcolonial settings, identity is shaped by both centripetal and centrifugal forces that simultaneously integrate and dis/integrate the subject.

POSTCOLONIAL NARRATIVE, THE HYBRID SUBJECT, AND THE INTERNATIONAL MARKET

Marking a reversal of the colonial differentiation between colonizer and native, anticolonial writing narrates a collective "national" identity which identifies and expels the presumedly "foreign." Despite its hybridity of form, contradictions between colonizer and colonized are recognized in nationalist writing and become the basis on which colonial domination and control is questioned and challenged. Thus the collective identity of anticolonial writing is national in the concrete sense that the struggle to end colonial domination universalizes identity within a particular set of geographic borders, for strategic reasons often coextensive with those of the districts of colonial administration. In postcolonial writing the narration of personal identity in a collective struggle against an "easily identifiable" foreign enemy is no longer the central theme. Instead, the hybridity that is repressed in anticolonial writing comes to the fore and national identity itself is recognized as both complicated and fractured. Foreign oppression may be seen to have its counterpart in domestic collaboration and corruption; domestic oppressions and difference displace the foreign enemy, and "we the people" becomes the site of difference, division, and struggle.

From the perspective of postcolonial history, the very formation of a unitary or self-contained national identity may itself appear problematic. There is an increasing recognition both of difference within the nation and of the overlaying and hybridizing of subjectivities through the nationalization and internationalization of culture. The postcolonial subject is both plural and divided, and a "realist" postcolonial autobiography positing a transparent relationship between the individual and the national collectivity becomes difficult if not impossible. While Frederic Jameson's argument that "third-world" literature is national allegory problematically sutures individual and nation in anticolonial writing, his position is altogether too constraining for postcolonial fiction and for Rushdie in particular.[3] In a subsequent issue of *Social Text* (1991) Aamir Mufti argues that

The role of the intellectual, as it appears in Rushdie's writings, involves ... going beyond a mere "telling of the experience of the collectivity itself," to a posing of specific challenges, directed at historical fictions of community and representation. (96)

Midnight's Children is constructed as the imagined autobiography of Saleem Sinai whose life—including his miraculous birth at the instant of India's independence—is proclaimed by Nehru himself to "mirror" the new nation's own (143).[4] The novel's content and form draw on the anticolonial autobiography, and rather than striving to represent the experience of a people under oppression in a "realistic" mode, the novel locates and disrupts claims to "truthful" representation.[5] We are told the story of Saleem's life by the mature Saleem character himself, and the chronological narrative of the life is delayed, interrupted, and sidetracked by various returns to the "present" and references to or prophecies of the "future." In this "present" of the frame, Saleem has an auditor, Padma, his consort/muse and representative of the illiterate Indian masses. In addition to his own meditations on the narrative, Saleem records Padma's reactions to the content and method of his storytelling. At the end of the novel, the story catches up with the frame, and we discover that Saleem is the manager of a chutney factory in present-day Bombay, with Padma his assistant, and in the closing pages, his wife. It is in the frame that the imaginative, re-creative processes of autobiographical narration—the processes which in anti- and postcolonial writing link individual and national identity—are directly explored.

The frame localizes Saleem's perspective, and simultaneously, Saleem's and Padma's metacommentary raises broader issues about the narration of Indian history to a national and international "postcolonial" audience. In the novel then, there is an individual, Saleem, that as "one of many" can contain and re-present "Indian experience" and, simultaneously, there are constant reminders of the problematics of this—or any—individual experience standing for the subcontinent. As we are given it, Saleem's life is fragmentary, partial, and incomplete— a self-conscious and evidently idiosyncratically flawed reconstruction of a faulty, if not deranged memory. In the frequently interrupting frame, the expectations of the auditor/reader to the violations of what Saleem calls "what-happens-nextism" are explicitly anticipated and addressed.

It is appropriate that Saleem compares himself in the frame to Scheherazade. In order to maintain the favor of Prince Shahryar and prolong her life, Scheherazade must make sure that her story will please her audience and entertain for 1001 nights. In putting himself in Scheherazade's place, Saleem invokes the expectation of an "Oriental" author providing exotic tales to the all-powerful reader:

In the renewed silence, I return to sheets of paper which smell just a little of turmeric, ready and willing to put out of its misery a narrative which I left yesterday hanging in mid-air—just as Scheherazade, depending for her very survival on leaving Prince Shahryar eaten up by curiosity, used to do night after night! (22)

Even the reference to turmeric, the essential spice of Indian cooking, plays on the notion that the attraction to the cosmopolitan reader of an Indian narrative in English is simply a matter of a desire for difference, a taste for a spicy, "colorful" dish. In this sense Saleem/Rushdie becomes not so much Scheherazade as the "Indian Punch," ironic Indian national spokesman, wrapped in the garb of British orientalist fancy.

In the frame, Rushdie parodies the place of the Indian novel in the international consumption of "third-world" cultural commodities and points to the enormous difficulty, perhaps impossibility, of escaping from established expectation and ways of knowing in conveying Indian experience to the West.[6] Saleem uses the expression "the chutnification of history" for his efforts to remember and reconstruct the past. He says he has "dedicated my latter days to the large-scale preparation of condiments" (38). In this sense, his narrative is a "preserve" in a double sense,

And my chutney and kasaundies are, after all, connected to my nocturnal scribblings—by day amongst pickle-vats, by night within these sheets, I spend my time at the great work of preserving. Memory, as well as fruit, is being saved. . . . (38)

If the "national" in the west is, above all, visual or aural—flags, military marches, national anthems—in *Midnight's Children*, the nation is playfully identified primarily through gustation and olfaction. The smell of Indian cooking and even of Padma's "coarse, peasant body" toys with orientalist stereotypes about India.[7] Saleem's enormous nose is said to "smell out" history, and, of course, the pickling of spices is both his daytime, and in the sense of the "chutnification of history," his nighttime occupation.

Both in *Midnight's Children* and elsewhere, Rushdie objects to the persistent emphasis on the purity of national tradition and the assignment of postcolonial writing within inappropriately confining

10 Rushdie becomes the "Indian Punch," ironic national spokesman, wrapped in the garb of British orientalist fancy. (*The Indian Charivari* in the manner of Punch, 1877).

national traditions. In an essay originally penned in 1983 and entitled, "'Commonwealth Literature' Does Not Exist," Rushdie writes:

[Commonwealth] books are almost always praised for using motifs and symbols out of the author's own national tradition, or when their form echoes some traditional form, obviously pre-English, and when the influences at work upon the writer can be seen to be wholly internal to the culture from which he "springs." Books which mix traditions, or which seek consciously to break with tradition, are often treated as highly suspect. (1991, 66)[8]

And,

"Authenticity" is the respectable child of old-fashioned exoticism. It demands that sources, forms, style, language and symbol all derive from a supposedly homogeneous and unbroken tradition. Or else. . . . Imagine a novel being eulogized for being "authentically English," or "authentically German." It would seem absurd. Yet such absurdities persist in the ghetto. (1991, 67)

In place of cultural purity or authenticity, Rushdie argues for a recognition of hybridity and cultural mixing that would move away from ghettoization.[9] Both in his novels and in his essays, he challenges the artificial fixation of identity and the restrictive containment of meaning.

POSTCOLONIAL IDENTITY AND ANTICOLONIAL RESISTANCE

In *Midnight's Children*, there is a dissonance with every phase of the traditional narration of anticolonial autobiography. Instead of beginning with an idyllic childhood steeped in "venerable native tradition," *Midnight's Children* opens on a disrupted and hybridized cultural heritage, extending generations before Saleem's birth. The long first section of the novel—Saleem is finally born on page 135—can thus be seen as a crucial complication of the anticolonial autobiographical narrative pattern. Rushdie cannot start a postcolonial novel with the unproblematic birth of a unitary and complete "Indian" subject but instead must explore the interrelationships and complicities inherent in the nationalist construction of Indian citizenship.

Thus, in a specific way, *Midnight's Children* picks up where the anticolonial autobiography leaves off. The opening scene of the novel is closely comparable to the closing scene of an autobiographical and anticolonial francophone novel by Cheikh Hamidou Kane, *Ambiguous Adventure*. Near the end of Kane's story, Samba Diallo, recently returned to the land of his childhood (Senegal) from a sojourn studying Western philosophy in Paris, appears to have given up the Islamic faith of his people. Although the moment is, as the title suggests, ambiguous, it is Samba's reluctance to pronounce the evening prayer that leads a loyal follower of the Diallobe's traditional teacher to strike him down and, apparently, kill him. *Ambiguous Adventure* finishes with Samba's death and a long hallucinatory scene where Samba's soul returns to its spiritual beginnings.

Hail! I have found again the taste of my mother's milk; my brother who has dwelt in the land of the shadows and of peace, I recognize you. Announcer of the end of exile, I salute you. (177)

Samba's confusion and death drive home Kane's message about the mixed blessing of assimilation, and the return of Samba's soul to Islam could be seen as the possible third stage of anticolonial autobiography as outlined above: the return to native tradition.

Just as in the closing of *Ambiguous Adventure*, in the opening of *Midnight's Children*, a contradiction between Islamic past and European education is manifest in a difficulty in pronouncing ritual prayers. Rather than the climax, however, the same scene in *Midnight's Children* initiates the story. Aadam Aziz, Saleem's grandfather, has recently returned to Kashmir after a medical education in Germany, and the narration begins with his hitting his nose on the ground while attempting to pray. At this moment in *Midnight's Children*, the break with tradition is *not* ambiguous, Aadam resolves "never again to kiss earth for any god or man" (4). This act marks an alienation between Aadam and his "ancestral valley," the site of "childhood springs in Paradise" (5):

Now returning he [Aadam Aziz] saw through travelled eyes. Instead of the beauty of the tiny valley circled by giant teeth, he noticed the narrowness, the proximity of the horizon; and felt sad, to be at home and feel so utterly enclosed. He also felt—inexplicably—as though the old place resented his educated, stethoscoped return. (5)

After his education abroad, Aziz views his homeland with the detachment of the European-assimilated "native intellectual," "knocked forever into that middle place, unable to worship a God in whose existence he could not wholly disbelieve. Permanent alteration: a hole" (6). Unlike the anticolonial *Ambiguous Adventure*, to be caught between East and West is in *Midnight's Children* not an ending but a beginning. It is the recognition of the break with a pure, contained "native" identity that brings the postcolonial subject into being. In this sense Aadam Aziz is, as his name suggests, the "first man," and his "fall" is established as necessary to the development of the complicated, hybridized nation to come.

The entire first section of the novel tracing Saleem's ancestry emphasizes national division rather than unity. Book One splices the anticolonial struggle into the countdown to national independence but does so in such a way as to prepare for a problematic postcolonial identity rather than to emphasize the development of a resistant nationalism. The violence of the British is present in the text, sharply recalled in *Midnight's Children* as Aadam Aziz witnesses the 1919 Jallianwallah Bagh massacre (where more than 1500 peaceful protesters honoring Gandhi's call for a work stoppage are killed or wounded by British machine-gun fire). Yet, for the most part, the broadly national events, the story, for instance, of the organization and struggle of Indian resistance, including Gandhi, Nehru and the Congress Party, and Jinnah and the Moslem league, are alluded to rather than narrated directly. (Just the opposite is true in the novel from Saleem's birth onwards, where it seems that every twist and turn in the fate of the nation's leaders is minutely experienced in Saleem's life.) In Book One then, instead of presenting a cohesive anticolonial nationalist movement, Rushdie emphasizes divisions among the Moslems and the anxious anticipation of partition. Rather than narrate national history, the first section intertwines Saleem's grandparents' and parents' lives with the increasingly intense intra-Moslem rivalry. For instance, Nadir Kahn, the first (and impotent) husband of Saleem's mother flees the murder of Mien Abdullah (organizer of separatist Moslems) and lives in hiding under the floor of Saleem's grandparents' house.

While Tim Brennan argues that Rushdie "excises" and "erases" "the story of Indian nationalism" (84), it would be more accurate to say that in the narration that takes place before independence is achieved, the nationalist struggle is seen from a particularist view, that of a Muslim family unsupportive of partition. Watching the unfolding of the nationalist movement from the perspective of a minority within a minority prepares the way for Rushdie's analysis of the impossibility of coherence in postcolonial Indian national identity.

FATHERING THE POSTCOLONIAL NATION

The complication and hybridization of Saleem's, and India's, identity is traced back in the novel to Aadam Aziz; yet it is Saleem's duplicitous birth and remarkably confused parentage that most vividly sets forth the contradictions and overlappings of postcolonial identity. Since the birth and parentage of Saleem and India are metonymically linked, examining Saleem's personal history opens onto Rushdie's critique of the new Indian state. Saleem's birth, like that of the nation, is not all that was promised; neither individual nor nation is who or what it seems.

As with India, Saleem's ancestry is complex and contradictory. His officially recognized parents, Ahmed Sinai and Amina Aziz, are an Islamic couple whose background suggests the regional diversity of the subcontinent. Amina's grandparents are from Kashmere; the couple met in Agra, and they live in Bombay. But Saleem's legal parents are not his "natural" ones. Well over a hundred pages into the novel we learn that Saleem was switched at birth by a nurse, Mary Pereira, anxious to please her radical boyfriend, Joseph D'Costa.[10] In this act, the wealthy Sinai baby is exchanged for the son of a poor Hindu couple, the street musician Wee Willie Winkie[11] and his wife Vanita. (In a pointed comment on the class inequality of Indian medical care, Vanita dies in childbirth while the doctor attends to the broken toe of the wealthy Ahmed Sinai.) Thus Saleem's parentage is not only geographically diverse but, like the presumed identity of the nation, it crosses lines of religion and class.[12]

And, still the proliferation of Saleem's parents continues. We discover that Wee Willie Winkie is not Saleem's natural father, either. Saleem was conceived in an extramarital liaison between Vanita and a British Anglo-Indian colonist, William Methwold. Saleem, then, is the biological child of an impoverished Indian mother and a wealthy, British colonist of an established Anglo-Indian family. The "true" parentage of Saleem, beneath the layers of appearance and subterfuge, is indicative of the identity of the Indian nation itself: beneath its claim to uniqueness and independence there is a hybridity, a heterogeneous combination of "Indian" and European elements.

Despite the fact that William Methwold's relationship to Saleem remains unrecognized by the other characters in the novel and that Methwold himself departs from the story from the moment of independence onward (about a third of the way into the story), Methwold is nonetheless and, perhaps all the more, a key figure.[13] Rushdie uses Methwold to satirize the adoption by Indian elite classes of the manners and customs of the departing British colonizers. Methwold is owner of the luxurious estates consisting of four mansions (significantly named after the great palaces of Europe) where Saleem's family takes up residence, and he handpicks the new ruling class, the Indian businessmen, military officers, scientists, and doctors who will preside over the "independent" nation. The sale of the property is made with one condition: the new tenants must leave everything in their homes just as they were under British rule and must repeat precisely all the customs of the former colonizer, including cocktail hour on the lawn every evening at six. Methwold's "little game" is effective:

They have all failed to notice what is happening: the Estate, Methwold's Estate, is changing them. Every evening at six they are out in their gardens, celebrating the cocktail hour, and when William Methwold comes to call they slip effortlessly into their imitation Oxford drawls; and they are learning about ceiling fans and gas cookers and the correct diet for budgerigars, and Methwold, supervising their transformation, is mumbling under his breath. . . . All is well. (113)

The scene comically renders the neocolonialist argument that the new national bourgeoisie imitates the former colonizers. It recalls Frantz Fanon's comments in the "Pitfalls of National Consciousness" (in *Wretched of the Earth*):

In the colonial countries, the spirit of indulgence is dominant at the core of the bourgeoisie; and this is because the national bourgeoisie identifies itself with the Western bourgeoisie, from which it has learnt its lessons. It follows the Western bourgeoisie along its path of negation and decadence without ever having emulated it in its first stages of exploration and invention. . . . (124)

11 Beneath its claim to uniqueness and independence there is a hybridity, a heterogeneous combination of "Indian" and European elements. (*General Jean François Allard and His Family*, 1838)

In the Indian context, the adoption of English manners has a history extending back at least as far as the intention expressed by Macaulay in his famous 1835 Minute, "We must at present do our best to form a class who may be interpreters between us and the millions we govern; a class of persons, Indian in blood and colour, but English in taste, in opinions, in morals, and in intellect."[14] The "Methwold effect" is completed when Saleem's father and the other businessmen of India begin literally to pale and turn white (212)—thus going one step further than Macaulay anticipated. (Ahmid says, "All the best people are white under the skin; I have merely given up pretending" [212]).

Throughout *Midnight's Children*, the Methwold estates are associated with neocolonialist perspectives. In view of the destruction and repression that begins to engulf the novel from about its midpoint on, there is even surrounding the estates a certain nostalgia for the colonial past. When Saleem leaves India to move with his family to Pakistan, the Methwold palaces are demolished, and yet Saleem recalls the film *Lost Horizon* and identifies the estates as a sort of "Shangri-La" (366). By the end of the novel, Saleem returns to Bombay and the location of his former home. Where once "the palaces of William Methwold stood wreathed in bougainvillaea and stared proudly out to sea," now there is "a great pink monster of a building, the roseate skyscraper obelisk of the Narlikar women, standing over and obliterating the circus-ring of childhood" (539). Thirty years after independence, the gracious estates that epitomized British rule are replaced with impersonal modern architecture of the sterile (and literally sterilized) Indian business class.[15]

Yet this barbed neocolonial interpretation is offset by the presence of Mary Pereira, engineer of the baby exchange and Saleem's ayah, living in one of the Narlikar apartments. Her success in the business of making chutney makes it possible for her to live in relative luxury in the building that occupies the very space where she had once slept on a servant's mat (546). Saleem travels to Mary's apartment where they both fantasize about the past. In the chaotic darkness of Indira Gandhi's emergency rule, the pattern of life established by Methwold would even appear to hold a certain attraction. Thus the anticolonial and anti-neocolonial arguments are penetrated by postcolonial possibilities that resist Manichean definition. If the Methwold estates and the "skyscraper obelisk" that takes their place outline the replacement of the colonial masters by the "businessism" (474) of a neocolonial elite, they also suggest the interpenetration or "leaking" of identity and the possibility of inventing new life even within oppressive structures of existence.

Straightening out Saleem's natural parents is no easier than sorting out Saleem's extensive and complex adoptive parentage, and both natural and adoptive parents have a role to play in Rushdie's investigation of national identity. Throughout the novel, Saleem ends up being taken in and protected by one adoptive "parent" after another until the list includes a failing Bombay film writer and film-star wife, a Pakistani general who engineers a coup d'etat, a Sikh snake-charming Communist living in the New Delhi streets, and Saleem's own ayah turned chutney entrepreneur in Bombay. Saleem's adoptive parents are a kind of *Fodor's* guide to the colorful and diverse characters of India (in fact, the snake charmer appears on Kodak posters all over India and is known as "Picture Singh"). Taken together, all these adoptive parents further the sense in which Saleem/India is the product of many influences. As with the Methwold estates, the free play in the adoption of parents is indicative of the novel's treatment of identity. Thus it is significant that Saleem's natural parents exit the text early and turn out to be inconsequential figures in Saleem's own life. In a strictly anticolonial novel, this sharp economic and cultural contradiction between Methwold and Vanita would be at center stage, but in Rushdie's postmodern text there is a kind of cultural mixing and crossing over, not so that the Anglo-English-colonizer/destitute-Indian-street-woman dichotomy doesn't matter but so that it is overlaid with other claims and relationships. The various adoptive parents are all public figures whose occupations are integral to national identity. Film producers, generals, snake charmers, rising entrepreneurs all have a part to play in one way or another in the multiple layering of postcolonial Indian experience. The colonizer is gone and his legacy is left behind now—the novel would appear to suggest—one must sort through the wreckage and explore the possibilities in the new, more complicated, and fluid context. Movement and the constant exchange of parents underscores the hybridity and complexity of Saleem's childhood and, by extension, points to the same features in the post-independence nation.

TEXTUALIZING THE NATIONAL BODY

Metaphors of the body are part of the discourse that has organized, unified, and legitimated various forms of social organization, and the language of the body continues to have a particular importance to the way the nation is understood. We speak of "the social body" the "body politic" the "head of state." Adjectives to describe the body are frequently applied to the nation-state: healthy/sick, youthful/aging, strong/weak. Through at least the eighteenth century in Europe the body may have been the crucial metaphor for understanding the functioning of the state; consider the medieval legal fiction of the king's two bodies, Hobbes' *Leviathan* or Rabelais' *Gargantua*.[16] Metaphors of the body serve to naturalize social organization, and stand in opposition to an understanding of the nation that emphasizes the historicity of its construction, the artificiality of relations of power, the heterogeneity of a "national people." In *Midnight's Children*, Rushdie uses Saleem's body to represent the nation, but by reversals, parody, and caricature he manages to rewrite the metaphor of nation as body in light of Indian beliefs and consistent with postcolonial history.

The nationalist image of India as a youthful, robust, and promising country is lampooned in the depiction of Saleem's deformed, ailing and unattractive person. As a baby, Saleem is a whining, ugly child with a misshapen, birthmarked face, a "monstrous" nose constantly "dripping," and an insatiable demand for attention. With his elongated nose, Saleem is said to resemble the elephant-headed Hindu god, Ganesh. Moreover, Saleem's facial features specifically incarnate the political map of the subcontinent. He is discolored by birthmarks on his face resembling the location of Pakistan/Bangladesh, "dark stains spread down my western hairline, a dark patch coloured my eastern ear" (144). He has a diminutive chin and enlarged temples, and his face is roughly triangular, like the shape of India itself.[17] His constantly battered body bears the marks of violence. He is deaf in one ear from being hit by his father, bald on the top of his head where a teacher pulled out his hair, missing a finger cut off by a slammed door, knocked unconscious by a flying spittoon, and "testerectomized" by Indira Gandhi's security forces. Near the end of the novel he is described as "nine-fingered, horn-templed, monk's tonsured, stain-faced, bow-legged, cucumber-nosed, castrated, and now prematurely aged," "a big-headed, top-heavy dwarf" (533-34). Saleem is practically a monster, almost a Caliban, in one sense the satirical embodiment of European discourse about the native Other.

Moreover, Rushdie's depiction of Saleem parodies the code of manliness and the idealization of the male body inherent in the European nationalist conception carried over to the "third world."

Discussing the rise of nationalism in Germany, Mosse describes this masculine code and traces it to an eighteenth-century neoclassical revival interpretation of the practices of Ancient Greece. Mosse emphasizes that the Classical model of the male form, found in sculpture, was de-eroticized in favor of a resolute ideal:

The ideal of masculinity, including its borrowed Greek standards of male beauty, was drafted by European nationalisms into service as national symbol or stereotype. The Greek ideal was stripped of any lingering eroticism, while its harmony, proportion, and transcendent beauty were stressed. Masculinity was expected to stand both for unchanging values in a changing age and for the dynamic but orderly process of change itself, guided by an appropriate purpose. (31)

If the nation implies purposeful and orderly change, Saleem's ugliness, and his tempest-tossed, picaresque victimization undermine the facile adoption of the Western notions of progress and modernization in India. Indeed, Saleem's impotence and helplessness are central to Rushdie's critique of the resolute manliness of nationalist discourse. Though Rushdie's characterization of India, like his characterization of Islam in *The Satanic Verses,* could be read as insulting, it is also evident that the "pristine manliness" of European nationalist discourse was for that matter never applicable in Europe (or specifically even in Germany) and has always been an ideological tool of those who are able to use discourses of the nation—or "modernization"—to serve their interests or legitimate their hold on power.

Despite the clever use Rushdie makes of the figures of body as nation, there is a fundamental irreconcilability between the metaphor of a coherently functioning, self-contained biological organism and the social and political mechanisms of the modern nation. This irreconcilability is evident throughout the novel, as Rushdie portrays the mature Saleem's body as "cracking up" and threatening to break apart. If as an infant his body expanded like the population of India, "I embarked upon an heroic program of self-enlargement" (145), as an adult it cannot seem to hold together. In the second paragraph, Saleem describes his body as "crumbling." In the second-to-the-last paragraph, Saleem's body "fissions," "cracks," and "explodes." The tension between the integrated and the disintegrating body is metaphorical for postcolonial nationhood. Aamir Mufti argues that

Saleem's disintegrating body and unfulfilled life highlight not so much the
failure as the impossibility of the national (liberal-democratic) project of
turning colonial subjects into democratic citizens under the direction of the
anglicized elite. (99)

As Saleem's body "cracks up," what is left behind is not just
"anonymous dust" but the story of his life, the autobiography he hopes
to pass on to the next generation. Thus unlike Caliban, Dulcanquellín,
or the characters of *Les bouts de bois de Dieu* who revolt directly,
Saleem's effort to hold together, his attempt to make meaningful
connection with the other citizens of India, is a project of writing.

I have begun to crack all over like an old jug—that my poor body,
singular, unlovely, buffeted by too much history subjected to drainage
above and drainage below . . . is coming apart at the seams. . . . I ask you
only to accept (as I have accepted) that I shall eventually crumble into
(approximately) six hundred and thirty million particles of anonymous,
and necessarily oblivious dust. That is why I have resolved to confide in
paper, before I forget. (We are a nation of forgetters.) (37)

As an alternative to metaphorical incorporation within a national body,
"confiding" the personal/national history "in paper" locates and
historicizes the inscription of identity. Identity, both personal and
national, is thus textual rather than bodily, something that is
constructed out of patterns of discourse, something that must be "read,"
interpreted, something which, like the space within the borders of
colonial administration, can be reinscribed.

NARRATING NATION TIME

Benedict Anderson argues that there was a profound change in the
apprehension of time necessary to think the modern nation:

What has come to take the place of the mediæval conception of
simultaneity-along-time is, to borrow again from [Walter] Benjamin, an
idea of "homogeneous, empty time," in which simultaneity is, as it were,
transverse, cross-time, marked not by prefiguring and fulfillment, but by
temporal coincidence, and measured by clock and calendar. (30)

As pointed out in the introduction, Anderson maintains that in European history "homogeneous, empty time" was embodied in two textual genres that arose during the Enlightenment along with the nation, the realist novel and the newspaper. The novel allows characters who may not know each other, or even have any direct relationship with each other, not merely to exist simultaneously but to be recognized by the omniscient reader as part of the same, synchronically understood society.

Thus it isn't surprising that *Midnight's Children* should be a novel preoccupied with the relationship of time and nation. From the beginning of *Midnight's Children*, the new nation is associated with a tyrannical clock time that is given a softening "Indian" twist: freedom comes precisely at the stroke of midnight, when "clock-hands joined palms in respectful greeting" (3). The midnight children are born "only partially the offspring of their parents—the children of midnight were also the children *of the time*: fathered, you understand by history" (emphasis in original, 137). Saleem speaks for all the midnight children when he says, "Thanks to the occult tyrannies of those blandly saluting clocks I had been mysteriously handcuffed to history, my destinies indissolubly chained to those of my country" (3). The chapter that counts down to Saleem's birth and the nation's moment of independence is titled "Tic Toc." In associating clock time so closely with the nation, Saleem even suggests that national "homogeneous" time could be partitioned: the clocks in Pakistan would run an hour ahead of their Indian counterparts (89).

Images of clocks and the mechanical measuring of time are constantly interrupted by other less "homogeneous" or "empty" measures, measures that assert Indian national difference. The clock time of the nation is "tyrannical" and "chaining" but is mediated by other modes of time, by mythological cycles, dynastic histories, even by discontinuous modes of narration. Saleem directly questions the uniformity of time, ". . . time is an unsteady affair, in my experience, not a thing to be relied upon." Later, ". . . time, in my experience, has been as variable and inconstant as Bombay's electric power supply. Just telephone the speaking clock if you don't believe me—tied to electricity, it's usually a few hours wrong. Unless we're the ones who are wrong . . . no people whose word for 'yesterday' is the same as their word for 'tomorrow' can be said to have a firm grip on the time" (123). This less chronometric, stereotypically oriental Hindu time is narrated as neither "homogeneous" nor "empty." Instead it is full of deities, colored with emotions, cyclical in vast millennial patterns. The rewriting of a chronometric "homogeneous" time is evident also in the particular way Rushdie/Saleem jumbles the sequence of narration. There is a constant multiplicity in the telling of the story, frequent interruption, a cutting, slicing, patching over of scenes, dialogue, and metanarrative, a moving backwards and forwards at the level of Saleem/Author and Padma/Auditor that violates a chronological progression of time. The free play of oral narrative and the associative operation of memory are techniques Rushdie draws on to develop alternatives to realist narration. Postcolonial time is constructed, like postcolonial national or individual identity, in hybrid, overlapping, and multiple layers.

This resistance to "national time" in the novel constantly locates Indian identity in a different apprehension of time that overlays the rational, modernizing framework of Enlightenment nationalism. Aruna Srivastava puts it this way:

> As he writes the novel, Saleem wrestles with a chronological view of history, passed on by the ruling British and now part of the Indian national consciousness, and (to him) a more ephemeral, (Mahatma) Gandhian, mythical view of history—properly and traditionally Indian, but suppressed by more "progressive" ideas about history and its relationship to time. (63)

There is a doubleness of time in the novel that expresses the paradox of nationalism itself in its claims to both universal form and particular identity. In the postcolonial treatment of time in *Midnight's Children* the "two timing" of the nation creates a tension that is not easily resolved by adoption of one time or another.

THE MIDNIGHT'S CHILDREN AND POSTCOLONIAL NATIONHOOD

The central trope for the novel's examination of nationhood are the midnight's children themselves. Born in the hour after midnight August 15, 1947—the moment of Indian independence—the midnight's children are graced with superhuman powers and fantastic abilities. As the elaborate conceit unfolds, it becomes apparent how perfectly suited it is to Rushdie's exploration of individual and national identity in postcolonial society. An interplay of possibility and disappointment is present in every aspect of the children's existence. It is evident, for instance, in their very number. In the first hour after midnight 1001 miraculously graced children are born and yet, apropos of the exigencies of Indian life, 420 die of malnutrition, disease, or misfortune before they reach their tenth birthday.

The magical abilities of the children are intriguingly suggestive of the promise held out in the founding of India. Plenitude is embodied in the Goanese girl with the gift of multiplying fish. The notion that the new nation will transform individual experience is both present and parodied in the boy that can increase or decrease his size at will, the child who can change sex when he/she wants to by dipping him/herself into water, the child who can turn into a wolf. There is Kerala, "a boy who had the ability of stepping into mirrors and re-emerging through any reflective surface in the land—through lakes and (with greater difficulty) the polished metal bodies of automobiles" (237). Kerala's easy mobility suggests personal freedom, and in connecting natural and manmade surfaces, lakes and automobiles, his talents emphasize the seamlessness of the nation's aspiration to unite natural and material possibility. And yet, despite the utopian dreams these children manifest, throughout the novel the magic and mythical vision of a "liberated" Indian nation is powerfully dispelled by the harsh realities of postcolonial history.

The tensions, disunity, and frustration of the decades after decolonization are explored by Rushdie in the tense relationships between the three most powerful children, Saleem, Parvati, and Shiva. Saleem himself is the most talented. Born on the very stroke of the hour, he has the greatest gift, the ability to enter into the minds of others, to become the "radio transmitter" through which all of the other children are able to communicate. Saleem explains that his head works like

a sort of national network, so that by opening my transformed mind to all the children I could turn it into a kind of forum in which they could talk to one another, through me. So in the early days of 1958, the five hundred and eighty-one children would assemble, for one hour, between midnight and one a.m., in the lok sabha or parliament of my brain. (271)

Saleem's attempt to form what he calls the "Midnight's Children's Conference" exemplifies Enlightenment notions of rational discourse and parliamentary government. His talent is the dream-come-true of

Fanon's European educated-native intellectual, and in terms of the anticolonial autobiographical pattern that underlies the text, the Midnight Children's Conference—where Salem enters into debate with the diverse children of India—can be identified as Saleem's imaginative enactment of the fourth stage of the intellectual's autobiography, the "return to the people."

If Saleem embodies the hope of a European-originated national idea, Parvati-the-Witch signifies Indian uniqueness and difference. Born into the magician's quarter of Old Delhi, she is given a stereotypically Indian legacy, "the genuine gifts of conjuration and sorcery." Her magical powers are employed in healing, protection, and escape, and she is Saleem's principal ally in his struggle with the third of the most important children of midnight, Saleem's arch rival, Shiva, the violent, materialistic, and ambitious child with knees powerful enough to crush opposing armies.

Saleem and Parvati are allegorical figures in the problematic drama of universal nationalist thought and particular postcolonial history. The marriage between Saleem and Parvati that occurs at her request three-quarters of the way through the book could be read as "acceptance" of the nationalist ideal. Yet the Saleem/Parvati relationship is never consummated; for when Saleem approaches Parvati, he is rendered impotent because he always sees an image of his sister. Pushing the reading of Saleem as the figure of nationalist thought and Parvati as that of Indian difference, the image of the sister masking the wife suggests the projection of European nationalism's perverse and insurmountable desire for its own kind. In short, the Saleem/Parvati relationship precisely underscores Partha Chatterjee's point that a nationalism based on Western Enlightenment is problematic for India because of the failure of this nationalism to recognize and appreciate Indian uniqueness and difference. Though Parvati casts her most powerful spells, Saleem remains unable to fulfill his marital responsibilities. In order to produce the next generation, she is obliged to seek her counterpart elsewhere. She turns, of course, to the other most powerful child of midnight, Shiva, a move clearly anticipated in Hindu mythology where Parvati is Shiva's consort. Later, Parvati returns to Saleem impregnated by Shiva. The child, Aadam Sinai, watched over by Saleem, is born in prophetic recurrence on the stroke of midnight, June 25th, 1975, "the precise instant of India's arrival at Emergency." The allegorical interpretation might be thought of as follows: India having attempted to find for itself a satisfying

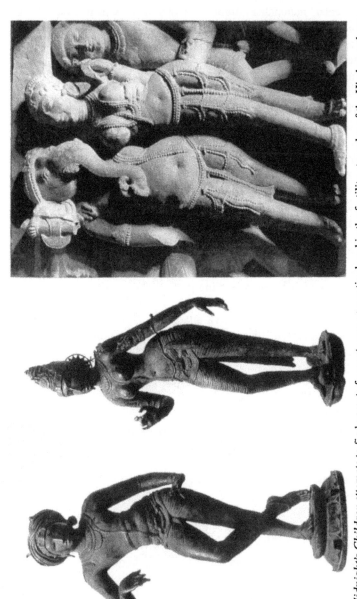

12 *Midnight's Children* attempts to find parents for contemporary nationhood in the fertility struggles of the Hindu pantheon. (Shiva and Consort, Ganesh and Consort)

"enlightened" nationalism, turns to its own more authentic mate in an Indian tradition that is violent, oppressive, and destructive but, simultaneously, fertile and generative. The child fathered by Shiva but adopted by Saleem is another "Adam," and the new generation of Indians is the fruit of the simultaneous acceptance/rejection of alien/indigenous nationality.

The disruption of nationalist aspirations by the disparities of economic class is a critical theme throughout the novel and is in sharpest focus in the Saleem/Shiva antagonism that gives *Midnight's Children* its strongest narrative tension. If in the midnight parliament Saleem is the spokesman for a progressive, universalizing nationalism, it is Shiva who points out that Saleem's position is explicitly formulated in terms that diffuse any class-based appeal or analysis. In convening the children, Saleem calls for a "third principle" to "drive between" "the endless duality of masses-and-classes, capital-and-labor, them-and-us" (306). He wants the children to let nothing "come between us," to "stick-together-through-thick-and-thin" (307). If this position sounds like the mediating pose of classic liberalism, Shiva's stance is starkly—and untheoretically—materialist.[18] Before he quits the conference in disgust, Shiva attacks what he considers the self-interested naivete of Saleem's notion of the possibility of a "third principle," of simple cooperation amongst the children.

No, little rich boy; there is no third principle; there is only money-and-poverty, and have-and-lack, and right-and-left; there is only me-against-the-world. The world is not ideas, rich boy, the world is not a place for dreamers or their dreams; the world, little Snotnose, is things. Things and their makers rule the world. (307)

Shiva's existence is a constant danger to Saleem's privilege, and his analysis of class difference threatens the conference/parliament Saleem convenes. Due to the chicanery of Mary Pereira, Saleem has, of course, taken Shiva's rightful place as child of wealth and privilege, and when Saleem learns the secret of his birth he resolves to keep it from Shiva. This effort "to erect a barrier around my new knowledge which could deny it to the children" leaves Saleem "afraid of Shiva" (339-40). Between Saleem and Shiva, there is then a profound class antagonism, the "political unconscious" of the nation itself. Saleem feels "guilty" that he should enjoy privileges and freedoms unavailable to the vast majority of Indian citizens, and he fears that the wrath of the Indian masses at this injustice would lead to a violent end to his position.

Despite the recognition of class antagonism, in Rushdie's narration of post-independence class identities, categories of class are persistently reinscribed within Hindu mythological principles. Madhusudhana Rao put this process in a classically orientalist formulation:

> The fatalistic disintegration of Saleem is, however, resolved in a timeless world of spiritual unification with the essential spirit and mind of India. (42)

As much as Rushdie himself might reject such a reading, it is possible to see how *Midnight's Children* suggests it. Consider Saleem's explanation of his evolving view of Shiva:

> He became for me, first a stabbing twinge of guilt; then an obsession; and finally. . . . He became a sort of principle; he came to represent, in my mind all the vengefulness and violence and simultaneous-love-and-hate-of-Things in the world; so that now even now, when I hear of drowned bodies floating like balloons on the Hooghly and exploding when nudged by passing boats; or trains set on fire, or politicians killed, or riots in Orissa or Punjab, it seems to me that the hand of Shiva lies heavily over all these things, dooming us to flounder endlessly amid murder rape greed war—that Shiva, in short, has made us who we are. (358)

While a mythic cycle of destruction and creation may suggest an ultimate triumph for Shiva in cosmic terms, it simultaneously renders unnecessary worldly political action. Despite Rushdie's self-expressed marxism, the persistent hybridization of secular and mythological worldviews in all his novels renders ambiguous questions of agency for political change.[19] Though class tension persists in *Midnight's Children*, there is an antipathy to political action or activism. The "revolutionary" of the early part of the novel is Joseph D'Costa, a dangerous bomb-throwing criminal. Language marchers kill Dr. Narlikar when he denigrates their cause, hurling him into the sea (210). The Communist Party meets in the filthy low-life Pioneer Café and its official candidate is the repulsive Nadir Khan (aka Nadir Qasim—sounds like Quisling?) whose once-fat face hangs in folds, and whose nearly bald head has hair "hanging lankly over his ears" (259). Neither the midnight's children nor the magician's ghetto marxists attempt organized or collective resistance. Instead, as Uma Parameswaran bluntly puts it, they "bury their talent in the ground instead of using it" ("Lest," 58).

Indeed, the last sections of the novel can be read within an orientalist interpretation of post-independence Indian history as the union of Indian nationalism with the subcontinent's supposed atavistic and destructive tendencies. There are ever-increasing upsurges of "ancient violence" as the novel progresses, including the language marchers, the massacres committed by the Indian army in their intervention in the Pakistan/Bangladesh war, and, above all, the repressive emergency declared by Indira Gandhi, identified in the novel simply as "the Widow." The conclusion of *Midnight's Children* is far from hopeful: it centers on Indira Gandhi and the national government's 1975 Emergency crackdown. Parvati is killed in a savage attack on the street magicians. Using the excuse of "civic beautification," a group of "Sanjay Youth Volunteers" who look identical to each other—and to the Gandhi family—lead a military charge on the Magician's ghetto. With Indian troops using Soviet weapons, Saleem asks ironically "What chance do Communist wizards have against socialist rifles?" (512). The midnight's children, the past expression of nationalist possibility, are now unorganized and disbursed. In his depiction of Indira Gandhi's attitude toward the children, Rushdie captures the paranoid view of the corrupt postcolonial leader assuming dictatorial power. Indira Gandhi imagines the innocent children as a

fearsome conspiracy which had to be broken at all costs—that gang of cut-throat desperadoes ... the grotesque aberrational monsters of independence, for whom a modern nation-state could have neither time nor compassion. (517)

Based on information a tortured Saleem provides to the interrogating Shiva (now a major in the Indian army), the remaining children are tracked down, incarcerated, and brutally sterilized as the nation devours its own children. The emergency brings an end to the children's procreative powers and terminates the hopes that were embodied in the nation's founding. Only at this point in the novel do we discover the double meaning of the midnight's children's name: their magical gifts are given in the midnight hour of independence, these same gifts are taken away during the prolonged midnight of "the Widow's" emergency rule. In keeping with the cyclical frame of history, there is left open, however, the mythical possibility of regeneration. Before he himself submits to voluntary sterilization, Shiva, the figure of both destruction and creation, consorts with women all across India, producing another generation of magical children yet to be born.

In the novel's last chapter, a new figure for the Indian nation takes the place of the Midnight's Children's Conference. Instead of a disputatious, ineffective parliament, there is the Midnite-Confidential Club, a corrupt and secret underground trysting place where the wealthy youth of Bombay steal for sexual titillation, illicit imported liquor and fabulous snake-charming contests. In this alternative metaphor of the postcolonial nation, neither India's independence struggle nor the fierce battles of contemporary national politics have any meaning. The sensual female attendant with eyes that are painted on her blind lids explains to Saleem and Picture Singh: "Here you are in a world without faces or names; here people have no memories, families or past; here is for *now*, for nothing except right now" (541). The Midnite-Confidential Club is Rushdie's figure for the corruption of Indian political culture. The rich indulge in fleeting sensual pleasures hypocritically denied to the rest of the population, and political contests are nothing more than a snake-charming sideshow where the masses are put into a trance. In the juxtaposition of the MC Conference and the MC Club, Rushdie starkly poses the disappointment of many postcolonial nations where the democratic aspirations of independence have been disregarded by a corrupt cosmopolitan elite.

The conclusion of the novel brings to a close the narration of postcolonial autobiography in terms entirely different from those of the heroic and inspiring narratives of anticolonial resistance. Instead of a participation in a social struggle directed toward national liberation, there is hopeless disintegration. The destruction of the Midnight's Children Conference and its replacement by the Midnite-Confidential Club represent the complete failure of the nationalist's dream. In Rushdie's bleak postcolonial vision, there is no "return to the people," no possibility of incorporating individual and national identity.

In attributing magical powers to the children Rushdie captures the exuberance of the birth of independent India, and he also mocks by exaggeration nationalism's messianic aspirations. Saleem describes the birth of the children as the climax of the progressive and modernizing history of the nation:

It was as though . . . history, arriving at a point of the highest significance
and promise, had chosen to sow, in the instant, the seeds of a future which
would genuinely differ from anything the world had seen up to that time.
(235)

Despite the possibilities inherent in the birth of the children, for
Rushdie they are also inscribed in the ancient mythical and magical
traditions of Indian culture and religion. The children live not only in
the time of the modern nation, but also in the Hindu millennium year of
Kali-Yuga, the age of darkness, and their tragic fate, the disappointing
conclusion of the novel and heartbreaking postcolonial history of India
itself set an important counterweight to the nationalist promise of
Enlightenment reason, rationalization, and social and economic
progress. If the children are poised like the Nietzchean superman on the
brink of overcoming the cycles of history, they are also caught in the
materialist realm and in the "eternal return" of the same. In the
fundamental duality of their existence the midnight's children, like all
Indian and perhaps all postcolonial citizens, have both traditional and
modern histories, and live in a time and space that is both progressive
and mythical. Saleem insists that despite their mythic qualities, their
inability to organize themselves and their ultimate defeat, the children
must not be dismissed as an impossibility or mere fantasy:

Midnight's children can be made to represent many things, according to
your point of view; they can be seen as the last throw of everything
antiquated and retrogressive in our myth-ridden nation, whose defeat was
entirely desirable in the context of a modernizing, twentieth-century
economy; or as the true hope of freedom, which is now forever
extinguished; but what they must not become is the bizarre creation of a
rambling, diseased mind. (240)

From Rushdie's perspective, the children's duality and hybridity cannot
be dismissed as "bizarre." It is something to welcome, even celebrate.
It is in this perspective and through the relationships and marvelous
talents of the children themselves that Rushdie explores the possibilities
and contradictions of the postcolonial Indian nation.

THE POSTCOLONIAL WRITER AND THE NATION

Salman Rushdie and his writing are at the epicenter of the complex and unstable global politics of the representation and reception of "the Orient" and the "third world." Though the Rushdie Affair itself has become an "international incident" with immediate life-and-death consequences, Rushdie's predicament differs more in degree than in kind from that of many postcolonial writers who use European languages to depict "third-world" nations. Postcolonial writing addresses widely differing audiences with divergent cultural, historical, and political memories. We know reading is context dependent; the case of *The Satanic Verses* indicates the extremes to which context affects interpretation.

Establishing the context of Rushdie's work is notoriously difficult. From one perspective Rushdie's novels can be read as part of the secular critique of Western orientalist discourse and the way such discourse has embodied the interests of European and American colonialism and neocolonialism. *Midnight's Children*, *Shame*, and *The Satanic Verses* are undeniably critical of simplistic or monolithic views of the Orient, India, Pakistan, or Islam. A recent analysis of postcolonial writing draws on one of Rushdie's essays for its title, *The Empire Writes Back*, and Rushdie's novels can be seen as a joco-serious "striking back" against colonizing power and discourse.

However, there are other perspectives from which to view Rushdie's writing. In the trilogy of his most successful novels, there is a profound concern with the cultural politics of India, Pakistan, and subcontinental migrant communities in England. Rushdie attempts to understand the hybrid complexity of postcolonial nations and peoples, non-Western and Western, modern and traditional. Furthermore, Rushdie addresses the profound tension in postcolonial nations between the high hopes of national independence and the disappointment of persistent political corruption, underdevelopment, factionalism, and neocolonialism. Given the frustrating history of independence, it is not surprising that Rushdie—and other postcolonial writers—increasingly challenge monolithic state authority and its supporting myths of coherent national progress and unified national identity.

As we have seen, *Midnight's Children* incorporates Indian beliefs and narrative practices, self-consciously caricaturizes orientalist depictions of the non-West, and disrupts realist narration associated with nationalism and modernization. However, *Midnight's Children*, like all of Rushdie's writing, is directed not only at Western orientalism. Aamir Mufti describes the critical consciousness of *Midnight's Children* as "double edged," "directed at both colonial culture and the myth of cultural authenticity and authority that replaced it" (100). Thus, from the perspective of the dedicated nationalist or the Islamic fundamentalist alert to colonialist history and repeated neocolonialist insult, Rushdie's writing is ambivalent, even threatening.[20] Of course Rushdie writes and publishes in English. While the only language for a legitimately "national" Indian literature, English is also the privileged tongue of the former colonial power. Neocolonial relationships, Western imperialism, and multinational corporate capitalism arrive with English and English arrives with them. Thus to use English in órder to harshly critique Indian or Pakistani culture, national leaders, or the Islamic faith, whatever advantages the language might offer, courts the misunderstanding of those who are oppressed by English, and it risks complicity in the unequal international circulation of culture and power. In this sense, *Midnight's Children* risks positioning Rushdie either as Indian Punch on the subcontinent or Baboo Jabberjee in the British Isles.

This political cartoon from an 1895 edition of *Punch* can be read as a depiction of the situation of the Indian writer in English. A well-dressed English-educated Indian, "Baboo Jabberjee, BA," on visiting Stratford remarks, "It was here, that the Swan of Avon was hatched" while a pretty English woman laughs at his ridiculousness. This cartoon bears comparison with another depiction of colonial encounter we have examined, the sixteenth-century etching of Vespucci encountering an Amerindian woman. In both, the colonizer's gaze determines the perspective of our view, and in both the Indians are in awe of and reverence toward the Europeans who provide him or her with their very identity, from the name "America" to the love of Shakespeare. Of course the reversal of gender roles is striking. Yet, in both cases, the male figure could be seen to represent emerging nationhood, legitimated or delegitimated by the regarding and attractive female, sexually available as Indian, sexually ridiculing as Englishwoman. This role of the nineteenth-century cartoon reminds us that Macaulay's efforts to create a class of Indians educated in English literature were never meant to "raise" this class to equality, and, today, the Indian writer's charm continues to be found in his representation to us of the "Other" in our own terms, in his "colorful" variation or, as Rushdie puts it, in his "chutnification."

"It was here," I said, reverently, "that the Swan of Avon was hatched!"

13 "Baboo Jabberjee BA," *Punch*, 1895

Indeed, Rushdie is acutely aware of the problem of the use of English in postcolonial writing, particularly so in *Midnight's Children,* a novel in which he attempts to narrate Indian national history. In a 1982 essay treating the novel, Rushdie responds to questions about the appropriateness of the choice of English. He argues like some African postcolonial writers that it is possible to "remake" English so that it need not be simply the language of the colonizer. Speaking of Indo-British writers, Rushdie says:

> Those of us who do use English do so in spite of our ambiguity towards it, or perhaps because of that, perhaps because we can find in that linguistic struggle a reflection of other struggles taking place in the real world, struggles between the cultures within ourselves and the influences at work upon our societies. To conquer English may be to complete the process of making ourselves free. (17)

The success of the effort to "conquer" English through English or through a "remade" version of English depends, above all, on the audience addressed. If the audience is already literate in a "standard" English, then the "remade" English may be defamiliarizing, may "write back" against empire. From the perspective of an Indian minority within the British population, Rushdie points out that the "forging of a British Indian identity [in] the English language is of central importance."[21]

But is it necessary to assume that because Rushdie writes in English that his audience must be an English-speaking or -reading one? There is always the activity of translation and, given the international exchange of cultural commodities and the international prominence of the English—as well as its national prominence in India—doesn't it make sense to anticipate that Rushdie's writing might also find an audience among non-English readers. Indeed, isn't that precisely what has happened with *The Satanic Verses?* Aamir Mufti argues that Rushdie's writing invites us to reconsider our received notions of readership. Mufti claims that the critic

> must account for forms of mass "consumption" other than "reading" in the narrower sense of that word. Extracts published in the print media, in English and in translation, commentary in print, on the airwaves, and from the pulpit, fantasticated representation in the popular cinema, rumors and

hearsay, such are the means by which the novel [*The Satanic Verses*] has achieved circulation in the Islamic world. (97)

Mufti's notion of audience goes beyond that of the "solitary bourgeois reader" and suggests a form of reading that might best be called "postmodern." This broader, even "postmodern" conception of reading would undo the argument that Rushdie's novels—and perhaps all postcolonial writing—have their influence only on European or cosmopolitan reading audiences. A postmodern conception of audience furthers the sense in which postcolonial writing need not always be read exclusively as a "writing back to empire" but as an active engagement in cultural and political discussion within the so-called "margins."[22] Furthermore *Midnight's Children* may have many readers that the text itself does not "imply." Thus, a postmodern conception of readership suggests that the notion that texts construct their own readership—or even authorship—needs to be re-evaluated within the highly complex global circulation of knowledge.

Throughout the metafictive narrative of *Midnight's Children*, Rushdie directly examines his positioning as teller of the Indian story, something that is of course impossible for the European-created Dulcanquellín and Caliban and not available within the socialist realism of *Les bouts de bois de Dieu*. The complex structure of *Midnight's Children*, the use of a comic, fallible, and clearly biased narrator, the presence of an illiterate peasant auditor, the elliptical use of language,—all of these are, as I have shown, involved in Rushdie's efforts to be self-conscious about the depiction of India, to move beyond the Baboo Jabberjee, BA role. Moreover and at the center of the novel, the failure of the Midnight's Children's Conference can be read as the failure of Indian writing in English. Able to reach only the most educated classes of the nation, writing in English is an elite, "magical" discourse that unites the disparate regional and cultural divisions of India but is unable to cut across the profound divisions of language, class, and caste. However, the novel's central metaphor for the examination of the position of the Indo-British writer writing about India is the "perforated sheet"—a figure which gives the first chapter its title.[23] In this chapter, Saleem's grandfather, a European-educated doctor, must examine an ailing young Islamic woman. Prohibited by the rules of purdah from looking at her directly, he is required by the woman's father to view his patient through a hole in a "perforated sheet":

You Europe-returned chappies forget certain things. Doctor Sahib, my
daughter is a decent girl, it goes without saying. She does not flaunt her
body under the noses of strange men. You will understand that you cannot
be permitted to see her, no, not in any circumstances; accordingly I have
required her to be positioned behind that sheet. She stands there, like a
good girl. (19)

Yet, by using a sheet with a hole cut in its center to allow the young
doctor to view his daughter's body, the young woman's father is not
simply following Islamic notions of modesty but also setting a snare to
catch the doctor's affections.

The peek-a-boo game of the perforated sheet suggests the
contradictions of Rushdie's representation of India. Despite his
childhood memories and frequent visits to India and Pakistan, living in
England, coming from an upper-class family, being a secular Muslim
have all been pointed out as separating Rushdie from the "truth" of the
subcontinent. It could be said that Rushdie's knowledge is partial and
piecemeal as if glimpsed through a hole in a sheet. Rushdie groups
himself with exile, emigrant, and expatriate writers who have an urge to
"look back":

But if we do look back, we must also do so in the knowledge—which
gives rise to profound uncertainties—that our physical alienation from
India almost inevitably means that we will not be capable of reclaiming
precisely the thing that was lost; that we will, in short, create fictions, not
actual cities or villages, but invisible ones, imaginary homelands, Indias of
the mind. (1991, 10)

As the metaphor of the sheet suggests, Rushdie's knowledge of
India is not only partial but also governed by an already established
code that equates the Western-educated with the all-knowing male and
India with the tantalizing exotic female. The sheet that both covers and
reveals the naked woman from the view is here simultaneously an
invocation of and a mocking of the familiar veil image, the established
metaphor for the problem of knowledge of the Other, particularly the
Islamic Other, in its relation to the West.[24] The veil/sheet is double
sided: as a symbol of the problem of writing in English, it suggests the
possibility of a means of control being converted, as the veil was in the
Algerian revolution, into a practice of resistance. In describing Indian
national history, Rushdie is positioned both inside an Orientalist point

of view and outside it, lifting the veil and putting it in place. By insistent "signifying" on classic orientalist figures such as the veil, the 1001 nights, Ali Bhaba and the Forty Thiefs—Saleem opens his narration by calling the "holey sheet" his "open sesame" (4)—Rushdie mocks "the colossal Western ego" that imagines, as the Germans tell Aziz, that "India—like radium—had been 'discovered' by the Europeans" (6). In place of this egotistic view, *Midnight's Children* proposes a diverse, heterogeneous conception of identity and knowledge. If this makes Rushdie sound like a European poststructuralist it should not surprise us. As postcolonial author, Rushdie both uses and plays with European traditions. Speaking of *Satanic Verses*, Gayatri Spivak comments:

> In post-coloniality, every metropolitan definition is dislodged. The general mode for the post-colonial is citation, re-inscription, re-routing the historical. *The Satanic Verses* cannot be placed within the European avant-garde, but the successes and failures of the European avant-garde are available to it. (79)

Spivak's point is that Rushdie's work must be seen within the frame of a global cultural politics broader than the poststructuralist project. In this light, *Midnight's Children* must be read not only as poststructuralist but as "resistance literature" that "writes back" to Empire *and* as an undermining of the theoretical grounds of a derivative nationalism that takes the Empire's place in the "third world."

The novel's construction of Indian identity resists imperialism and derivative nationalism, yet its depiction of resistance is peculiarly individualistic. Saleem's recurrent gesture is to project his identity on to India and to imagine India as coextensive with himself—almost as if, like Caliban or the Indian Punch, Saleem can not escape his position in the European imaginary. Despite attention to the complexity and interconnection of identity, *Midnight's Children*'s autobiographical treatment of history risks solipsism in its conflation of self with nation. By this strategy, collective forms of definition or resistance are dismissed or left unexplored. In contrast with *Les bouts de bois de Dieu*'s extensive portrayal of the mobilization of working and peasant classes in Africa, there is little reference in *Midnight's Children* to social, cultural, or political organization among the oppressed or impoverished in India. The communist magicians are swept away without a fuss. Throughout the novel, threats to the power of ruling classes or the national government are only mythical or imaginary. Communication between the midnight's children themselves doesn't extend beyond the magical telepathic interchange that takes place in Saleem's head. Saleem's feeble and compromised effort to form a parliament dissipates because the children are more interested in selfish concerns than in the pressing problems of the commonweal.

Ironically, in pointing out the complexity and heterogeneity within national identity, Rushdie fails to investigate the multiple social and institutional practices that produce/narrate this heterogeneity. If a national agency is oppressive, what other agencies—what other forms of identity—are available? The answer to such a question, of course, depends on a local understanding of social and cultural struggle, an understanding *Midnight's Children* appears to lack. Thus, the view of Indian society in the novel feels like a tourist's view or, perhaps more precisely, a migrant's view.[25] In *Shame*, Rushdie has written:

> As for me: I, too, like all migrants, am a fantasist. I build imaginary countries and try to impose them on the ones that exist. I, too, face the problem of history: what to retain, what to dump, how to hold on to what memory insists on relinquishing, how to deal with change. (92)

In *Midnight's Children*, history is imperfectly remembered, and the specificity of experience is easily displaced by a vision of an anonymous national public, the "one two three, four hundred million five hundred six" that finally trample Saleem underfoot (552). As autobiography, *Midnight's Children* is the recollection of a life—or in Saleem's terms, the chutnification of history—with the ostensible purpose of conveying the past to later generations.[26] And yet, despite the ambition to pass on the aspirations crystalized in the moment of independence, there is in *Midnight's Children* an overwhelming hopelessness. By rendering Saleem as a picaresque pathetic/comic figure the possibilities for social involvement are restricted. By failing to narrate any meaningful, interconnected agency, the aspirations of Indian nationalism are shown to lack foundation, perhaps, as some critics maintain, the aspirations are even betrayed.[27]

Near the middle of the *Midnight's Children*, there is a scene that provides another, more disturbing figure for Rushdie's relationship to India than that of the "perforated sheet." Saleem's friends, forbidden by their parents to leave their wealthy estate on a hill above the city, watch an enormous, two-day long march of striking workers, small shopkeepers, and native-language advocates. Trying to get the attention of Evie, an American "Annie Oakley" with whom he is infatuated, Saleem rides her bike round and round her and uses his special power to read her thoughts. Offended, she grabs his bike and hurls it toward the march. Out of control, a terrified Saleem rushes toward the marchers. They catch him and ask the "little laad-sahib" ("little princeling," "young nawab," 228) to speak in their language. He utters the only phrase he knows in Gujarati, a rhyme about "thrashing you to hell." The marchers take up the chant and are inspired by it to kill rival marchers.

Like Saleem on his bicycle, Rushdie is outside direct political involvement, distanced from India by reason of geography and "above" the marchers in terms of social class. Apparently more interested in things Western than in the vital issues in the streets, when he approaches India he is out of control, crashing into a scene he does not understand and which he effects in ways he is unable to anticipate. In light of the controversy over *Satanic Verses*, the scene of the marchers, unable to understand Saleem's English but taking up and turning into a deadly battle cry Saleem's fumbled Gujarati becomes eerily familiar.

Of course, Saleem is a character created by Rushdie and the bicycle scene, like all the reflection in *Midnight's Children* on language and political action, is within Rushdie's own self-critical narration. While at least one critic has read the connection between Saleem and Rushdie in the bicycle scene as unconscious on Rushdie's part, it is also possible to consider it as self-conscious parody, still another example of Rushdie understanding and pointing to the problematics of his own position *vis-à-vis* the nation.[28]

Frantz Fanon wrote twenty-five years ago about the necessary assumption of of white masks by those with dark skin who sought to assimilate to the colonial order and fulfill the intentions of the colonial education we have been examining throughout *Making Subject(s)*. In 1989 in *The Satanic Verses*, Rushdie describes the experience of Salahuddin Chamchawala, a young man who, like Rushdie himself, was transplanted from India to England at thirteen years of age,

On winter nights he, who had never slept beneath more than a sheet, lay beneath mountains of wool and felt like a figure in an ancient myth, condemned by the gods to have a boulder pressing down upon his chest; but never mind, he would be English, even if his classmates giggled at his voice and excluded him from their secrets, because these exclusions only increased his determination, and that was when he began to act, to find masks that these fellows would recognize, paleface masks, clown-masks, until he fooled them into thinking he was *okay*, he was *people-like-us*. (43)

The adoption of "paleface" and "clown-masks" allows Salahuddin to take on an already scripted identity so as to "fool" his English classmates into thinking that he is "people-like-us." Rushdie makes clear that writing in English as an Indian migrant demands the use of images, techniques, and forms that will be recognized by his metropolitan audience and that can be inverted to serve other purposes. Salahuddin's mimicry should be familiar to us, as it is a standard theme not only of postcolonial writing but of minority texts as well. In African American literature, for instance, consider the crisis of identity experienced by Ralph Ellison's invisible man or by Paule Marshall's Avey Johnson, the main character in her 1983 novel *Praisesong for the Widow*.

If postcolonial hybridity is the strength of Rushdie's writing it is also its weakness. Rushdie's novels can be read as espousing a facile postmodernism, where political commitment is embodied simply as a politics of individual expression and free play.[29] Yet in exploring postcolonial hybridity, Rushdie's work should also be seen within the context of a global cultural politics. In this larger frame *Midnight's Children* is both "resistance literature" that "writes back" to empire and it is scathing critique of the corrupt nationalism and absolutist ideology that has taken the empire's place in the "third world."

Rushdie's continuing peek-a-boo on the international stage, the murder of his Japanese translator, his guarded speeches and appearances remind us that at the time of this writing the Iranian *fatwa* decree is still in force and Rushdie himself is in partial hiding. In *Midnight's Children*, Saleem describes his fear of Shiva in terms that today have an ominous ring:

I'm still terrified of him. There is unfinished business between us, and I spend my days quivering at the thought that . . . roused to wrath by the irrecoverable loss of his past, he might come looking for me to exact a stifling revenge. . . . (529)

Rushdie's writing and the tragic "Rushdie Affair" indicate that a retreat into privacy is not a postcolonial option. In the final words of *Midnight's Children*,

> it is the privilege and the curse of midnight's children to be both masters and victims of their times, to forsake privacy and be sucked into the annihilating whirlpool of the multitudes, and to be unable to live or die in peace. (552)

CHAPTER 6

Conclusion

As far as I understand it, the notion of textuality should be related to the notion of the worlding of a world on a supposedly uninscribed territory. When I say this, I am thinking basically about the imperialist project which had to assume that the earth that it territorialized was in fact previously uninscribed. So then a world, on a simple level of cartography, inscribed what was presumed to be uninscribed. Now this worlding actually is also a texting, textualizing, a making into art, a making into an object to be understood.

Gayatri Spivak

As comparative literature engages with the three processes of globalization, democratization, and decolonization, the effect is a broadening of subject matter which calls for shifts, among other things, in priorities and modes of accountability.

Mary Louise Pratt

The postcolonial era is marked by the universal existence of the nation-state, the political, social, and cultural expression that "worlds" our world. Both imperial nationalism and anticolonial national resistance are relational terms that construct "national peoples" and justify institutions of governance. This book has examined the fundamental legitimation of the nation-state apparatus by exploring the making of national identities in literary texts written during the crucial periods of nation formation. In the process we have seen that the literary works that are most important to nationhood have certain features in common. Early Modern English and Spanish dramas and twentieth-century "third world" novels incorporate a variety of social classes within a single imaginative structure. The theater of Shakespeare and Lope brings together a cross-section of types and characters on the same stage. When the colonized subject is present, as in *El nuevo mundo* and *The Tempest*, the framework becomes explicitly imperial. Likewise the twentieth-century postcolonial novels examined here depict disparate characters within simultaneous time and space. While *Les bouts de bois de Dieu*'s inclusion of different locations and individuals narrates a nationally unified resistance, in *Midnight's Children* the story of an individual life magically attempts to take in India's social diversity.

Both the dramas and the novels we have examined demonstrate a close link between colonialism and nationalism. Columbus and Prospero are both patriarchal male figures whose power and control extend over national and imperial subjects. Significantly, "founding mothers" are absent from these stories of emerging European imperial nationhood. On the other side, colonized male subjects seem to undergo a narrative "sex change operation," as their resistant or competitive maleness is converted to an idealized passive and cooperative "femaleness." Simultaneously native female subjects in *El nuevo mundo* are depicted as "traitorously" welcoming the European male colonizer. Columbus' voyage to the New World becomes, in a play written one hundred years after the event, a glorification of Spanish national accomplishment. Absolutist rule over non-Europeans is also extended to European subjects in *The Tempest*. Renaissance science/magic from the colonies becomes formal knowledge in the administrative service of state and empire. The exercise of power through spectacle, surveillance, and discipline produces differentiated individual subjects within an imperial and absolutist order. While these plays have much in common, the movement from Lope de Vega to Shakespeare manifests a transition from religious inscriptions to Enlightenment ones, from the consecrated to the protoscientific. This is evident both in the derivation and legitimation of Columbus' or Prospero's power and in the portrayal of colonized natives. In Lope, Native Americans appear as integrated communities with established religious practices; in Shakespeare, Caliban is presented as an individual marvel or curiosity—a marketable museum display.

These plays construct identities through the relationship of empire and nation, yet their legitimation of national and imperial authority is conflictive and incomplete. In both works rebellions against authority are planned, executed, and, in the end, put down. Legitimate grievances are sympathetically portrayed, but in both works the powerful emerging frameworks of imperial nationalism contain subversion. In Lope, a *deus ex machina* justifies colonial rule and sanctifies nationalism. In Shakespeare, scholarly and "scientific" absolutism overrides comic and carnivalesque energy that threatens to unite English lower classes and indigenous natives. Though treason can be spoken in these works of European colonialism, native and citizen rebellion is ideologically foreclosed.

Anti- and postcolonial novels open up this closure and self-consciously complicate the codes of European colonial discourse; yet they also—like the great canonical works—participate in the making of national subjects. In the anticolonial novel power is derived and legitimated through the elaboration of a national people whose developing activity and consciousness are responsive to political and economic domination. In *Les bouts de bois de Dieu* authority is developed in a present—and future—oriented struggle against colonial domination and neocolonial co-optation. Women play a central and equal role, and there emerges a resistant female subjectivity that both extends and transforms African femininity. In Rushdie's postcolonial work, authority is sufficiently broken up, questioned, and unraveled so that the European-derived nation-state form itself becomes suspect. The masculine gender coding of nationalist discourse is mocked as *Midnight's Children* lampoons the manliness of the new nation in the pathetic persona of Saleem Sinai. Anticolonial nationalism serves as the starting point for a new national ruling class trained to imitate the lifestyle of the former colonial masters, and the imposition of Indira Gandhi's Emergency indicates the degree to which national administration loses legitimacy.

In the Renaissance plays, differences within the emerging national "Self"—differences of ethnicity, class, religion, and gender—are projected onto a colonized Other in a process which simultaneously "purifies" European national subjects and legitimates rule over the colonies. In *El nuevo mundo*, the Indians turn out to be an imaginative construction shaped primarily from the heterogeneity of *Spanish* society, and, in *The Tempest*, the figure of Caliban serves as a screen for the merging of *English* discourses on Native Americans, African slaves, European wild men, reluctant school children, and drunken servants. While nativist anticolonial literature, on the other hand, may operate by a reversal of this process, the postcolonial novels resist straightforward or simple identity integrations and projections. The African and Indian works examined here do not accept radical, essential, or nativistic separations between Self and Other. Instead, *Les*

14 Identity formed in struggle. (French Involved in Timucuan Wars, Theodor de Bry, 1591)

bouts de bois de Dieu depicts the hybrid, syncretic *incorporation* of European economic, cultural, and political practices by self-aware Africans who simultaneously resist European domination. Even more overtly, *Midnight's Children* examines the tremendously complex cross-bred ancestry of modern India, the "leakage" between Western and Eastern cultures, and the ever-greater difficulty of fixing identity once and for all in the postcolonial world.

The problems and possibilities posed by the use of European languages to represent non-European cultural identities in all these works is tied to their sophisticated process of cultural syncretization. The Renaissance dramas purport to present cultural Others, although the results are pastiche projections emerging from existing European discourses. When the subaltern attempts to speak, the voice that emerges is complicated and overdetermined by an existing colonial discourse. The problem of European languages and literary forms as vehicles for African or Indian national culture is explicitly foregrounded by the works we have examined. *Les bouts de bois de Dieu*'s capacity to express an African national culture in the French language is shown to depend on the language's relationship to cultural and political struggles that remain ongoing in Senegal. In *Midnight's Children*, there is a self-conscious critique (in the metaphor of the sheet) of the problem of describing India in a novel written in English.

Nations don't emerge like Athena out of Zeus's head, fully formed, armed, and ready for action. The close reading of literary texts in their respective historical and cultural situations demonstrates that in neither European nor "third world" context is there a primordial, ahistorical, or otherwise "originary" national people. "The people" must learn who they are, and national subjects must be formulated in specifiable and relational discourses. Our reading of literary texts from the Spanish and English Renaissance and from postcolonial Senegal and India reinforces Althusser's point that this process of education constitutes an "ideological" apparatus. In all the texts we have considered, educational processes themselves play a central role in the development of subjection to nation and empire. In *El nuevo mundo*, a Spanish colonizer teaches Dulcanquellín how to model his conduct on that of the Spanish monarch. Prospero's education of Caliban offers a case study of how to train the subservient colonial subject, while his treatment of the shipwrecked Europeans is designed to teach them to accept his authority. If the Renaissance dramas depict the education of colonial subjects, the twentieth-century novels continue to suggest the

15 Identity as syncretic incorporation. ("Les Amoureux," Gora Mbengue, Glass, India ink, paint, Senegal, 1983)

centrality of education and, even more fully, manifest the ambivalences and contradictions that such education produces. *Les bouts de bois de Dieu* depicts a revolutionary form of national education taking place outside of the formal educational system during the process of anticolonial resistance. It comparatively illustrates the way a colonial education produces Africans who serve merely as intermediaries between French rulers and indigenous populations. The inherent dilemma of all colonial education for the native is elaborated in *Midnight's Children* in the cultural distance created between Aadam Aziz and India—a distance that is amplified by the difficulties of exiled author and narrator to render Indian identity in a novel in English.

We have come to see that the discourses that form supposedly independent nations are, in fact, international and reiterative. Ironically, nationalism draws on the circulation of forms, institutions, and relationships in a global economic and cultural system. The speed-up of globalization in recent years—via new communication technologies, dramatically improved transportation, internationalization of finance and manufacturing, and so on—has led some scholars to begin to explore the possibility of emerging "post-nationalist" forms for culture and identity. Rather than a uniform modernization or even "Americanization" of the world, Frederick Buell, for example, argues that globalization serves to juxtapose cultural differences, indeed, even increase and proliferate them:

> Worldwide interconnectedness does not result in the creation of a "global society." It yields, on the one hand, a decentered set of subnational and supranational interactions—from capital transfers and population movements to the transmission of information—and these interactions help multiply, invent, and disseminate cultural differences, rather than overcome them. On the other, it challenges existing nation-states to reformulate their cultural identities for a more complexly interconnected era, a process that has been marked by both fundamentalist attempts to reconsolidate borders and new kinds of internationalization that render those borders startlingly porous. (10-11)

This book has demonstrated that even from their beginning in the Renaissance, imperial nation-state systems and concomitant national cultures have been formulated in relation to "international" Others in ways that both establish and threaten borders of culture and identity. For their age, the characters of Columbus and Prospero could be seen as "cosmopolitan" national figures and, in the juxtaposition of radical differences and the pastiche formation of native American identities in Lope's and Shakespeare's plays, there is something that we might even describe as "postmodern."

Yet the texts we have examined, especially as we have moved into the postcolonial era, are increasingly conscious of national identity as itself something to be made, shaped, even reconstructed. Identity fashioning becomes increasingly cross-culturally jumbled, and distinctions between Self and Other become less Manichean. The Europeans in Shakespeare's and Lope's New World plays clearly believe in their difference from the natives they encounter. The Africans struggling against French authority in *Les bouts de bois de Dieu*, are fully aware of differences that distinguish them from Europeans but simultaneously find ways to incorporate and integrate European customs, language, and education into their own institutions and worldview. While class, ethnic, religious, and gender differences divide Rushdie's India, the overlaying, seepage, and confusion of identity render suspect fixed cultural determinations.

There may be something hopeful about the radical juxtapositions and imbrications of a postmodern world. Perhaps in the recognition of layerings and difference is a glimmer of postnationalism, an anodyne to our own century, probably the most jingoistic and violent of human history. But such an opportunity will have meaning only as long as it provides a space to address the contradictions and uneven development of past and present. More than thirty years ago Octavio Paz concluded *El laberinto de la soledad*, his study of Mexican national character, with the phrase "Somos contemporáneos de todos los hombres" (We [Mexicans] are contemporaries of all men). His (masculinist) declaration asserted the "catching up" of the "third world" to the "first." In the 1990s sharp distinctions between "first" and "third worlds" have become more difficult or even impossible to sustain. "Postcoloniality" and "postmodernism" are terms that can now be seen to describe both the previous "margin" and the previous "center." Rather than thinking of the "third world" as needing to "catch up" with the first, it might be more accurate to see the globe's future in the "third world" rather than the "first." Intimate juxtaposition of wealth and poverty, startling new technologies and resurgent traditionalism, dependency of local markets on international capital, governments chronically underfunded while state decision-making is dominated by entrenched interests, desperate migrations bringing diverse ethnic and linguistic backgrounds more and more into troubled contact—all of these previously defining features of "third world" experience are becoming more and more familiar in the "first."

In *Making Subject(s)* I have argued that the discipline of comparative literature needs to look to its previous "margins" in order to better understand its historic "center" as well as its likely future directions. In this process, the postcolonial analysis I have utilized in reading both European and "third world" works is positioned to play an especially vital part. Emily Apter argues that,

With its interrogation of cultural subjectivity and attention to the tenuous bonds between identity and national language, postcolonialism quite naturally inherits the mantle of comparative literature's historical agency. (86)

As an experiment in comparative literature, this book demonstrates that it is not enough to simply juxtapose texts from different traditions, but it is also necessary to closely examine the historical, cultural, linguistic, and political relations that bind them together in mutually defining ways. Comparative literature should not treat "third-world" texts the way Columbus treated Caribbean islanders, i.e., incorporating their differences within an existing ideological framework. S.P. Mohanty points to the simultaneous reconstitution of cultural frames that must take place in any meaningful cultural encounter.

Two systems of understanding encounter each other to the very extent that both are contextualized as forms of life; this encounter leaves open the possibility of a fundamental change in both. (16)

In thinking about the "place" of minority literature, Cornel West maintains it should not simply be added on to an expanded canon. Any incorporation of minority literature, he argues, needs to include "a wholesome reconsideration of the canon already in place" (19). In seeking to apply questions that have begun to be raised about national identity in emergent literatures in Africa and India to such central figures in the European canon such as Lope and Shakespeare, *Making Subject(s)* hopes to contribute to such a "wholesome reconsideration."

Notes

1 INTRODUCTION

1. See Ahmad 4-6 and Minh-ha 97-100.

2. Spivak, "Can" *passim*.

3. Kwame Anthony Appiah (1991) describes "postmodern" "African" art combining indigenous and European traditions as a commodity designed to serve the consumption demands of Western elites rather than an "authentic" African cultural expression.

4. In the following passage Armstrong outlines a form of Early Modern hegemony where secular languages, systems of pedagogy, and the practice of writing are understood as indispensable to the development of identities:

> Religious organizations are important for ethnic identity because in premodern conditions such organizations penetrate the masses of a population to a degree that few administrations of large polities can attain.... Because both Islam and Christianity assert a duty to proselytize, both missionary activity and sectarian advocacy require forms of communication accessible to the masses... Preaching and written exhortation have necessarily been in popular languages. Religious activity therefore contrasts with the heavy emphasis on high cultural values embodied in traditional elite languages used by imperial administrative personnel. As a result of these factors, religious organizations are not only more penetrative than imperial administrations; the former greatly stimulate the use and written codification of popular languages, especially during periods of intense sectarian controversy. (238)

5. Anderson 68.

6. Macaulay 729.

2 OTHER-FASHIONING

1. An MLA computer search produced references to two articles (Dille and Weiner). In 1980 a French edition of the play included relevant notes and introduction (Lemartinel). A chapter of Robert Shannon's 1985 Ph.D. dissertation (published in 1989) is the only attempt to treat the play thoroughly. Shannon makes a source-influence study of the relation of specific conquest narratives to three Lope plays: "I hope to identify in the play the sources which Lope has followed in the process of artistic creation and where he has departed from the lead in order to reveal, perhaps, his own personal observation" (8). Shannon believes that Lope drew on the accounts of both Gómara and Oviedo in *El nuevo mundo*, but followed neither one very closely. Shannon's interest in Lope's "personal" perspective, his treatment of the conquest accounts as independent of Spanish discourse and transparently "real," and his apparent acceptance of the position he ascribes to Lope (". . . that the spiritual direction of the Conquest is of far greater importance and will, in the end, triumph and stand as Spain's overwhelming achievement in America" [91-2]) limit his analysis. Shannon is presently working on a bilingual critical edition of the play.

According to Glen Dille's investigation there are only a dozen extant Spanish Golden Age plays on the subject of Columbus. Dille doesn't specify how many of the twelve depict Native Americans. Menéndez y Pelayo in his scholarly introduction to the play (1900) calls it "la más antigua producción dramatica consagrada al descubrimento del Nuevo Mundo" [the oldest dramatic production dedicated to the discovery of the New World].

2. "The audience witnessing a national history play at the public theater comes to feel that its own history is being performed. In a sense, such a belief is a corporatist illusion, especially since the crown's interests were not ultimately national. But it is also a progressive insistence on the right of the populace to judge the ruling class's exercise of state power. In this respect the national history play in the public theater inherently subverts aristocratic ideology" (221). Reactions to Cohen by Hispanists can be found in Zahareas.

3. All quotations from *El nuevo mundo* are from the *Real Academia* edition. All translations are my own.

4. Shannon compares Dulcanquellín to "an idealized Christian king" and finds him "a symbol of tyranny, egotism, and moral and social corruption" (91). Shannon bases his view on Dulcanquellín's waging war on Haiti, abducting Tacuana, and, his occasional lapses of certainty about the Christian faith. The second point may be the most persuasive, although Shannon may be said to overstate the case. Nonetheless, to the extent that Dulcanquellín is *different*, he is so in ways that suggest his unfitness as a ruler *in idealized Spanish terms*. Shannon's reading provides a more direct justification for Spanish colonialism than one that emphasizes likeness and familiarity.

5. Armstrong argues that the relationship of Moslems and Christians led both groups to emphasize the Other in their process of Self-definition.

Indeed, their common origins as well as their geographical proximity made the Islamic and the Christian civilizations the major negative reference points for one another. In this respect, the two civilizations resembled on a grand scale ethnic groups that commonly define themselves by reference to out-groups. All Moslems conceived themselves to be united, at least in contrast to neighboring Christians. Christians, usually on the defensive, often adopted a similar minimal identity criterion. In this way, the two great religious civilizations interacted over the centuries to perpetuate and to redefine each other's identity in terms that may be characterized as "supraethnic" (90).

6. Henry Louis Gates Jr. argues that the "talking book" is the signal trope of African American literature.

7. Walter D. Mignolo comments in his essay "Literacy and Colonization: The New World Experience":

> It is interesting to point out in connection with the topic of literacy and colonization, first, the attribution of "low" degrees of language development to human communities, and second, that human societies were ranked in the chain of being according to their lack or possession of alphabetic writing. (77)

8. Gómez-Moriana 97-8 and Armstrong 266.

9. The humorous treatment of cannibalism is not a reason to dismiss the importance of it, however. Hulme notes that cannibalism is often treated with humor "'Cannibalism' can hardly, it seems, be discussed—or indeed practiced—without laughter. This certainly sets it apart from incest and from other taboos on the mutilation of the body. It need hardly be said that the presence of laughter is by no means an indication of triviality" (81-2).

10. Prescott uses this line as an epigram in his famous history.

11. The attempted control of subversion by a totalizing system is by no means limited to the Spanish. By drawing connections between documents from the Plymouth Colony and Shakespeare's *Henry* plays, Stephen Greenblatt, in *Shakespearean Negotiations*, shows that by recording the potentially disturbing voice of the Other within the discourse of the culture in power, subversive ideas can be contained. In the case of *El nuevo mundo*, where the other is not something recorded in a document of direct contact, but instead is written of years later and in the traditions of a well-established genre, any subversion suggested by an Other can be all the more thoroughly neutralized. That the *comedia* functions in this way is acknowledged even by those who criticize a sociological approach to its interpretation. A case in point would be Charlotte Stern's comment that "in fact, the *comedia* exhibits a remarkable capacity for absorbing and neutralizing dissident views" (11).

12. Malinche has many counterparts including, in North America Pocahantas and Sacajawea.

13. The connection with Malinche was first made for me by Anuncia Escala.

14. Thus Jean Franco describes national identity as "a problem of *male* identity" (131).

15. In the writing about Columbus and, in the scholarly work that does exist on *El nuevo mundo*, the famous "discoverer's" treatment of the indigenous peoples continues to be characterized as "pacific" or even "humane." Jack Weiner writes in 1983: "Y Lope precisamente da a *El nuevo mundo descubierto por Cristóbal Colón* un carácter de obra hagiográfica porque nuestro dramaturgo reconoce la importancia y los métodos de Colón para tratar con los indígenas pacífica y humanamente" [And Lope gives *El nuevo mundo* a hagiographic character precisely because he recognizes the importance and the methods used by Columbus to treat the indigenous people peacefully and humanely] (67). Yet "sailing the ocean blue" entailed more than the hardship and romance of discovery: Columbus himself initiated the New World slave trade, taking five hundred slaves to Spain (two hundred dying *en route*); the Spanish under Columbus systematically cut off the hands of Indians who did not produce the gold Columbus imagined was in their possession. Columbus's actions were, of course, a mere prologue to a genocide that consumed 70 million people (Todorov 133).

16. I refer to *The Prince* in general, although it offers a particularly pertinent passage:

Nothing brings a prince more prestige than the accomplishments of great deeds and giving uncommon examples of himself. In our time there is King Ferdinand of Aragon, the present King of Spain. The latter can practically be called a new prince for from being a weak king he has become, through fame and glory, the first king of the Christians; and if you consider his actions, you will find all of them to be great and some extraordinary. In the beginning of his reign he laid siege to Granada: and that undertaking was the foundation of his state [. . .] Besides this, in order to be able to undertake even greater campaigns, always making use of religion, he turned toward a pious cruelty, expelling and eliminating the *marranos* from his Kingdom. There could not be a more pitiless or more uncommon example from the latter. Under the same mantle of religion he attacked Africa; he carried out the Italian Campaign; he recently attacked France; and in the manner he has always performed and carried out great projects which have always kept his subjects in a state of suspense and admiration and intent on their outcome. And these moves of his have followed so closely one upon another and in such a way that he has never allowed people time and opportunity in between those moves to be able to quietly counter them. (cited in Gómez-Moriana 99)

3 IMAGI/NATIVE NATION

1. Recognizing her affinity to the protagonist of Shakespeare's play in a performance that coincided with an attempted treason by Essex in 1601.

2. Extracts from the letter are included in both Frank Kermode's 1954 Arden edition and Stephen Orgel's 1987 Oxford edition of the play. On other pamphlets, see Kermode xxvi to xxx; and Vaughan and Vaughan 41-50.

3. Vaughan and Vaughan 38.

4. Hulme also traces the association of cannibalism and non-Christians to the depiction of Jews in Europe (85).

5. The Europeans were unaware of the ousting of the Mongols from China by the Ming Dynasty (in 1368). The designations "Arawak" and "Carib" and the distinctions made between them are tied to a colonialist anthropology (see Retamar 6-8 and Hulme, chapter 2). Hulme connects the European accusation of cannibalism to the Christian communion:

Boundaries of community are often created by accusing those outside
the boundary of the very practice on which the integrity of that
community is founded. This is at one and the same time a psychic
process -- involving repression and projection -- and an ideological
process -- whereby the success of the projection confirms the need
for the community to defend itself against the projected threat,
thereby closing the circle and perpetuating it. This is . . . the central
regulating mechanism of colonial discourse. (85)

6. This discussion is indebted to Hulme 15-23.

7. The most complete tracing of the various possibilities of sources for
Caliban is Vaughan and Vaughan. Brown makes the case for Ireland: "Given
the importance of the colonization of Ireland for British expansionist, together
with its complex discursive formation . . . it is surprising that such scant
attention has been paid to such material in relation to *The Tempest*" (49).

8. All references to the play are to the 1987 Oxford edition.

9. Hulme 41-2.

10. Vaughan and Vaughan 14.

11. The encounter of two clowns in Shakespeare, as with Speed and
Launce in *Two Gentlemen of Verona*, is a moment for both particular mirth and
sharp awareness of social pecking order.

12. Stephano's subsequent action is prophetic of the next four hundred
years of colonialism in the New World: "He shall taste of my bottle. If he have
never drunk wine afore, it will go near to remove his fit. If I can recover him
and keep him tame, I will not take too much for him; he shall pay for him that
hath him, and that soundly" (II, ii, 72-5).

The expense of alcohol to "tame" the Indian is a sound investment.
Caliban indicates that Stephano's ploy is effective:

"That's a brave god, and bears celestial liquor. I will kneel to him." (II, ii,
112-3) [and] "I'll swear upon that bottle to be thy true subject, for the liquor is
not earthly" (119-120).

13. Caliban's fate at the end of the play is open. Many productions leave
Caliban in possession of the island, though such a move can be as imperialist as
any (see Griffith's analysis of the 1904 production directed by Beerbohm Tree
169-70). My choice would be to follow the only suggestions the text does give
us and have the play end with Caliban taken off to Europe in a cage or chains

where he will be put on exhibit. Why should such a valuable commodity be left behind?

14. Semonin, "Nature's", 6.

15. Orgel 37.

16. The first conjoining of the words "British" and "empire" took place in the latter part of the sixteenth century (Hulme 90).

17. Siegel 106.

18. The only speakers of the Island Carib language still alive are Central American descendants of escaped slaves.

19. R.A.D. Grant in an extended scholarly essay in *Shakespeare Studies* (1983) explicitly treats the "ethical bearing and moral significance" of the play "uncontaminated by historical circumstance" and offers a different interpretation of the morality of the relationship of Prospero and Caliban. After considering whether or not to equate Prospero with God (concluding "It is clear that many of the attributes of divinity on which providential thought concentrates are recapitulated in human form by Prospero" [240]) he notices with approval that "In Shakespeare's conception there is an unmistakable contempt, if not for the lower orders per se, at any rate for the kind of society they would create if left to themselves" (249). He comments that "Prospero's reduction of him [Caliban] to slave status is thus doubly justified: rationally, on Hobbesian grounds of self-defense, and morally, from breach of trust and ingratitude" (251). Grant seems to understand the implications of his position, indicating at the outset that "I have not, for example, concealed my impatience with many current moral and political assumptions" (236).

20. In its broadest outlines the analysis here depends on Adorno's argument in *Dialectic of Enlightenment* that Enlightenment reason and empirical science are part of domination in modern capitalist society in much the same way that magic and myth dominated precapitalist societies. As much as he intends to restore Enlightenment thought, Adorno reads Enlightenment as making an exclusive claim on knowledge and justifying the hierarchical ordering and "rationalizing" of society.

21. In his study of Renaissance magic, John Mebane writes,

> Compared to modern scientists, Renaissance magicians operated within a cosmological framework which seems fantastic, and which had to be rejected before genuine science could evolve. Nonetheless, in daring to believe that the human mind could guide and command the creative forces of nature, they asserted important attitudes and

values which eventually contributed to the evolution of genuine science. Hermetic magicians and Paraclesians often proclaimed the overthrow of the traditional authorities which had imposed strict limits upon the search for truth; together with the mechanical artisans with which they frequently allied themselves, they are among Bacon's immediate predecessors in emphasizing experience, rather than mere citation of Galen or Aristotle, as the appropriate test of assertions about nature. Perhaps most importantly, they predicted that the imminent renewal of all of human knowledge would bring with it the reform of human society and of human nature itself. (7)

22. Examining the construction of national subjects has not been part of the scholarship on *The Tempest*. Curt Breight (1990) connects the play to a dark reading of the politics of the English nation-state (see discussion below). Walter Cohen does not emphasize the emergence of national identity in his discussion of the play. For Cohen *The Tempest* suggests the historically progressive possibilities of a marxist class struggle. Admitting the "ethnocentric" "attitude" of Shakespeare in regard to colonialism, Cohen says Prospero and his magic represent the possibility of bourgeois science combining with prebourgeois feudal peasant (utopian) energies:

In *The Tempest*, Prospero's prototechnical magic offers precisely the mechanism by which Gonzalo's dream might someday come into being. The fusion of feudal communism and bourgeois science points beyond the two main modes of production of Shakespeare's England and indeed of postclassical European history as a whole. (404)

23. Peter Greenaway's 1991 film *Prospero's Books* offers an interpretation of the play that foregrounds the importance of Renaissance science and learning by emphasizing the content of Renaissance books, particularly the development of investigative science. Interspersed throughout the film are illustrations from Renaissance studies of anatomy, architecture, nature, and foreign lands. Prospero is shown teaching Miranda out of a volume on different kinds of plants. Magic and science are richly connected as pages of books blow through scenes with Caliban, as white horses appear in Prospero's library, as anatomical drawings made by the dissection of the human body are juxtaposed with images of four-legged creatures and unicorns.

24. By accepting Prospero's separation of knowledge and power (in the abjuration of his magic) some scholars fail to recognize the way in which Prospero's book-learned magic is necessary to his rule on the island. Paul A. Cantor for instance argues in his article "Prospero's Republic: The Politics of Shakespeare's *The Tempest*" (1981) that Prospero's disinterested separation of knowledge and politics is precisely what makes him an ideal philosopher-king: "His final disposition to philosophy guarantees that he will remain aware of facts of life beyond the political, and this larger perspective helps to moderate whatever ambition he develops" (254). Cantor argues that the play is basically about "Prospero learning to be tough when he has to" (244), and he follows Platonic logic to its Machiavellian conclusion without so much as a wince, approving that "in the deepest sense he [Prospero] has to refrain from sharing the truths he has learned about rule with other men, for these truths, if spread throughout society, would undermine his power to rule" (251).

25. Foucault's argument about the development of the systems of discipline that precede the Panopticon helps to close this significant time gap. Foucault finds the precursor to the Panopticon to be the elaborate city-wide regimentation and system of inspection established during a seventeenth-century plague (see epigram to this chapter [Foucault, 205]).

The most extended Foucaultian treatment of Shakespeare is by Christopher Pye in *The Regal Phantasm: Shakespeare and the Politics of Spectacle* (1990). Though Pye doesn't analyze *The Tempest*, he does make contributions to the understanding of the histories and of *Macbeth*. While emphasizing the role of spectacle in the exercise of power, Pye does not examine the way in which modern systems of discipline produce individual identity.

26. Cressy 2.

27. Orme 18.

28. Consider Bianca in *Taming of the Shrew* who was educated in her home by the tutors hired by her father.

29. Hunt, in his study of Prospero as a teacher, compares him positively to Belarius (of *Love's Labour Lost*):

A close comparison of Prospero's pastoral instruction with that of his counterpart Belarius not only clarifies the effectiveness of the magician's art but also directs our attention to its best working. When his teaching requires an angry persona, Prospero, after all, self-sacrificially risks his reputation as a kind father. (Hunt 38)

Orgel makes the case that Prospero's power is exercised over children.

> Prospero's magic power is exemplified, on the whole, as power
> over children: his daughter Miranda, the bad child Caliban, the
> obedient but impatient Ariel, the adolescent Ferdinand, the wicked
> younger brother Antonio, and indeed, the shipwreck victims as a
> whole, who are treated like a group of bad children. (60)

30. Breight makes a similar argument but doesn't carry it far: "The
reeducation of all the aristocrats thus necessitates something more extensive
and explicit than the private taming of Antonio and Sebastian" (17).

31. Two centuries later the links between propriety and nationalism were
both more explicit and more closely tied to the class antagonism of the
industrial era. Nonetheless, George Mosse's analysis of respectability and
nationalism has resonances with *The Tempest,*

> In order to establish controls, to impose restraint and moderation,
> society needed to reinforce the practical techniques of physicians,
> educators, and police. But their methods had to be informed by an
> ideal if they were to be effective, to support normality and contain
> sexual passions. In most timely fashion, nationalism came to the
> rescue. It absorbed and sanctioned middle-class manners and morals
> and played a crucial part in spreading respectability to all classes of
> the population, however much these classes hated and despised one
> another. (9)

32. Nash 279.

33. Gillies 677.

34. "It is only a slight exaggeration, I think, to suggest that Europeans had,
for centuries, rehearsed their encounter with the peoples of the New World,
acting out, in their response to the legendary Wild Man, their mingled attraction
and repulsion, longing and hatred." (Greenblatt, *Learning* 21) This analysis
counters the view that the natives could only understand the European
colonizer as the return of one of their own gods.

35. This process has its analogue in the development of English literature
as a mode of instruction in India and its *subsequent* incorporation as a mode of
instruction in England (see Viswanathan). Hawkes draws on the

Caliban/Prospero relationship in his examination of the early twentieth century national institutionalization of literary study in England.

36. Greenblatt puts it more subtly: *"The Tempest* utterly rejects the uniformation view of the human race, the view that would later triumph in the Enlightenment and prevail in the west to this day. All men, the play seems to suggest, are *not* alike, strip away the adornments of culture and you will *not* reach a single human essence" (26).

37. Cressy 92. "The ferule was a sort of flat ruler widened at the inflicting end into a shape resembling that of a pear . . . with a . . . hole in the middle to raise blisters" *(OED)*. In the etymology of the word "ferule" the *Oxford English Dictionary* quotes Ben Jonson. In 1636 he wrote, "From the rodde, or ferule, I would have them free."

38. *Marvelous.* Todorov makes a similar point in *The Conquest of America.*

39. The development of a technology of social control in the colonies that can be used back home is the focus of Gauri Viswanathan's work on the development of English literature.

40. A work that situates the rebellion of the jester and drunken butler within the context of the "masterless man" is A.L. Beier's *Masterless Men: The Vagrancy Problem in England 1560-1640.* For a discussion of the pedagogical possibilities of this work see my article, "Homelessness" 1991.

41. Breight doesn't list Walter Cohen in his sources, but much the same idea is present in Cohen's *Drama of a Nation:*

> Any drama of state performed in the public theater automatically
> converted a heterogeneous and, it seems, largely popular audience
> into judges of national issues, a position from which most of its
> members were excluded in the world of political affairs. (183)

42. For Paul Brown, *"The Tempest* is not simply a reflection of colonialist practices but an intervention in an ambivalent and even contradictory discourse" (48).

43. In this sense the utopian possibilities of the play are inscribed in the same discourse that delineates control and manipulation. The best exploration of the ambivalence of colonialist discourse in the play is Brown: By constructing a native subject, like Caliban, who takes literally the colonialist discourse that describes the savage realm as a pastoral space lacking governance, Shakespeare is able to make "powerlessness represent a *desire for*

powerlessness" (66). Though Brown does not make the point, the implication is that the reiteration of the pastoral image of Native American society by Native Americans themselves may be an adoption of colonialist discourse rather than a refusal of it, albeit an adoption that might serve as a form of what Homi Bhabha calls "mimicry."

44. Mebane makes similar connections between Renaissance science, magic and power, yet his view of Prospero is entirely benign.

> It is quite natural that in *The Tempest*, the most fully realized of the romances, Shakespeare would focus upon the figure of the magus, the most fully developed expression of Renaissance hopes for the development of humankind's moral, intellectual, and spiritual potential. Through years of study, contemplation, and reflection upon his experience, Prospero has brought his own soul into harmony with the cosmic order, and consequently his art is a means through which God's will is accomplished. ... By mastering his passions and cultivating the forces of nature, Prospero has obtained the power to command the forces of nature, and in the course of the play he brings all of the other characters under his control. But the most impressive of his feats—indeed, the one to which all of his other powers serve as means to an end—is his power to bring others toward the same self-knowledge he has found within himself. (176-7)

4 PEDAGOGICAL AND PERFORMATIVE NATIONALISM

1. A point made by Anthony Appiah (*In My Father's House* 149). Neil Lazarus makes a similar case in his discussion of Armah.

2. Amilcar Cabral also emphasizes the importance of national culture to the liberation struggle. In *Return to the Source* Cabral states:

> A people who free themselves from foreign domination will not be culturally free unless, without understanding the importance of positive contributions from the oppressor's culture and other cultures, they return to the upward paths of their own culture. The latter is nourished by the living reality of the environment and rejects harmful influences as much as any kind of subjections to foreign cultures. We

see therefore that if imperialist domination has the vital need to practise cultural oppression, national liberation is necessarily *an act of culture*. (in Jeyifo 12)

3. Fanon's notion of national culture can be viewed within the history of the marxist debates on "the national question." Since Lenin identified the "right of nations to self-determination," the revolutionary role of anticolonial nationalism became a central concern of Marxist thinkers during the Third International. Fanon's conception of national culture is also indebted to Otto Bauer and Antonio Gramsci. Bauer emphasized the importance to liberation struggles of the cultural and historical community of the nation. Gramsci's concept of the "national popular" underscores the significance of the participation of intellectuals in the struggle for cultural hegemony. (For a more detailed discussion of the history of the concept of nation in Marxist thought, see Munck.)

4. While Achebe resists the colonialist rewriting of the past, he is alert to the danger Fanon cites of romanticizing African tribal society. JanMohamed points out:

Achebe's nostalgia must be distinguished from the romantic ethnology of the Nègritude movement, for, unlike the latter, he neither portrays an idealized, monolithic, homogenized, and pasteurized "African" past, nor does he valorize indigenous cultures by reversing the old colonial manichean allegory as, for instance, Léopold Senghor does. (181)

5. Lazarus says:

The conflation of independence with revolution is the product of a utopian conceptualization of the national liberation struggle; that in spite of the fact that the overall thrust of his work committed him to a more pragmatic emphasis, Fanon was often—and paradigmatically— drawn to phrase his ideas in messianic terms; and what was present as a tension in his work was "resolved," in a squarely messianic conceptualization of national liberation, in terms of which decolonization was interpreted as a *revolutionary* process and the independence ceremony was taken to signal that the revolution has been won, rather than merely begun. (12)

6. In drawing his conclusions Lazarus draws on the work of Ngugi. Although Lazarus does not extensively address francophone writing, it is significant for the present study that he differentiates Ousmane Sembène from other writers of the same generation. Lazarus considers Sembène a "rare exception," an African writer who was not influenced by the self-interested ideology of African national bourgeoisie (11).

7. Chinua Achebe explains that he dreams in both Ibo and English. In his essay "The Writer and His Community" (found in *Hopes*), he points out some of the problems of writing in English in a country which is largely illiterate and in which English is a minority tongue. Yet he maintains that if English were abolished in Nigeria the country would be seriously divided over the question of what language to put in its place. (60)

8. In Ngugi, *Decolonizing* 8.

9. In Ngugi, *Decolonizing* 8

10. Bakhtin describes double-voiced discourse as

> another's speech in another's language [that] serves two speakers at the same time and expresses simultaneously two different intentions: the direct intention of the character who is speaking, and the refracted intention of the author ... Examples of this would be comic, ironic, or parodic discourse.... A potential dialogue is embedded in them, one as yet unfolded, a concentrated dialogue of two voices, two world views, two languages. (324-5).

Bakhtin's discussion of dialogism focuses primarily on the relationship of different sociolects within a national language, but his theory has particular relevance to the appropriation of European languages by "third world" authors.

11. All translations from texts other than *Les bouts de bois de Dieu* are my own.

12. For an elaboration of this argument, see Tire.

13. Film allowed access to a larger audience:

> Although Senegal is the eldest African daughter of France, whose influence has been pervasive since the seventeenth century, and although it is probably the African country where the French language is most widely spread, the writers of the fifties could only reach a European readership and a paper-thin layer of highly educated black intellectuals. They could not hope to reach what is

conventionally and somewhat repulsively called "the masses," that is, the millions of ordinary individuals, illiterate peasants and semi-literate clerks, not to mention the urban workers, still exploited by foreign companies, the unemployed and the beggars. To these Sembène managed to convey his message with movies, where he made abundant use of vernacular languages. (Gérard and Laurent 134)

14. Schipper 565.

15. Ngugi examines these issues in *Writers and Politics*.

16. In describing the ties between Senegal and Soudan, Foltz notes:"Among the labor leaders, many of the Senegalese, as well as all the Soudanese, had originally been associated with the RDA-affiliated UGTAN [Union Générale des Travailleurs d'Afrique Noire]" (152).

17. English quotations are from the Price translation.

18. The union of the workers on the Dakar-Niger line and the struggle for control over their labor in Sembène's portrait of colonized Africa recall Marx's famous description of the rapid transformation of European history:

Now and then the workers are victorious, but only for a time. The real fruit of their battles lies, not in the immediate result, but in the ever-expanding union of the workers. This union is helped on by the improved means of communication that are created by modern industry and that place the workers of different localities in contact with one another. It was just this contact that was needed to centralize the numerous local struggles, all of the same character, into one national struggle. And that union, to attain which the burgers of the Middle Ages, with their miserable highways, required centuries, the modern proletarians, thanks to railways, achieve in a few years. (481)

19. The Wolof are the largest group of the Senegambians of the coast districts of Senegal and Gambia. Their language is understood by most of the peoples of Senegal and Mali. The Bambara are the largest group of the Mande peoples, located East and inland from the Senegambians in Senegal, Mali, Guinea and Gambia.

20. Le Blanc is thought to be crazy by the other colonials, "Un vrai coup de bambou!" (275) ["suffering a severe case of sunstroke" (178)]. Moreover, as long as he is in the colonial world, Manichean divisions assert themselves and,

despite his best efforts, LeBlanc is unable to befriend Africans, "Il avait fini par faire de lui un être déchu dont les Noirs riaient et que les Blancs méprisaient" (259) ["He had become a narrow, bitter person, laughed at by the blacks and mistrusted by the whites" (166)]. The failure of Le Blanc's efforts at cross-racial friendship recalls the famous closing lines of Forster's *Passage to India*, where "the sky itself whispers 'no, not yet'" to the possibility of friendship between Fielding and Aziz.

21. Years after the novel was written Sembene stated:

My work as a writer is narrowly associated with the struggle for real independence. In Africa we first thought that in 1960 with Independence paradise would come. Now we know better. The whites have left indeed, but those in power now behave in exactly the same way. (Schipper, 567)

22. Jean Franco describes a similar pattern in Mexico:

Women were especially crucial to the imagined community as mothers of the new men and as guardians of private life, which from Independence onward was increasingly seen as a shelter from political turmoil. Two aspects of the recodification of gender deserve special attention; the carving out of a territory of domestic stability and decency from which all low elements were expelled, and the displacement of the religious onto the national, which once again made "purity" the responsibility of women. (81)

23. In other contexts Sembène is a critic of polygamy, see *Xala*.

24. African women writers often challenge the treatment of women in "modern" Africa by contrasting modern society with traditional cultures that offered women respect, responsibility and a measure of freedom. For an examination of women in modern society in Mariama Ba's *So Long a Letter*, Buchi Emecheta's *Joys of Motherhood*, and Ama Ata Aidoo's *Our Sister Killjoy*. To consider the vital roles for women in tribal life, see Flora Nwapa's *Efuru* and Buchi Emecheta's short stories. In Bessie Head's *A Question of Power*, the protagonist makes a "return" to a rural culture that demonstrates the same theme.

25. In Senègal, for instance, only 6% of the school-age population in 1949 was enrolled in the French schools (Boahen, 23).

26. See Crowder.

27. The career of Léopold Senghor, the first black *professeur agrégé*, member of the French Assembly, poet, founder along with Aimé Césaire of the *nègritude* movement, and first president of Senegal is exemplary. See Markovitz.

28. Toni Morrison makes a similar argument about her character Sula (343-4).

29. For further discussion of Menchú and education, see my book *Teaching and Testimony*.

30. See Brench 112

31. In Senegal, there is a history of complicity between the French and most of the mallams, Imams and even some of the important marabouts dating back to the early conquests (see Boahen, 20-22). In the novel the Imams tell the assembled women:

> Dieu nous fait coexister avec les toubabs français, et ceux-ci nous apprennent à fabriquer ce dont nous avons besoin, nous ne devons pas nous révolter contre cette volonté de Dieu dont les connaissances sont un mystére por nous. (196)

> God has decided that we should live side by side with the French *toubabs*, and the French are teaching us things we have not known and showing us how to make the things we need. It is not up to us to rebel against the will of God, even when the reasons for that will are a mystery to us. (124)

32. This is a particularly interesting passage because it contrasts the construction of individuality between African and European societies. One is valorized by familial relations and family honor, the other by the legalistic construction of individual identity reinforced by the trial that identifies individual guilt and responsibility.

33. Harrow describes the effect in this way: "Sembène's shift of the action from Bamako to Thies to Dakar serves to give a global impression of the effects of the strike action—dramatically it enables him to leave the action suspended as he picks up the thread first in one place and then in another" (485).

34. In a 1991 *Critical Inquiry* article, Anthony Appiah elaborates the distinction Lazarus begins to draw between those African novelists who wrote

immediately before and after the independence struggle and the current period of African writing. Appiah argues that the African novel is a hybridized construction, produced and circulated in an international market of cultural commodities dominated by the West. Thus the particular position of the African intellectual writer must be considered before taking the African novel as able to "speak for" an African population. Appiah points out that the first generation of African novels were part of a modernist and realist effort to legitimate nationalism as an anticolonial project:

> These early novels [the generation of *Things Fall Apart* and *L'Enfant noir*] seem to belong to the world of eighteenth- and nineteenth-century literary nationalism: they are theorized as the imaginative recreation of a common cultural past that is crafted into a shared tradition by the writer. They are in the tradition of Sir Walter Scott, whose *Minstrelsy of the Scottish Border* was intended, as he said in the introduction, to "contribute somewhat to the history of my native country; the peculiar features of whose manners and character are daily melting and dissolving into those of her sister and ally." The novels of this first state are thus realist legitimations of nationalism; they authorize a "return to traditions" while at the same time recognizing the demands of a Weberian rationalized modernity. (Appiah, 349)

Appiah argues further that the current second stage of African writing represents a critique of the first stage and "identifies the realist novel as part of the tactic of nationalist legitimation." In the present era, the African nation-state founded in anticolonial struggle is often despotic, corrupt, and not at all *post*colonial, despite a change in the composition of the ruling class.

5 (DIS)INTEGRATING NATION AND SELF

1. Tim Brennan points out the enormous demands placed on the reader of Rushdie's fiction:

> Flourishing in a highly developed literary tradition of several millennia, working off of a set of standard invocations and stories from a voluminous array of epics and holy books, the novels can

require an extraordinary immersion in literary and historical background: Vedic, Puranic and epic traditions with their centuries-long Sanskrit commentary; the civilizations of Mohenjo-Daro, the Aryans, the empires of the Mauryans, Mughals and British; an uncanny mixture of village television programmes, nationwide Hindi cinema-viewings and oral storytelling; and, on top of this, the grafting on to this intellectual legacy of the British canon itself. (79-80)

2. The evolution of the "native intellectual" is clearly for the *male* writer. For female anticolonial writers, childhood experience is likely to appear "split," thus a desire for edenic return is less likely, and the post-independence disappointment seems less surprising to women writers.

3. Rushdie has indicated his intention to resist straightforward allegorical interpretation. In a 1983 lecture/interview he states:

I didn't want to write a book which could be conventionally translated as allegory, because it seems to me that in India allegory is a kind of disease. You know, everything, all texts, all statements, are interpreted allegorically. There is an assumption that every story is really another story which you haven't quite told, and what you have to do is to translate the story that you have told into the story you haven't told. (3)

4. In discussing *Midnight's Children* Uma Parameswaran makes the more general point that "writing history as autobiography is another way of connecting the individual component of society with the collective stream of history" ("Handcuffed," 40).

5. Keith Wilson puts this in aesthetic terms: "From the first principles of his narrative, Rushdie confronts directly the fallibility of the artist, the partialness of his vision, and the imperfection of the work of art" (26).

6. Timothy Brennan points out that claims of "third-world" authenticity are part of the inevitable book marketing strategies.

Operating within a *world* literature whose traditional national boundaries are meaningless, writers like Fuentes and Rushdie also possess "calling-cards" in the international book markets because of

their authentic native attachment to a specific Third-World locale.
(60)

7. Indeed, exoticizing the nation's diet reaches remarkable extremes as
food is considered in *Midnight's Children* to carry a personal and spiritual
power. Simply eating Saleem's grandmother's food invigorates the personality
of his parents:

> Amina began to feel the emotions of other people's food seeping into
> her--because Reverend Mother doled out the curries and meatballs of
> intransigence, dishes imbued with the personality of their creator;
> Amina ate the first salans of stubbornness in the birianis of
> determination. (164)

8. Homi Bhabha makes a similar point that is not confined to critics of
commonwealth literature:

> *Out of many one*: nowhere has this founding dictum of the political
> society of the modern nation—its spatial expression of a unitary
> people—found a more intriguing *image* of itself than in those diverse
> languages of literary criticism that seek to portray the great power of
> the idea of the nation in the disclosures of its everyday life. (294)

9. In discussing *The Satanic Verses* Rushdie writes:

> *The Satanic Verses* celebrates hybridity, impurity, intermingling, the
> transformation that comes of new and unexpected combinations of
> human beings, cultures, ideas, politics, movies, songs. It rejoices in
> mongrelization and fears the absolutism of the Pure. *Mélange*,
> hotchpotch, a bit of this and a bit of that is *how newness enters the
> world.* It is the great possibility that mass migration gives the world,
> and I have tried to embrace it. (1991, 394)

The same sentiment forms the utopian conclusion of Rushdie's young adult
novel, *Haroun and the Sea of Stories*. The war between the dark and light side
of the planet of Kahani ends with "a peace in which Night and Day, Speech and
Silence, would no longer be separated into Zones by Twilight Strips and Walls
of Force" (191).

10. If Aadam Aziz is the first of the new men, Rushdie further grafts on Judeo-Christian traditions with the names Mary and Joseph to suggest, and ironically undercut, Saleem's—and the nation's—place as savior.

11. The name Wee Willie Winkie is familiar from English nursery rhymes. He "runs through the town, upstairs and downstairs in his night gown," and the name is appropriate in one way as Wee Willie Winkie cries "Are the children in their beds?" In a perhaps obscure reference, "Wee Willie Winkie" is also the name of a Kipling (1888) short story about the son of a British officer in India who saves an English woman with a twisted ankle from Pushto "bad men." (See *The Mandalay Edition of the Works of Kipling: Wee Willie Winkie and Other Stories*, New York: Doubleday, 1927, 233-246.)

12. Even excepting the 350 years of contact with the British, Indian culture has, of course, long been highly complex and hybrid. Ganesh N. Devy points out that

> an Indian is inevitably bicultural and lives within a bilingual or even multilingual cultural idiom. He is born with a skill to switch his culture-code according to the needs of his social situation. And even when he lives within an organic and native social context, he at once lives with many main-stream cultural traditions and several sub-stream cultural currents. (346)

Devy comments:

> In India there has been such a complex inter-relationship between various social, linguistic, racial and religious cultures, and these distinguishable sub-cultures are so numerous that it is virtually impossible to fit them in a common formula of sociological, linguistic or ethnic cultural structure. (345)

In an interview discussing *Midnight's Children* and *Shame*, Rushdie says:

> My view is that the Indian tradition has always been, and still is, a mixed tradition. The idea that there is such a thing as a pure Indian tradition is a kind of fallacy, the nature of Indian culture has always been multiplicity and plurality and mingling. (10)

13. Methwold's ancestor, "the first William Methwold" was the East India Company Officer who in 1633 imagined that Bombay could be a British fort to control the West of India. (Saleem describes the hybrid character of the city's name, from both the Portuguese "Bom Bahia" and the Hindu goddess Mumbadevi [106].)

14. "Minute of the 2nd of February, 1835" in Thomas Babington Macaulay. *Macaulay: Prose and Poetry.* Selected by G.M. Young. Cambridge: Harvard UP, 1952, 729.

15. The Narlikar women are former patients of Dr. Narlikar, gynecologist and birth control advocate.

16. In Kantorowicz's classic study, *The King's Two Bodies,* the notion of a relationship between the state and the person of the king involves images of sickness and health not dissimilar to Rushdie's treatment of Saleem/India. Kantorowicz quotes an Elizabethan legal document:

> For the king has in him two Bodies, *viz.,* a Body natural, and a Body politic. His body natural (if it be considered in itself) is a body mortal, subject to all Infirmities that come by nature or Accident, to the Imbecility of Infancy or old Age, and to the like Defects that happen to the natural bodies of other People. But his Body politic is a Body that cannot be seen or handled, consisting of Policy and Government, and constituted for the Direction of the People, and the Management of the public weal, and this Body is utterly void of Infancy, and old Age, and other natural Defects and Imbecilities, which the Body natural is subject to . . . .(7)

The significant difference between Rushdie's portrayal of Saleem and the medieval version, of course, is that the conceit works not as a justification of state power but a questioning of it: there is no ideological guarantee of health or agelessness for the Indian nation.

17. Saleem's name indirectly suggests Indian geography. The Sinai peninsula has a geometric similarity to the shape of India, is a land of many conquests held, in the present, as a colony.

18. Aamir Mufti links Saleem's position with Nehru:

> The shadow of Nehru, the totemic intellectual of Indian nationalism, hangs over Saleem's life, and his attempts to discover and impose a "third principle" . . . are deeply informed by the pedagogic and

mediating role that the intellectual-politician is meant to play within
the narrative of Indian nationalism. (99)

19. Kumkum Sangari makes a related point:

The narrative embraces all mythologies in an effort to activate an
essentially plural or secular conception of Indianness; it even appears
at times to grasp Indianness as if it were a torrent of religious, class,
and regional diversity rather than a complex articulation of cultural
difference, contradiction, and political use that can scarcely be
idealized. (180)

Given Timothy Brennan's denunciation of Rushdie as a "cosmopolitan" writer,
it is almost surprising that he sees Rushdie's use of myth as a self-aware attack
on "false consciousness."

Although much of *Midnight's Children* unfolds within a modern and
political mode, repeatedly recalling the sectarian violence of contemporary
Indian political life and the class tensions against which any national unity is
artificially constructed, it is nevertheless designed to suggest the living
presence of India's mythical past, not as "vital tradition" but as false
consciousness. (101)

Farther on, Brennan balances his view:

The use of Hindu mythology—despite Rushdie's rejection of its
superstitious aspects and the supposed *sacredness* of national
traditions—is in this way both sardonic and sincere. (113)

20. Speaking of Said's *Orientalism* Rushdie himself has written: "Let me
add only that stereotypes are easier to shrug off if yours is not the culture being
stereotyped; or, at the very least, if your culture has the power to counterpunch
against the stereotype" (*Imaginary*, 89).

21. Feroza Jussawalla argues that the novel appears to be addressed to
"Western readers who would derive pleasure from the hybrid mixtures of
language and situation" (38) and that Rushdie's language is "cliched,
stereotypical speech of the Eurasian, 'niggerized' class" (39). Her stand seems
rather contradictory, however. She also says that "a large part of the dialect is
captured from the Goan and Anglo-Indian English spoken around Bombay"
and that Rushdie is "eminently successful in capturing the cadences of Urdu

and the wry irony and humor that mark Urdu speech" (40). She finds Rushdie's style both "so familiar" that it is "tedious" and so "excessive" that it "erects a Chinese wall of language" (41). While rejecting an emphasis on stylistic experimentation in Indo-English writing, she also believes Rushdie doesn't show a "nationalistic concern for Indianizing English or showing how well an Indian can imitate a contemporary model." Instead she views Rushdie as "writing in a style he has contempt for--parodying a parody" (41).

22. Perhaps this partly explains why several of Rushdie's Indian critics make extensive efforts to summarize and restate the narrative action of *Midnight's Children*. See for instance Naik, Narayan, and Singh.

23. Batty reads the metaphor of the perforated sheet universally as a figure for the functioning of narrative itself:

> Narrative is a perforated sheet, concealing the whole while revealing a part; it is a temporal medium, like episodic cinema, which tantalizes us with its trailers but only ever partially fulfils our expectations . . . (61)

Keith Wilson makes a similar argument:

> *Midnight's Children* is, then, a novel centrally concerned with the imperfections of any narrative act, the compromises which govern the relationship of a writer with a reader who is hungry for linearity, and the impossibility of rendering a reality—however much concerned with public history—that is not petrified into false and subjective form at the point at which an artist attempts to render it. (30)

24. The connection between Naseem and the subcontinent is strengthened in the next chapter where she is described as a "partitioned woman" (23).

25. Sudha Pai argues that the most fruitful way to read *Midnight's Children* is as an expression of the viewpoint of the expatriate: "*Midnight's Children* is a self-conscious expression of the expatriate writer's way of grasping and rendering the truth of historical reality . . ." (36). Spivak puts the tension between native and migrant status in Rushdie's writing this way: "Writing as a migrant, Rushdie still militates against privileging the migrant or the exilic voice narrowly conceived, even as he fails in that very effort" (82).

26. Speaking of his adopted son, Saleem tells Mary "I did it for him" (547).

27. Brennan and Talal Asad would be in this category. The most interesting response to their position is Mufti. While Spivak makes a case that the postcolonial position must "distance" itself from national agency, she never implies that these aspirations can be left behind:

> It is only if we acknowledge the heterogeneous desire for that great rational abstraction—agency in a nation—that we post-colonials will be able to take a distance from it. (94)

28. Cronin does not credit Rushdie with a self-consciousness of how this scene operates metaphorically. Cronin makes a case that Indian writing in English is "irrevocably separated from India" (202). Aamir Mufti's broader notion of reading erodes Cronin's position.

29. Kumkum Sangari makes just this point:

> The writing that emerges from this position [postmodern skepticism], however critical it may be of colonial discourses, gloomily disempowers the "nation" as an enabling idea and relocates the impulses for change as everywhere and nowhere. (183)

Bibliography

Achebe, Chinua. *Hopes and Impediments: Selected Essays.* New York: Doubleday, 1989.

———. *No Longer at Ease.* London: Heinemann, 1960.

———. *Things Fall Apart.* New York: Fawcett, 1969.

Adamson, David. "Authority and Illusion: Power of Prospero's Book." *Comitatus* 20 (1989): 9-19.

Adorno, Rolena. "Colonial Spanish American Literary Studies: 1982-1992." *Revista Interamerica de Bibliographia* 38.2 (1988): 167-176.

Adorno, Theodor W., and Max Horkheimer. *Dialectic of Enlightenment.* Trans. John Cumming. New York: Continuum, 1989.

Ahmad, Aijaz. "Jameson's Rhetoric of Otherness and the 'National Allegory.'" *Social Text* 17 (Fall 1987): 3-25.

———. *In Theory: Classes, Nations, Literatures.* London: Verso, 1992.

Aidoo, Ama Ata. *Our Sister Killjoy.* Essex: Longman, 1977.

Alarcón, Norma. "Chicana's Feminist Literature: A RE-Vison Through Malintzin/ or Malintzin: Putting Flesh Back on the Object." *This Bridge Called My Back.* New York: Kitchen Table, 1983.

Alter, Robert. "The Novel and the Sense of the Past." *Salmagundi* 68 (1985): 91-106.

Althusser, Louis. "Ideology and Ideological State Apparatuses." In *Lenin and Philosophy.* New York: Monthly Review Press, 1971, 127-86.

Anderson, Benedict. *Imagined Communities: Reflections on the Origin and Spread of Nationalism.* London: Verso, 1983.

Appiah, Kwame Anthony. "Is the Post- in Postmodernism the Post- in Postcolonial?" *Critical Inquiry* 17 (Winter 1991): 336-357.

———. *In My Father's House: Africa in the Philosophy of Culture.* New York: Oxford UP, 1993.

Apter, Emily. "Comparative Exile: Competing Margins in the History of Comparative Literature." *Comparative Literature in the Era of Multiculturalism.* Ed. Charles Bernheimer. Baltimore: Johns Hopkins UP, 1995. 86-96.

Archer, John. *Sovereignty and Intelligence: Spying and Court Culture in the English Renaissance.* Stanford: Stanford UP, 1993.

Armstrong, John A. *Nations Before Nationalism.* Chapel Hill: U of North Carolina P, 1982.

Asad, Talal. "A Comment on Aijaz Ahmad's *In Theory.*" *Public Culture* 6.1 (1993): 31-39.

Bakhtin, M.M. *The Dialogic Imagination.* Trans. Caryl Emerson and Michael Holquist. Austin: U of Texas P, 1981.

Barker, Francis and Peter Hulme. "Nymphs and Reapers Heavily Vanish: The Discursive Con-texts of *The Tempest.*" *Alternative Shakespeares.* Ed. John Drakakis. London: Methuen, 1985. 191-205.

Barthes, Roland. "Mythologies." *A Barthes Reader.* Ed. Susan Sontag. New York: Hill and Wang, 1982.

———. *S/Z.* Trans. Richard Miller. New York: Hill and Wang, 1974.

Batty, Nancy E. "The Art of Suspense: Rushdie's 1001 (Mid-)Nights." *Ariel* 18.3 (1987): 49-65.

Beier, A. L. *Masterless Men: The Vagrancy Problem in England 1560-1640.* New York: Methuen, 1985.

Berrian, Brenda F. "Through Her Prism of Social and Political Contexts: Sembène's Female Characters in *Tribal Scars.*" *Ngambika: Studies of Women in African Literature.* Trenton: African World, 1986.

Beverley, John. "The Margin at the Center: On *Testimonio.*" *Modern Fiction Studies* 35.1 (1989): 11-28.

Bhabha, Homi K. "The Other Question: Difference, Discrimination, and the Discourse of Colonialism." In *Literature, Politics and Theory.* London: Methuen, 1986.

———. "DissemiNation: Time, Narrative, and the Margins of the Modern Nation." In *Nation and Narration.* Ed. Homi Bhabha. London: Routledge, 1990.

———. *The Location of Culture.* New York: Routledge, 1994.

Boahen, A. Adu. "Introduction." *God's Bits of Wood.* New York: Anchor, 1970.

Bohannan, Paul, and Philip Curtin. *Africa and Africans.* Revised Edition. New York: Natural History Press, 1971.

Brantlinger, Patrick. "Victorians and Africans: The Genealogy of the Myth of the Dark Continent." *"Race," Writing and Difference*. Ed. Henry Louis Gates. Chicago: U of Chicago P, 1985.

Breight, Curt. "Treason doth never prosper": *The Tempest* and the Discourse of Treason." *Shakespeare Quarterly* 41.1 (1990): 1-28.

Brench, A.C. *The Novelist Inheritance in French Africa*. London: Oxford UP, 1967.

Brennan, Timothy. "The National Longing for Form." *Nation and Narration*. Ed. Homi Bhabha. London: Routledge, 1990.

———. *Salman Rushdie and the Third World: Myths of the Nation*. New York: St. Martin's Press, 1989.

Brown, Paul. "'This thing of darkness I acknowledge mine': *The Tempest* and the Discourse of Colonialism." *Political Shakespeare: New Essays in Cultural Materialism*. Ed. Jonathan Dollimore and Alan Sinfield. Ithaca: Cornell UP, 1985. 48-71.

Buell, Frederick. *National Culture and the New Global System*. Baltimore: Johns Hopkins UP, 1994.

Burshatin, Israel. "The Moor in the Text: Metaphor, Emblem, and Silence." *"Race," Writing and Difference*. Ed. Henry Louis Gates Jr. Chicago: U of Chicago P, 1985.

Cabral, Amilcar. *Return to the Source: Selected Speeches*. New York: Monthly Review Press, 1973.

Cantor, Paul A. "Prospero's Republic: The Politics of Shakespeare's *The Tempest.*" *Shakespeare as Political Thinker*. Ed. John Alvis and Thomas G. West. Durham: Carolina Academic P, 1981.

Carey-Webb, Allen. "Homelessness and Language Arts: Contexts and Connections," *English Journal* (Nov. 1991), 22-28.

Carey-Webb, Allen, and Stephen Benz, eds. *Teaching and Testimony: Rigoberta Menchú and the North American Classroom*. New York: SUNY P, 1996.

Cartelli, Thomas. "Prospero in Africa: *The Tempest* as Colonialist Text and Pretext." *Shakespeare Reproduced: The Text in History and Ideology*. Ed. Jean Howard and Marion O'Conner. London: Methuen, 1987. 99-115.

Caufield, Mina Davis. "Imperialism, the Family, and Cultures of Resistance." *Socialist Revolution* 20 (October 1974).

Chatterjee, Partha. *Nationalist Thought and the Colonial World: A Derivative Discourse*. Delhi: Oxford UP, 1986.

Cohen, Walter. *Drama of a Nation: Public Theater in Renaissance England and Spain.* Ithaca: Cornell UP, 1985.

Cressy, David. *Education in Tudor and Stewart England.* New York: St. Martin's, 1975.

Cronin, Richard. "The Indian English Novel: *Kim* and *Midnight's Children.*" *Modern Fiction Studies* 33.2 (1987): 201-13.

Crowder, Michael. *Senegal: A Study of French Assimilation Policy.* London: Methuen, 1967.

de Certeau, Michel. *Heterologies: Discourse on the Other.* Trans. Brian Massumi. Minneapolis: U of Minnesota P, 1986.

Dangarembga, Tsitsi. *Nervous Conditions: A Novel.* Seattle: Seal Press, 1988.

Devy, Ganesh N. "The Multicultural Context of Indian Literature in English." *Crisis and Creativity in the New Literatures in English.* Ed. Geoffrey Davis and Hena Maes-Jelinek. Amsterdam; Atlanta: Rodopi, 1990. 345-354.

Dille, Glen F. "The Plays of Cervantes, Lope, Calderón and the New World." *LA CHISPA: Selected Proceedings.* New Orleans: Tulane U, 1987.

———. "El descubrimiento y la conquista de América en la comedia del Siglo de Oro." *Hispania* 71 (1988): 492-502.

Elliot, J.H. *Spain and Its World: 1500-1700.* New Haven: Yale UP, 1989.

Emecheta, Buchi. *The Joys of Motherhood.* New York: Braziller, 1979.

Fanon, Frantz. *Black Skin, White Masks: The Experiences of a Black Man in a White World.* New York: Grove Press, 1967.

———. *The Wretched of the Earth.* Trans. Constance Farrington. New York: Grove Press, 1961.

Fokkema, Aleid. "English Ideas of Indianness: The Reception of Salman Rushdie." *Crisis and Creativity in the New Literatures in English.* Ed. Geoffrey Davis and Hena Maes-Jelinek. Amsterdam; Atlanta: Rodopi, 1990. 355-368.

Foltz, William J. *From French West Africa to the Mali Federation.* New Haven: Yale UP, 1965.

Forster, E.M. *A Passage to India.* New York: Knopf, 1991.

Foucault, Michel. *Discipline and Punish: The Birth of the Prison.* Trans. Alan Sheridan. New York: Vintage Books, 1979.

Franco, Jean. *Plotting Women: Gender and Representation in Mexico.* New York: Columbia UP, 1989.

Freire, Paulo. *Pedagogy of the Oppressed.* New York: Continuum, 1987.

Gates, Henry Louis Jr. *The Signifying Monkey: A Theory of African American Criticism.* New York: Oxford, 1988.

Gellner, Ernest. *Nations and Nationalism.* Ithaca: Cornell UP, 1983.

Gérard, Albert. "Literature, Language, Nation and the Commonwealth." *Crisis and Creativity in the New Literatures in English.* Ed. Geoffrey Davis and Hena Maes-Jelinek. Amsterdam; Atlanta: Rodopi, 1990. 93-102.

Gérard, Albert and Jeannine Laurent. "Sembene's Progeny: A New Trend in the Sengalese Novel." *STCL* 4.2 (Spring 1980): 133-188.

Gillies, John. "Shakespeare's Virginia Masque." *ELH* 53.4 (1986): 673-707.

Gómez-Moriana, Antonio. "Narration in the Chronicles of the New World." Trans. Jane E. Gregg and James V. Romano. *1492-1992: Re/Discovering Colonial Writing.* Minneapolis: Prisma Institute, 1989. 97-119.

Gonzáles-Echevarría, Roberto. "America Conquered." *The Yale Review* 74 (1985): 281-91.

Grant, R.A.D. "Providence, Authority, and the Moral Life in *The Tempest.*" *Shakespeare Studies,* 16 (1983): 235-263.

Greenblatt, Stephen. *Learning to Curse: Essays in Early Modern Culture.* New York: Routledge, 1990.

– – –. *Marvelous Possessions: The Wonder of the New World.* Chicago: U Chicago P, 1991.

– – –. *Renaissance Self-Fashioning: From More to Shakespeare.* Chicago: U of Chicago P, 1980.

– – –. *Shakespearean Negotiations: The Circulation of Social Energy in Renaissance England.* Berkeley: U of California P, 1988.

Griffiths, Trevor. "'This Island's mine': Caliban and Colonialism." *Yearbook of English Studies* 13 (1983): 159-80.

Harlow, Barbara. *Resistance Literature.* New York: Methuen, 1987.

Harrow, Kenneth W. "Art and Ideology in *Les bouts de bois de Dieu*: Realism's Artifices." *The French Review* 62.3 (1989): 483-493.

Hawkes, Terence. "Swisser-Swatter: Making a Man of English Letters." *Alternative Shakespeares.* Ed. John Drakakis. London: Methuen, 1985. 26-46.

Head, Bessie. *A Question of Power.* London: Heinemann, 1974.

Helgerson, Richard. *Forms of Nationhood: The Elizabethan Writing of England.* Chicago: U of Chicago P, 1992.

Hill, Christopher. *The Pelican History of Britain: Volume 2 1530-1780 Reformation to Revolution.* Harmondsworth: Penguin, 1971.

Hobsbawm, Eric. *Nations and Nationalism Since 1780: Programme, Myth, Reality.* Cambridge: Cambridge UP, 1990.

Hulme, Peter. *Colonial Encounters: Europe and the Native Caribbean 1492-1797.* London: Methuen, 1986.

Hunt, Maurice. "Belarius and Prospero: Two Pastoral Schoolmasters." *Lamar Journal of the Humanities* 15.2 (1989): 29-41.

Jameson, Fredric. "Third-World Literature in the Era of Multinational Capitalism." *Social Text* 15 (Fall 1986): 65-88.

JanMohamed, Abdul. "The Economy of Manichean Allegory: The Function of Racial Difference in Colonialist Literature." *"Race," Writing and Difference.* Ed. Henry Louis Gates. Chicago: U of Chicago P, 1985.

— — —. *Manichean Aesthetics: The Politics of Literature in Colonial Africa.* Amherst: U of Massachusetts P, 1983.

Jara, René, and Nicholas Spadaccini. "Introduction: Allegorizing the New World." *1492-1992: Re/Discovering Colonial Writing.* Minneapolis: Prisma Institute, 1989. 9-50.

— — —. *Amerindian Images and the Legacy of Columbus.* Minneapolis: U of Minnesota P, 1992.

Jayawardena, Kumari, Ed. *Feminism and Nationalism in the Third World.* London: Zed, 1986.

Jeyifo, Biodun. "Class Perspectives in the Analysis of Contemporary African Culture and Literature: The Issues Involved." *Odu: Journal of West African Studies* 23 (1983): 1-15.

Jussawalla, Feroza. "Beyond Indianness: The Stylistic Concerns of 'Midnight's Children.'" *The Journal of Indian Writing in English* 12.2 (1984): 26-47.

Kane, Hamidou. *Ambiguous Adventure.* London: Heinemann, 1972.

Kantorowicz, Ernst H. *The King's Two Bodies: A Study in Medieval Political Theology.* Princeton: Princeton UP, 1957.

Kay, Dennis C. "Gonzalo's 'Lasting Pillars': *The Tempest,* V.i.208." *Shakespeare Quarterly* 35.3 (1984): 322-4.

Kesteloot, Lilyan. *Anthologie Negro-Africaine.* Marabout: Alleur, 1967.

Laclau, Ernesto and Chantal Mouffe. *Hegemony and Socialist Strategy: Towards a Radical Democratic Politics.* London: Verso, 1985.

Lazarus, Neil. *Resistance in Postcolonial African Fiction.* New Haven: Yale UP, 1990.

Lévi-Strauss, Claude. *Tristes Tropiques.* Trans. John and Doreen Weightman. New York: Atheneum, 1973.

Macaulay, Thomas Babington. "Minute of the 2nd of February, 1835" in *Macaulay: Prose and Poetry.* Selected by G.M. Young. Cambridge: Harvard UP, 1952.

Malak, Amin. "Reading the Crisis: The Polemics of Salman Rushdie's *The Satanic Verses.*" *Ariel* 20.4 (1989): 176-186.

Mannoni, Octave. *Prospero and Caliban: The Psychology of Colonization.* Trans. Pamela Powesland. Ann Arbor: U Michigan P, 1990.

Markovitz, Irving Leonard. *Léopold Sédar Senghor and the Politics of Nègritude.* New York: Atheneum, 1969.

Marx, Karl, and Friedrich Engels. "Manifesto of the Communist Party." *The Marx-Engels Reader.* Second Edition. Ed. Robert Tucker. New York: Norton, 1978.

McDonald, Russ. "Reading *The Tempest.*" *Shakespeare Survey* 43 (1991): 15-28.

Mebane, John S. *Renaissance Magic and the Return of the Golden Age: The Occult Tradition and Marlowe, Jonson, and Shakespeare.* Lincoln: U of Nebraska P, 1989.

Menchú, Rigoberta with Elizabeth Burgos Debray. *Me llamo Rigoberta Menchú y así me nació la conciencia.* Mexico City: Siglo Veintiuno 1985.

Menéndez y Pelayo. "Observaciones Preliminares." In *Obras de Lope de Vega.* Madrid: La Real Academia Espanola, 1900.

Mignolo, Walter D. "Literacy and Colonization: The New World Experience." *1492-1992: Re/Discovering Colonial Writing.* Minneapolis: Prisma Institute, 1989. 51-96.

Minh-ha, Trinh T. *Woman, Native, Other: Writing, Postcoloniality, and Feminism.* Indiana UP: Bloomington, 1989.

Mohanty, S.P. "Us and Them: On the Philosophical Bases of Political Criticism." *Yale Journal of Criticism* 2.2 (1989): 1-31.

Morrison, Toni. "Rootedness: The Ancestor as Foundation." *Black Women Writers.* Ed. Mari Evans. New York: Doubleday, 1984. 339-345.

Mosse, George L. "Mass Politics and the Political Liturgy of Nationalism." In *Nationalism: The Nature and Evolution of an Idea.* Ed. Eugene Kamenka. Australian National UP: Canberra, 1975. 39-54.

———. *Nationalism and Sexuality: Respectability and Abnormal Sexuality in Modern Europe.* New York: Howard Fertig, 1985.

Mufti, Aamir. "Reading the Rushdie Affair: An Essay on Islam and Politics." *Social Text* 19.4 (1991): 95-116.

Mukherhjee, Arun P. "The Vocabulary of the 'Universal': Cultural Imperialism and Western Literary Criticism." *World Literature Written in English* 26.2 (1986): 343-53.

Munck, Ronaldo. *The Difficult Dialogue: Marxism and Nationalism.* Zed: London, 1986.

Naik, M.K. "A Life of Fragments: The Fate of Identity in *Midnight's Children.*" *The Indian Literary Review* 3.3 (1985): 63-68.

Narayan, Shyamala A. "*Midnight's Children.*" *The Literary Criterion* 18.3 (1983): 23-32.

Nash, Thomas. *Works.* Oxford: Blackwell, 1958.

Ngugi wa Thiong'o. *Decolonizing the Mind: The Politics of Language in African Fiction.* London: James Currey, 1986.

———. *Devil on the Cross.* Trans. Ngugi wa Thiong'o. London: Heinemann, 1982.

———. *A Grain of Wheat.* London: Heinemann, 1975.

———. *Petals of Blood.* London: Heinemann, 1977.

———. *Writers and Poltics.* London: Heinemann, 1981.

Nixon, Rob. "Caribbean and African Appropriations of *The Tempest.*" *Critical Inquiry* 13 (1987): 557-578.

Nwapa, Flora. *Efuru.* London: Heinemann, 1978.

Ojo, S. Ade. "Revolt, Violence and Duty in Ousmane Sembene's *God's Bits of Wood.*" *Nigeria Magazine* 53.3 (1985): 58-68.

Orgel, Stephen. "Prospero's Wife." *Rewriting the Renaissance: The Discourses of Sexual Difference in Early Modern Europe.* Ed. Margaret W. Ferguson, Maureen Quilligan, and Nancy J. Vickers. Chicago: U of Chicago P, 1986.

Orme, Nicholas. *Education and Society in Medieval and Renaissance England.* London: Hambledon Press, 1989.

Pai, Sudha. "Expatriot Concerns in Salman Rushdie's *Midnight's Children.*" *The Literary Criterion* 4.23 (1988): 36-41.

Parameswaran, Uma. "Handcuffed to History: Salman Rushdie's Art." *Ariel* 14.4 (1983): 34-45.

———. "'Lest He Returning Chide': Saleem Sinai's Inaction in Salman Rushdie's *Midnight's Children.*" *The Literary Criterion* 18.3 (1983): 57-66.

———. "Salman Rushdie in Indo-English Literature." *The Journal of Indian Writing in English* 12.2 (1984): 15-25.

Paz, Octavio. *El laberinto de la soledad*. Mexico D.F.: Fondo de Cultura Economica, 1959.

Prasad, Madhava. "On the Question of a Theory of (Third World) Literature." *Social Text.* 31/32 (1992): 57-83.

Pratt, Mary Louise. "Comparative Literature and Global Citizenship." *Comparative Literature in the Era of Multiculturalism.* Ed. Charles Bernheimer. Baltimore: Johns Hopkins UP, 1995. 58-65.

Pye, Christopher. *The Regal Phantasm: Shakespeare and the Politics of Spectacle.* London: Routledge, 1990.

Rao, Madhusudhana M. "Quest for Identity: A Study of the Narrative in Rushdie's *Midnight's Children.*" *The Literary Criterion* 25.4 (1990): 42-51.

Retamar, Roberto Fernández. "Caliban: Notes Toward a Discussion of Culture in Our America." *Caliban and Other Essays.* Trans. Edward Baker. Minneapolis: U Minnesota P, 1989.

Rushdie, Salman. *Haroun and the Sea of Stories.* London: Granta/Viking, 1990.

— — —. *Imaginary Homelands: Essays and Criticism 1981-1991.* London: Granta/Viking, 1991.

— — —. *Midnight's Children.* New York: Avon, 1982.

— — —. "*Midnight's Children* and *Shame.*" Interview. *Kunapipi* 7.1 (1985): 1-19.

— — —. *The Satanic Verses.* New York: Viking, 1989.

— — —. *Shame.* New York: Knopf, 1983.

Said, Edward. *Orientalism.* New York: Vintage, 1979.

— — —. *Culture and Imperialism.* New York: Vintage, 1993.

Sangari, Kumkum. "The Politics of the Possible." *Cultural Critique* (Fall 1987): 157-186.

Schipper, Mineke. "Towards a Definition of Realism in the African Context." *New Literary History* 16.3 (Spring, 1985): 559-575.

Sembène, Ousmane. *The End of Empire.* London: Heinemann, 1982.

— — —. *God's Bits of Wood.* Trans. Francis Price. London: Heinemann, 1962.

— — —. "Interview." *L'Afrique litteraire* 49 (1980): 111-126.

— — —. *Les bouts de bois de Dieu.* Paris: Presses Pocket, 1960.

— — —. *Xala.* Trans Clive Wake. Westport: Lawrence Hill, 1976.

Semonin, Paul. "Monsters in the Marketplace: The Exhibiting of Human Oddities in Early Modern England." *Freakmaking: Constituting*

Corporeal and Cultural Others. Ed. Rosemarie Garland Thomson. New York: New York UP, 1996. 69-81.

——. "'Nature's Nation': Natural History as Nationalism in the New Republic." *Northwest Review* 30.2 (1992): 6-41.

Seton-Watson, Hugh. *Nations and States: An Enquiry into the Origins of Nations and the Politics of Nationalism.* London: Methuen, 1977.

Shakespeare, William. *The Tempest.* Ed. Frank Kermode. Cambridge: Harvard UP, 1954.

——. *The Tempest.* Ed. Stephen Orgel. New York: Oxford UP, 1987.

Shannon, Robert. *Visions of the New World in the Drama of Lope de Vega.* New York: Peter Lang, 1989.

Siegel, Paul N. "Historical Ironies in 'The Tempest.'" *Shakespeare Jahrbuch* 119 (1983): 104-111.

Singh, Sushila. "Salman Rushdie's *Midnight's Children*: Rethinking the Life and Times in Modern India." *Panjab University Research Bulletin* 16.1 (1985): 55-67.

Spivak, Gayatri. "Can the Subaltern Speak." *Marxism and the Interpretation of Culture.* Eds. Cary Nelson and Lawrence Grossberg. Urbana: U of Illinois P, 1988.

Sprinker, Michael. "The National Question: Said, Ahmad, Jameson." *Public Culture* 6.1 (1993): 3-30.

——. "Reading *The Satanic Verses.*" *Public Culture* 2.1 (1989): 79-99.

Srivastava, Aruna. "'The Empire Writes Back': Language and History in *Shame* and *Midnight's Children.*" *Ariel* 20.4 (1989): 62-78.

Stern, Charlotte. "Lope de Vega, Propagandist?" *Bulletin of the Comediantes* 34.1 (1982): 1-36.

Swann, Joseph. "'East Is East and West Is West'? Salman Rushdie's *Midnight's Children* as an Indian Novel." *World Literature Written in English* 26.2 (1986): 353-62.

Swietlicki, Catherine. "Lope's Dialogic Imagination: Writing Other Voices of 'Monolithic' Spain." *Bulletin of the Comediantes* 40.2 (1988): 205-226.

Tire, Alioune. "Oulof ou français le choix de Sembène." *Notre libraire* 81 (1985): 43-50.

Todorov, Tzvetan. *The Conquest of America: The Question of the Other.* Trans. Richard Howard. New York: Harper & Row, 1984.

Vaughan, Alden T. "Caliban in the 'Third World': Shakespeare's Savage as Sociopolitical Symbol." *The Massachusetts Review* 29.2 (1988): 289-313.

— — —. "Shakespeare's Indian: The Americanization of Caliban." *Shakespeare Quarterly* 39.2 (1988): 137-153.

Vaughan, Alden T., and Virginia Mason Vaughan. *Shakespeare's Caliban: A Cultural History.* Cambridge: Cambridge UP, 1991.

Vega Carpio, Lope de. *The Discovery of the New World by Christopher Columbus.* Trans. Frieda Fligelman. Berkeley: Gillick, 1940.

— — —. *El nuevo mundo descubierto por Cristóbal Colón.* E. J. Lemartinel and C. Minguet. Paris: Presses Universitaries de Lille, 1980.

— — —. *El nuevo mundo descubierto por Cristóbal Colón.* In *Obras de Lope de Vega.* Madrid: La Real Academia Española, 1900.

Viswanathan, Gauri. *Masks of Conquest: Literary Study and British Rule in India.* New York: Columbia UP, 1989.

Wallace, Karen Smyley. "Women and Alienation: Analysis of the Works of Two Francophone African Writers." *Ngambika: Studies of Women in African Literature.* Trenton: African World, 1986.

Weiner, Jack. "La guerra y la paz espirituales in tres comedias de Lope." *Revista de Estudios Hispanicos* 17 (1983): 65-79.

Wernham, R.B. *Before the Armada: The Emergence of the English Nation 1485-1588.* New York: Harcourt Brace, 1966.

West, Cornel. "Minority Discourse and the Pitfalls of Canon Formation." *The Yale Journal of Criticism* (1987): 193-201.

Wilson, Keith. "*Midnight's Children* and Reader Responsibility." *Critical Quarterly* 26.3: 23-37.

Zahareas, Anthony N., ed. *Special Number: Plays and Playhouses in Imperial Decadence. Hispanic Issues.* Minneapolis: Institute of Ideologies and Literature, 1985.

Zinn, Howard. *A People's History of the United States.* New York: Harper & Row, 1980.

Index